Atlantic Canada

A Concise History

Margaret R. Conrad and James K. Hiller

OXFORD

UNIVERSITY PRESS

OXFORD
UNIVERSITY PRESS

70 Wynford Drive, Don Mills, Ontario M3C 1J9
www.oup.com/ca

Oxford University Press is a department of the University of Oxford.
It furthers the University's objective of excellence in research, scholarship,
and education by publishing worldwide in

Oxford   New York

Auckland   Cape Town   Dar es Salaam   Hong Kong   Karachi   Kuala Lumpur
Madrid   Melbourne   Mexico City   Nairobi   New Delhi   Shanghai   Taipei   Toronto

With offices in

Argentina   Austria   Brazil   Chile   Czech Republic   France   Greece   Guatemala
Hungary   Italy   Japan   Poland   Portugal   Singapore   South Korea   Switzerland
Thailand   Turkey   Ukraine   Vietnam

Oxford is a trade mark of Oxford University Press
in the UK and in certain other countries

Published in Canada
by Oxford University Press

Library and Archives Canada Cataloguing in Publication

Conrad, Margaret
Atlantic Canada: a concise history/Margaret R. Conrad and James K. Hiller.

Includes bibliographical references and index.

ISBN-13: 978-0-19-541829-3
ISBN-10: 0-19-541829-8

1. Atlantic Provinces—History—Textbooks.   I. Hiller, J.K. (James K.), 1942–   II. Title.
FC2005.C65 2006   971.5   C2005-906438-2

Cover and text design: Brett Miller
Cover image: Department of Mines and Resources/
Library and Archives Canada/PA-020699

This book is printed on permanent (acid-free) paper ∞.
Printed in Canada

Contents

Introduction   v

Chapter 1   Beginnings   1

Chapter 2   Aboriginal Peoples   12

Chapter 3   European Encounters, 1000–1598   22

Chapter 4   Colonial Experiments, 1598–1632   34

Chapter 5   Colonial Communities, 1632–1713   46

Chapter 6   Renegotiating the Atlantic Region, 1713–63   60

Chapter 7   Community Formation, 1749–1815   77

Chapter 8   Maturing Colonial Societies, 1815–60   94

Chapter 9   Confronting Confederation, 1860–73   112

Chapter 10   The Industrial Challenge, 1873–1901   128

Chapter 11   The Promise and Peril of a New Century, 1901–19   145

Chapter 12   Between the Wars, 1919–39   162

Chapter 13   The Emergence of an Atlantic Region, 1939–49   178

Chapter 14   The Real Golden Age? 1949–75   191

Chapter 15   The Atlantic Region in a Global Context, 1975–2005   210

Selected Bibliography   224

Notes   231

Index   237

Introduction

This book is a successor to *Atlantic Canada: A Region in the Making* (2001), but it does not replace that profusely illustrated volume, which was written for a general readership. This version aims to provide university students with an expanded, reorganized, and updated text and bibliography, together with biographies, documents, and inserts that provide more detail on important themes in the main body of the narrative. We have also adopted a more utilitarian title: *Atlantic Canada: A Concise History*.

For our purposes, 'Atlantic Canada' means Newfoundland and Labrador as well as the Maritime provinces of New Brunswick, Nova Scotia, and Prince Edward Island. The boundaries of these provinces have been defined over the years by diplomats, lawyers, and politicians, and do not include all the areas of eastern Canada that might be considered 'Atlantic'. Artificial as they might be, existing political boundaries frame the history explored in this book.

Those boundaries enclose a huge region: 539,101 square kilometres of land and fresh water, extending over 17 degrees of longitude and latitude, with 16,000 kilometres of shoreline. Landscapes vary from the dramatic Torngat Mountains of northern Labrador to the quiet farmlands of Prince Edward Island and the Annapolis Valley, to the forests of New Brunswick. Climates vary as well, subarctic or cool where the Labrador Current comes near the coast, more temperate in southern areas.

Geographically diverse, Atlantic Canada contains its own distinct sub-regions—Labrador and Cape Breton, for instance—as well as regions defined not so much by geography as by other loyalties: Acadie, Africadia, Mi'kma'ki. Although the population is deeply rooted and possesses a strong sense of place—it is said that an Atlantic Canadian would rather be at home than in Heaven—loyalties and identities remain local or provincial, not regional. People rarely say 'I'm an Atlantic Canadian' in the way that people on the Prairies say 'I'm a Westerner.'

Nevertheless, we believe that to emphasize the differences between the provinces and sub-regions of Atlantic Canada is to obscure essential similarities. We see 'Atlantic Canada' as something more than the artificial geopolitical construct announced in 1949, when Newfoundland joined Confederation. Its peoples have, and have had, much in common. The challenge in writing this book has been to find these common historical threads while reflecting the region's diversity, and to ensure that all parts of the region, and all its peoples, receive adequate attention. Readers can judge for themselves how successful this balancing act has been.

For all that, Atlantic Canada is still 'a region in the making'. The federal government and big business treat the four provinces as a single unit with Halifax as its capital, and the region has responded to such pressures not by discussing political union, but by developing greater internal collaboration and cooperation. This is most evident in the Maritimes. Newfoundland—officially 'Newfoundland and Labrador' since 2001—remains to some extent a cuckoo in the nest. There are those on both sides of the Cabot Strait who will maintain that the island of Newfoundland has no significant affinities with other parts of the region. For its part, Labrador sees itself as distinct from both Newfoundland and the Maritimes.

Our primary goal in writing this book is to make the history of Atlantic Canada better known to the citizens of the four provinces. We also hope that it will appeal to Canadians elsewhere, who all too often display a woeful ignorance of Atlantic Canada and its people, treating both the region and its history as marginal and unimportant. Making available a synthesis of the region's long and remarkable history may provide a corrective, and can help Atlantic Canadians develop an accurate and assured sense of who they are.

Over the past 35 years an avalanche of lively historical literature has transformed our knowledge of the region's past. Many of the scholars who have contributed to that literature are, or were once, our colleagues and students, and to them we are deeply indebted. Historians outside the university have also made valuable contributions, as have the archivists who have collected the documents and images that make historical research possible.

In our lifetime, the study of Atlantic Canadian history developed in a collegial and collaborative atmosphere and became an exciting field of inquiry. It now supports regular conferences and a range of journals, of which the flagship is *Acadiensis*, founded in 1971. This text is inevitably selective in its coverage, but we hope that it will spark the interest of our readers and stimulate them to learn more about the place we call Atlantic Canada.

Margaret R. Conrad
James K. Miller
October 2005

Chapter One

Beginnings

In 1855, J. William Dawson, a native of Pictou County, Nova Scotia, published a book entitled *Acadian Geology*. In it he reflected on a time 350 million years earlier when 'multitudes of large animals now extinct' inhabited the Maritimes and 'submerged tropical forests' laid the foundations for the region's rich coal deposits. Dawson was a pioneer in the emerging fields of geology and paleontology, two of the sciences that, in the nineteenth century, were transforming everything people had hitherto believed about the earth and its inhabitants. A strict Presbyterian, he refused to accept the theory of evolution as expounded by his famous contemporary Charles Darwin. Dawson nevertheless helped to advance new scientific ideas about the origins of the earth and the emergence of an 'Atlantic region'.

The Making of the Atlantic Region

In Dawson's time most people living in the British North American colonies subscribed to a biblical interpretation of the origins of the universe. God, they believed, had created heaven and earth in six days—some thought 4004 years before the birth of Christ—and placed Adam and Eve in the Garden of Eden, from which they were eventually expelled to people an imperfect world.

Aboriginal creation stories also attributed the earth's origins to powerful gods. According to Mi'kmaq beliefs, Kji-kinap made the world and breathed life into a large, flat stone that he named Kluskap (Glooscap). With the help of a young man and a young woman, Kluskap cleaned out the silt-choked river beds, made the trees grow, summoned birds and animals from the Sky World, and shaped various geological features. Like the Christian God, Kluskap established a gendered social order. 'I am going to marry you together,' he told the two young people who helped him to form the earth. 'You will live together and have children, and they will have children. Go and make yourselves a wigwam. The man can go out into the forest and hunt animals. The woman can cook them.'[1]

The implications of the scientific view of creation that now dominates most textbooks also take a leap of faith to grasp. In the 1830s, Abraham Gesner, another Nova Scotia-born scientist, had discovered fossils in the Bay of Fundy region. These drew the attention of Charles Lyell, the British founder of modern geology. In 1852 Lyell and Dawson explored the cliffs around Joggins on Chignecto Bay, where they found the earliest reptilian remains discovered in North America

Timeline

1 billion–750 million years BP	Supercontinent Rodinia dominates the earth.
350–200 million years BP	Supercontinent Pangaea, with its coal-forming swamps, dominates the earth; fish and reptiles flourish.
200 million years BP	Pangaea begins to break up, creating the Americas, Eurasia, and Africa.
66 million years BP	Mass extinction of earth's species, including the dinosaurs, perhaps as a result of the impact of an asteroid or meteorite.
2 million–10,000 years BP	Ice Age grips the earth.
20,000 years BP	Glaciers from the last ice age begin to melt.
10,600 years BP	Approximate date of the Paleo-Indian site at Debert: the first known human habitation in the Atlantic region.
10,000–2500 BP	Archaic cultures inhabit the Maritimes and Newfoundland.
4000 BP	Paleo-Eskimos arrive in Labrador.
2500 BP	Woodland (Ceramic) cultures begin to dominate the Maritime region.
2000 BP	Dorset people arrive in Labrador and spread to the island of Newfoundland.
1250–1450 CE	Thule culture arrives in Labrador.

to that time. These findings helped to confirm the view that the earth and its inhabitants were far older than the Book of Genesis suggested.

Scientists now think that the earth is at least 4.5 billion years old, and explain the creation of continents and oceans through the theory of plate tectonics. According to this theory, continents are in constant movement, colliding and breaking apart as they float on the planet's soft, molten interior. When a supercontinent breaks apart into smaller continents, oceans form between them; when those continents collide, the earth's crust buckles to form mountain chains, and pieces of ocean crust, arcs of volcanic islands, and continental fragments litter the landscape. These redistributed elements are called 'terranes'. The Atlantic region represents a collage of such terranes, welded to each other over millions of years of continental movement.[2]

The eastern part of the Canadian Shield dates from the period when several continental fragments came together to create the supercontinent of Rodinia. While all of Labrador is composed of ancient rocks from a mountain-building collision, known as the Grenville Orogeny, the southern boundary of this landform also slips into the Gulf of St Lawrence and parts of Newfoundland. The recent discovery of a fragment (called the Blair River block) of the Grenville Orogen near the northern tip of Cape Breton testifies to the dramatic geological processes that have occurred in the region over billions of years. Indeed, Atlantic Canada boasts some of the earth's oldest landforms: at Saglek Bay in Labrador, for instance, rocks have been found that date back some 3.6 billion years.

Rodinia broke apart into smaller continents about 750 million years ago. As the cycle of continental drift continued, the Atlantic region took shape at the centre of a continent named Pangaea, which itself was formed when ancient continental plates—Laurentia to the west and Gondwana to the east—collided. Evidence of the collision can be seen in many parts of the Atlantic region, but most notably in the section of the Appalachian mountain chain that includes Gros Morne National Park, on the west coast of Newfoundland. In 1987 UNESCO declared Gros Morne a World Heritage Site in recognition of its geological importance.

Two hundred million years ago, the two plates that had formed Pangaea again separated and the space between them was filled by the present Atlantic Ocean. In the break-up, fragments of Gondwana remained attached to Laurentia, including the Eastern Zone of Newfoundland, much of Nova Scotia (the Megumba Zone), and parts of New Brunswick and the northeastern United States. The terrain stretching from northern Africa to Scandinavia bears striking resemblances to the Atlantic shores of the Maritimes and Newfoundland because they were once part of the same land mass.

In the 200 million years since Pangaea divided and the North Atlantic continent began drifting northward, adjustments of the earth's crust and the forces of erosion have eaten away the once rugged mountains of the Appalachian chain and built up the continental shelf, with its rich reserves of oil and natural gas. Water flowing from mountains along the coastal margins and the interior of the continent created the Gulf of St Lawrence, carved out the Cabot Strait and Strait of Belle Isle, and laid down the iron-rich sandstone deposits that are responsible for the red soils of Prince Edward Island. Where water drained into basins creating lakes, life forms emerged. One such lake occupied what is now Albert County in New Brunswick. Lake Albert once teemed with fish and algae, and it is their remains, locked up in the lake sediments, that are the source of the hydrocarbons still being extracted from an oil and gas field near Moncton.

The exposed rocks along the Bay of Fundy reveal dramatic evidence of the last 360 million years of the earth's history. During what is known as the Carboniferous period (286 to 360 million years ago), the region was subjected to repeated buckling and faulting. When the buckling and sediment accumulation were slow, the vegetation that grew on the river flood plains was preserved as coal beds; when these processes occurred more rapidly, forests were drowned, trapping reptiles in hollow tree stumps. The reptiles that Dawson and Lyell discovered in drowned forests were the ancestors of the dinosaurs that would dominate the region for nearly 200 million years until they suddenly became extinct—perhaps as a result of an asteroid or meteorite hitting the earth—some 66 million years ago.

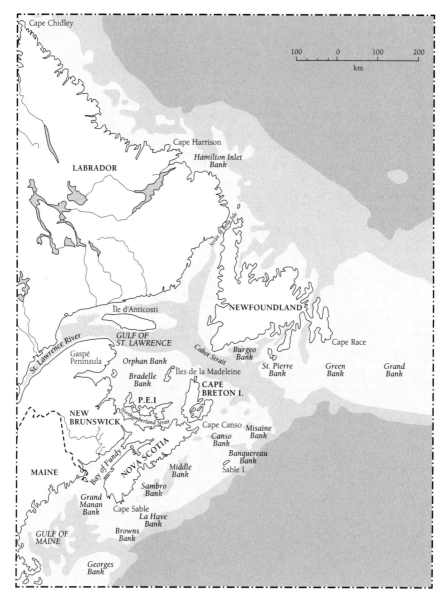

The continental shelf and fishing banks. Adapted from Innis, *The Cod Fishery*, 7.

The final shaping and scraping of the Atlantic landscape occurred during the last Ice Age, which gripped the continent from 2 million to 10,000 years ago. During the Wisconsinan glaciation (75,000 to 10,000 years ago), the Laurentide Ice Sheet gradually expanded to cover most of what is now Canada, including Labrador and the tip of Newfoundland's Northern Peninsula. The rest of Newfoundland and the Maritimes were covered by an independent ice cap, which

'Reptiles of the Coal Period', an illustration from the 1891 edition of J.W. Dawson's *Acadian Geology*.

formed part of the Appalachian Glacier Complex. Ice flowed over earlier river valleys, cut deep valleys and fiords, and dumped boulders, gravel, and fine sand throughout the region. Erratics—glacial debris dropped by the moving ice cap—still litter the landscape in some areas, including along the road to Peggy's Cove, Nova Scotia.

About 20,000 years ago the glaciers of the last ice age began to melt. The sea level rose, fell, and rose again as the ice retreated and the land rebounded from the weight of the glaciers. Prince Edward Island began as three islands; later it was connected to the mainland by a land bridge. In periods when the sea level was low, sections of the continental shelf and much of what is now the undersea coast, including the Bay of Fundy, lay exposed. The Atlantic region took the geological form we recognize today as recently as 3,000 years ago.

The First Peoples

The early history of human habitation in the Atlantic region is difficult to determine because many areas of coastal settlement have sunk below sea level, and the region's acidic soils tend to destroy any organic materials that have not been submerged. As a result there are few sites that offer evidence of continuous occupation over long stretches of time. Archaeological discoveries in recent years have enabled us to imagine the broad outline of the region's early human history, but we may never know the full story.[3]

The earliest North American peoples are called Paleo-Indians. Hunting species such as mammoths, mastodons, and longhorn bison, they moved across the continent from the south and west as the retreating glaciers permitted, adapting their culture to the changing climate, animal species, and vegetation. The oldest

Rock formations at Hopewell, Albert County, New Brunswick. These 'flower pots', carved by the high tides of the Bay of Fundy, are left exposed at low tide. They became popular tourist attractions in the nineteenth century. PANB, New Brunswick Travel Bureau, P93AL-14.

discovered remains of human settlement in the region were found near Debert, Nova Scotia, in the 1960s. Dated to about 10,600 years ago, the site is believed to be a seasonal encampment near a caribou trail passing through the Cobequid Bay region. Although these Paleo-Indians may have relied primarily on caribou for survival, their descendants pursued diverse hunting, fishing, and gathering subsistence patterns, gradually making their way to the rich maritime life of the Strait of Belle Isle, where archaeological evidence dating back nearly 9,000 years has been found at Pinware Hill in southern Labrador.

Paleo-Indian culture, based on chipped stone technology, gave way to a sequence of what are termed Archaic cultures, distinguished from their predecessors by the fact that their stone tools were ground and polished. While it is believed that Archaic peoples inhabited the region from 10,000 to 2,500 years ago, until recently very little was known about the first 5,000 years of their occupation. Because of evidence found near lakes and rivers and from drowned coastal sites in the Bay of Fundy and off Prince Edward Island, archaeologists now agree that the Early and Middle Archaic cultures they have identified in New England also existed in the Maritimes. By the late Archaic period, beginning about 5,000 years ago, there were two distinct groups inhabiting the Atlantic region: the Interior Late Archaic and the Coastal Late Archaic.

The Interior Late Archaic peoples represented an eastern version of the Laurentian tradition that extended from the Great Lakes to the shores of what are now Maine and New Brunswick. The Coastal Late Archaic marks a distinct phase in what the archaeologist James Tuck calls a Maritime Archaic tradition.[4] With local variants, it extended from Maine to Northern Labrador and from Newfoundland to the Gulf of St Lawrence, and reflects a continuous occupation of coastal areas from the Paleo-Indian period to European settlement. There has been considerable debate on this issue, in part because time and tides have eroded areas where these people once lived. B.J. Bourque, for instance, maintains that the Late Archaic in the southwestern Maritimes and Maine represents a separate cultural tradition, which he calls the 'Moorehead phase'.[5]

The evidence is firmer in Labrador and Newfoundland, where archaeologists have been able to document an unbroken Maritime Archaic tradition running from 7,500 to 3,500 years ago. Surviving artifacts from sites such as L'Anse Amour and Port au Choix indicate that a Northern Branch of that tradition spread from the Strait of Belle Isle along the coast of Labrador, eventually reaching Saglek and Ramah bays. The Southern Branch people occupied southern Labrador and were the first humans to colonize the island of Newfoundland, where they established themselves some 5,000 years ago (perhaps even earlier), spreading around the entire coastline with the possible exception of the Avalon Peninsula.

There is also evidence that people belonging to the Broad Point (or Susquehanna) culture, first defined in the Middle Atlantic states of North America, moved into the southwestern extremes of the Maritimes in the late Archaic period. What makes them distinct, apart from the broad points of their artifacts, is the fact that they cremated their dead and buried their ashes and bone fragments in pits. The Broad Point peoples seem not to have penetrated much beyond southwestern New Brunswick and the Yarmouth–Tusket region of Nova Scotia.

Whatever their specific traditions, all Archaic cultures depended—as their Paleo-Indian predecessors had—on some combination of hunting, fishing, and gathering. Their highly mobile communities consisted of bands made up of a few related families, 50 people on the average. Although they carved out territorial jurisdictions, there was probably significant cultural exchange between the sea-based and interior peoples who shared the region's bounty. Surviving tools suggest that they adapted their resources of stone and bone to the job at hand. In the sea-based societies, people fashioned toggling harpoons to spear seals and swordfish, which they then killed using lances tipped with bone and ground slate points. Animals were butchered with stone knives and the skins dressed with bone scrapers. From the bones of small birds and animals people crafted fine needles and awls with which to make shelters, clothing, footwear, and carrying bags. Ground and polished axes, adzes, and gouges were used to fashion wooden spear shafts, traps, and other hunting equipment, as well as wooden bowls, dugout canoes, house frames, and small decorative objects.

Archaic peoples had highly developed spiritual beliefs, burying their dead accompanied by red ochre, tools, weapons, and decorative objects, in cemeteries. If the surviving carved charms, tokens, and amulets are any indication, the Archaic peoples living in the Atlantic region had great respect for the fish, sea birds, whales, and seals on which they depended for survival. At Port au Choix, for example, some of the graves included the remains of a particular bird species, which may have served to identify family lines.

Climatic Change and Cultural Adaptation

Population movements and cultural evolution in the Maritimes appear to be linked to climatic change. About 3,500 years ago, rising sea levels and cooling temperatures encouraged greater reliance on shellfish and fur-bearing animals, and the adoption of new practices and technologies from other cultures. The Maritime Archaic culture as such disappeared. About 2,500 years ago, absorbing influences and perhaps immigrants from the south and west, the Maritime peoples moved into the Woodland (or Ceramic) period, characterized in part by the use of clay pottery. Modern Maliseet and Mi'kmaq have almost certainly descended from the Woodland peoples who predominated in the Maritimes between 500 and 2,500 years ago.

The appearance of ceramics may be an indication that Archaic peoples borrowed technology from adjacent cultures in the New England and St Lawrence regions to meet changing circumstances. The notion of cultural borrowing would allow for more continuous human occupation of the region than has hitherto been considered possible. Such a theory is supported by burial mound sites found on the Red Bank Reserve on the Miramichi and at Skora, near Halifax. Similar to sites associated with the Adena in Ohio, they suggest either that people from the interior of the continent swept through the region 3,000 years ago or that Maritime Archaic people had learned new ways to inter their dead relatives.

Most Woodland sites are located along the coast or on rivers where fish were abundant. From the available evidence, there seems to have been considerable continuity in the seasonal rhythms. For example, some bands in eastern New Brunswick made regular late-winter expeditions to Prince Edward Island to catch sea mammals. While most bands were highly mobile, the discovery of more than a hundred semi-subterranean pit-houses in the Passamaquoddy Bay area suggests that people living there were based in the same village for most of the year. These pit-houses were conical structures framed with poles or saplings covered with skins or sheets of bark, and sometimes banked with a mixture of shells and soil, presumably to keep out the cold.

The peoples of southeastern New Brunswick developed somewhat different cultural patterns, but they shared with their neighbours a dependence on shellfish and the use of clay pots. Shell middens—accumulations of discarded shells of clams, quahogs, mussels, and occasionally scallops or oysters—are found throughout the region and offer valuable evidence about the evolution of Woodland material culture. At a midden site at Sellar's Cove, on the shores of St Margaret's Bay, Nova Scotia, remains from nearly the entire span of the Woodland period indicate that pottery techniques declined, perhaps because people were becoming more mobile. By the time of European contact, both the semi-permanent dwellings along the coast and pottery had disappeared, for reasons that have yet to be fully explained.

Mobility was greatly advanced by the use of birchbark for making dishes, bas-

Archaeological sites in the Atlantic region. Adapted from Buckner and Reid, *The Atlantic Region to Confederation*, 4.

kets, and especially canoes. Ribs for canoes were made from cedar and thwarts from maple or other hardwoods. Woodland peoples appear to have used their canoes primarily for river and coastal travel, but they were clearly able to navigate the Northumberland Strait, the Strait of Canso, and perhaps the Cabot Strait as well. Before the arrival of Europeans, the region's Aboriginal peoples had also adopted the bow and arrow.

Dorset Paleo-Eskimo artifacts, 1,300 to 2,000 years old, from Port au Choix in northwestern Newfoundland. Clockwise from top left: a bone harpoon head tipped with a stone end-blade, two typical Dorset triangular end-blades, two end-scrapers, two ground nephrite engraving tools, a chipped-stone knife, three microblades, and a bone point. At the bottom is a segment of a whalebone sled-runner, and above that a stone awl. M.A.P. Renouf, MUN.

Newfoundland and Labrador experienced the same climatic shift that affected the Maritimes, but received successive immigrants from the north rather than the south and west.[6] The first of these were the Groswater Paleo-Eskimos, who arrived in coastal Labrador nearly 4,000 years ago and later spread to the island of Newfoundland, replacing the Maritime Archaic people. In turn, their culture was replaced about 2,000 years ago by the Late Paleo-Eskimo, usually called Dorset, who probably originated in the Hudson Bay–Foxe Basin area. They disappeared from the island of Newfoundland by the ninth century and from Labrador by 1300. Skilled in crafting stone, bone, and ivory tools, the Dorset people produced distinctive soapstone lamps and cooking vessels as well as whalebone 'shoes' to protect the runners on their sleds, which they probably hauled themselves.

The direct ancestors of the modern Labrador Inuit were the Thule, the last major group to migrate there from the western Arctic. Adept at catching whales with their large toggling harpoons, kayaks, and umiaks, they moved quickly across the High Arctic. Their success was facilitated by a warming trend about 1,000 years ago, which reduced the sea ice and drew both bowhead and right whales into the northern waters. Arriving in the extreme north of Labrador between 1250 and 1450, they reached Saglek by 1500, and soon after that encountered Europeans in the Strait of Belle Isle.

Since the material culture of the Thule has been well preserved, we know more about their lifestyles than those of most early peoples in the region. The typical house was an oval-shaped, semi-subterranean structure with three levels, entered through a tunnel leading to a slightly elevated flagstone floor. At the rear was a raised sleeping platform. A low earthen exterior wall supported a whalebone interior frame, which was covered with baleen and sod to create a domed roof. It seems likely that the Thule people also built igloos—although it is impossible to trace their fast-disappearing remains. The Thule had teams of dogs trained to pull their sleds. By 1500 right whales were the main stay of their diet, supplemented by the sea mammals, birds, fish, land animals, and wild berries that flourished in the region.

The origins of the modern Labrador Innu are imperfectly understood, but have been traced back about 1,000 years to a tradition known to archaeologists as Recent Indian, whose remains have been found at Point Revenge. On the island of Newfoundland, the Little Passage people, named for the site near Gaultois on Newfoundland's south coast, were also Recent Indians and the direct ancestors of the Beothuk.

Conclusion

The history of the peoples of Atlantic Canada before European contact shifts constantly as new archaeological evidence emerges and gives rise to new theories. Many questions remain unanswered, but it is now possible to trace the main outlines of a story of continuous human occupation beginning with the arrival of Paleo-Indians over 10,000 years ago. What we can say for certain is that archaeologists have opened a fascinating window on past cultures in the Atlantic region, which has a long history of peoples encountering environmental change, new technologies, and new populations.

Chapter Two

Aboriginal Peoples

With the arrival of Europeans in the later fifteenth century, a much more detailed picture of Aboriginal societies begins to emerge. Europeans were intrigued by the 'New World' that they had found, and many of them wrote meticulous descriptions of its peoples and their ways of life. While their accounts must be treated with caution, they add an important dimension to the story told by the surviving material culture and the oral traditions of indigenous peoples.

In the Atlantic region the newcomers encountered at least five cultural groups, which they called Eskimo and Montagnais–Naskapi in Labrador, Beothuk in Newfoundland, Micmac and Malecite in the Maritimes. These were not necessarily the names that those peoples used to identify themselves. In recent years, for example, northern people have objected to 'Eskimo', whose origins are obscure; they prefer to be called 'Inuit', meaning simply 'the people'—a term that many Aboriginal groups used at the time of contact to distinguish themselves from the other creatures with whom they shared the land. More recently, Aboriginal peoples have begun adopting names and spellings that reflect their own language structures rather than imposed Europeanized versions. Thus 'Micmac' becomes 'Mi'kmaq', 'Malecite' becomes 'Maliseet' (or Wulstukwiuk) and 'Montagnais–Naskapi' becomes simply 'Innu'.

When Cabot embarked on his first transatlantic voyage, the human population of the Americas was no less varied than that of Europe.[1] Natives of the Atlantic region lived on the eastern edge of a world that included complex empires, city-states, confederacies, and chiefdoms, as well as band communities like their own. The Labrador Inuit were the easternmost branch of a culture stretching across the Arctic, while the Mi'kmaq, Maliseet, Beothuk, and Innu belonged to the Algonkian language group, which occupied an extensive territory from the Atlantic to the Rockies. Essentially communal societies, they were largely self-sufficient, though in contact with each other.

All pre-contact peoples in the Americas shared a worldview according to which humans were part of a cosmological order that included the land and its animals, the stars, and the sea. The universe functioned harmoniously only when natural forces were in balance—a condition maintained by elaborate rituals. Because of their strong spiritual beliefs, most of the surviving evidence of pre-contact Aboriginal societies takes the form of burial sites, not monuments to the living. What today would be called the natural and social sciences were highly devel-

Aboriginal peoples in the sixteenth century.

oped. Before the arrival of Europeans, North Americans had calculated the movement of the sun and stars and understood a great deal about the medicinal properties of plants.

As primarily hunter-gatherers, the peoples of the Atlantic region followed a seasonal round that allowed them to make the most effective use possible of the resources around them. They shared characteristics with other northeastern Woodland cultures that dominated present-day New England and Québec, but also had access to the region's rich ocean resources. Although long winters, especially in Newfoundland and Labrador, sometimes made survival difficult, the Aboriginal peoples of the Atlantic region were relatively affluent by the standards of northern North America at the time of European contact.

The Mi'kmaq and Maliseet of the Maritimes

The Mi'kmaq were the most numerous of the Aboriginal groups living in the Atlantic region in 1500. While estimates of their numbers at the time of contact range from 3,500 to 200,000, the scholarly consensus now suggests a figure of about 12,000–15,000.[2] The extended family, sometimes supplemented by a few unrelated individuals, was the basic unit of Mi'kmaq society. Headed by a chief or sakamow, this unit formed the summer village that could number as many as 200 people, but broke up into smaller groups during the winter. Summer was also a time for Mi'kmaq leaders to come together to consult among themselves on matters of common interest.

By the eighteenth century the Mi'kmaq were divided into seven districts, each governed by a chief who presided over a council of chiefs from each district's communities. This form of political organization may only have developed in response to European trade, but the significance of chiefs seems to have been deeply rooted in Mi'kmaq society. Nicolas Denys, a French fur trader who spent several decades in the Maritimes in the seventeenth century, noted that the Mi'kmaq greatly valued the genealogical traditions that linked them to a line of 'ancient chiefs' stretching back more than twenty generations.[3]

Although ocean resources featured prominently in the Mi'kmaq diet, the moose played an important role in the Mi'kmaq economy. Every part of the animal was used. Its meat was eaten fresh and dried, its bones rendered a highly nutritious moose butter, called *cacamos*, and the skin was fashioned into clothing, moccasins, carrying bags, and snowshoe webbing. Antlers and bones were turned into tools, weapons, and needles. Moose brains were used in tanning skins, dewclaws became rattles, shin bones were carved into dice, tendons served as thread, hair was used in embroidery, and hoofs yielded an ingredient used to treat epilepsy. While moose were killed throughout the year, they were most easily caught in the winter, when snowdrifts impeded their escape from hunters speeding along on snowshoes.

Mi'kmaq men were skilled at hunting, using dogs to help them track down their prey, which were then dispatched with spears and arrows. Fish were so plentiful that they were easy to catch with three-pronged spears, loosely woven nets, and weirs. The Mi'kmaq method for trapping migrating birds was particularly ingenious. Under the cover of darkness, men floated their canoes among a flock of ducks or geese; they would then light torches, which confused the birds and caused them to circle the light, enabling the hunters to knock them down with long poles.

Oral History

> To preserve the fire, especially in winter, we would entrust it to the care of our war-chief's women, who took turns to preserve the spark, using half-rotten pine wood covered with ash. Sometimes this fire lasted up to three moons. When it lasted the span of three moons, the fire became sacred and magical to us, and we showered with a thousand praises the chief's woman who had been the fire's guardian during the last days of the third moon. We would all gather together and, so that no member of the families which had camped there since the autumn should be absent, we sent out young men to fetch those who were missing. Then, when our numbers were complete, we would gather round and, without regard to age or rank, light our pipes at the fire. We would suck in the smoke and keep it in our mouths, and one by one we would puff it into the face of the woman who had last preserved the spark, telling her that she was worthy above all to share in the benign influence of the Father of Light, the Sun, because she had so skilfully preserved his emanations.[4]

It is now widely recognized that oral traditions are more reliable than text-bound historians used to believe. Certainly this account of a Mi'kmaq cultural tradition, recorded in the 1740s on what is now Prince Edward Island, is powerfully evocative; it also reveals more than any inert artifact could about the problems that a Maritime winter posed for the region's indigenous people. At the same time, it leaves many unanswered questions. We have no way of knowing, for example, whether the practice described here was still current in the 1740s, or how widespread it may have been. Moreover, although the account is attributed to Chief Arguimaut (L'kimu), it was preserved for posterity by a Roman Catholic missionary, the Abbé Pierre Maillard. The evidence of ethnographers is rarely accepted without scrutiny today, and we must not lose our critical perspective when we discover a rare archival document, even (or perhaps especially) one written by a priest. The Europeans who first came into contact with Aboriginal peoples had a Christian world view, a sense of cultural superiority, and a gendered perspective that often led them to misinterpret—perhaps deliberately, perhaps unconsciously—what they heard and saw. For all its seeming authenticity, this oral account must be treated like any other historical evidence: as the product of a particular time and place, with no greater claim to truth than any other kind of evidence.

By the time of European contact the Mi'kmaq no longer used clay pots to cook their food, but fashioned watertight containers from birchbark stitched with spruce roots and sealed with spruce gum; heated stones from the fire would be placed in the pot until its contents boiled.

Europeans frequently commented on Mi'kmaq gender roles, courtship practices, and family relationships. According to Chrestien Le Clercq, a Récollet missionary in the Gaspé region in the second half of the seventeenth century, the Mi'kmaq were patriarchal, subordinating women and 'mooseless' younger males to the authority of adult men:

> The women have no command among the Indians. They must needs obey the orders of their husbands. They have no rights in councils, nor in the public feasts. It is the same, as to this, with the young men who have not yet killed any moose, the death of which opens the portal to the honours of the Gaspesian nation, and gives to the young men the right to assist at public and private assemblies. One is always a young man, that is to say, one has no more rights than the children, the women, and the girls, as long as he has not killed a moose.[5]

Polygamy was practised, Le Clercq reported, and marriages were easily dissolved, especially when no children were involved. The method of carrying infants drew Le Clercq's particular attention. 'In place of a cradle, they make the children rest upon a little board, which they cover with the skins of beaver or with some other furs.' Both the cradleboard and the infant's clothing were adorned with beadwork, porcupine quills, and painted designs, which Le Clercq believed were used 'to beautify it, and to render it just so much the finer in proportion as they love their children'.

Like all Aboriginal peoples in the Atlantic region, the Mi'kmaq had a complex world view that helped them to explain their existence. They considered the sun and moon to be the ancestors of 'People', who lived on the Earth, which was part of a spiritual universe made up of Six Worlds. In addition to the Earth World, there was the World beneath the Water, the World beneath the Earth, the World above the Sky, and the World above the Earth. After death, the People went to the Ghost World, which a very few managed to visit while still living.

The Mi'kmaq universe formed itself out of Power, which was manifested in people, animals, plants, and phenomena such as winds, weather, seasons, and directions. Not only could one form of power change into another—a person into a wolf, or a stone into a person—but the character or state of mind of the power force could also change, from good to evil, for instance, or strong to weak. This notion of power made for an unpredictable universe, but it encouraged people to acquire and use power responsibly through proper behaviour.

At the time of contact, people with special spiritual powers played a major role in articulating the Mi'kmaq sense of the world and the appropriate ways of living in it. Legends helped to remind people of spiritual truths and signs representing spiritual phenomena, such as the sun, were often incorporated as intricate designs on clothing, adornments, and other material possessions. Believing that dreams and trances helped them to contact spirit powers, the Mi'kmaq placed great emphasis on developing ways to achieve altered states of consciousness and paid close attention to the knowledge revealed in their dreams.

The Maliseet, who lived in what is now southwestern New Brunswick and

This engraving of an 'homme Acadien' shows a Mi'kmaq marked with various symbols, including both a sun and crosses. LAC, c-21112.

northeastern Maine, shared many characteristics with the Mi'kmaq. According to Mi'kmaq lore, the Maliseet were a break-away tribe, but the Maliseet believe their differences are rooted in deeper cultural patterns. In the early contact period, the Maliseet were distinguished from other Aboriginal groups in the Atlantic region by the fact that they grew corn and may have done so before the arrival of Europeans.

Both Native oral history and early European records suggest that there was conflict between the Maliseet and their Mi'kmaq neighbours, but we have no way of knowing the extent of the enmity in the pre-contact period. What is clear is that when the Mi'kmaq gained access to European weapons, they used their military advantage to expand their control over the Gaspé Peninsula as well as portions of the Saint John River watershed, which had traditionally been Maliseet territory.[6] By the seventeenth century, the Mi'kmaq were scoring victories over the Abenaki as far south as the Saco River in Maine.

Whether the Mi'kmaq were present in southern Newfoundland (Ktaqmkuk) before the sixteenth century is disputed. Some scholars who accept the validity of

Mi'kmaq oral tradition believe that Mi'kmaq crossed the Cabot Strait and hunted on the island. Others note that there is no archaeological evidence to support this claim, and argue that the crossing would not have been possible before the Mi'kmaq acquired European boats.

The Beothuk, Innu, and Inuit of Newfoundland and Labrador

Until recently not a great deal was known about the Beothuk, an Algonkian people who chose to remain apart from Europeans and became extinct in the 1820s. Perhaps numbering as many as 2,000 in 1500, they were among the first Aboriginal people that Europeans encountered in North America. Because they painted themselves with red ochre, they may have inspired the term 'Red Indian'. For food and clothing the Beothuk depended heavily on caribou, which they hunted during the herds' fall migrations, although marine resources such as seals, seabirds, fish, and shellfish were also important. Moving frequently to accommodate the seasonal round, the Beothuk travelled long distances in distinctive, light-weight birchbark canoes and lived in easily assembled wigwams—sometimes conical, sometimes oval or multi-sided—covered with hides or birchbark.

The Beothuk were probably in contact with the Innu, who by 1500 were living on the south coast and interior of Labrador, but they tended to stay away from the Inuit. For the most part based in the coastal area north of Hamilton Inlet, the Inuit moved farther south on a seasonal basis, especially after Europeans arrived in the Strait of Belle Isle. The Innu relied heavily on what the interior could provide, principally caribou and a variety of freshwater fish, which they caught in the winter and spring. During the summer months they gathered on the coast in large groups to hunt whales, seals, and saltwater fish before breaking into small bands to winter in the interior.

Like other Aboriginal groups in the region, the Innu shared the rewards of a successful hunt and encouraged egalitarian values. Open displays of anger were repressed, decisions were made through discussion and consensus, and conformity was encouraged through joking and ridicule. Patience and good humour were considered important virtues. In contrast to Europeans, who practised a harsh discipline aimed largely at breaking children's will, the Innu spared their children physical punishment. Although gender roles were clearly defined, Europeans remarked on the independence and relative power of Innu women, who dominated the life-sustaining lodge hearth, controlled the distribution of food, and readily left husbands who were not good providers.

The Labrador Inuit were primarily a coastal people, though caribou were also important to them for both food and clothing. During the fall and winter the people lived in semi-subterranean sod houses at the mouths of fiords, the men hunting whales and seals from their kayaks and umiaks until the sea froze, when they would hunt seals through the ice. In the spring some Inuit fished through lake ice, while others built snow houses on the outer islands and lived on seals, fish, and mussels. In early summer everyone moved to the islands, where skin tents replaced

Before her death in 1829, Shanawdithit, the last surviving Beothuk on the island of Newfoundland, drew these images depicting aspects of her culture. LAC, c-28544.

sod huts and snow houses. In July the Inuit congregated at places where salmon was plentiful, before migrating inland to hunt caribou.

The success of the hunt was assisted by shamans, or *angakut*, who mediated between the human and spirit worlds. In 1772 the Moravian missionaries at Nain reported that a female shaman 'fell into a trance, when her soul took a tour through the inland parts, where she saw a vast quantity of Rain Deer. Upon this the Esquimaux went to the inlet as directed by her, where they saw and got many deer'.[7] Shamans also treated sickness, which was thought to be caused by evil spirits, and in general helped Inuit to make sense of their lives and deaths.

One of the earliest European images of North America is a woodcut of an Inuit mother and daughter, probably from Labrador, who were captured by French fishermen and taken to Europe in 1566. The fact that kidnappers had killed the woman's husband before taking their captives foreshadowed the hostile relations that quickly developed between Inuit and newcomers. Writing in the early seventeenth century, Samuel de Champlain noted that the Inuit were 'very malicious . . . [attacking] fishermen, who in self defence arm small vessels to protect the boats which put to sea to fish cod'.[8] In later years the French would be slow to establish fishing and sealing stations on the Labrador coast, in part because of their justified fear of the Inuit.

The Capture of an Inuit Woman and her Child

Printed in Augsburg in 1567, this woodcut is the first known European depiction of Inuit drawn from life. The woman and child had been put on exhibition in Europe after being captured on the Labrador coast the previous year. From W.C. Sturtevant, 'The First Inuit Depiction by Europeans', *Etudes Inuit Studies* 4, 1–2 (1980), 47–9.

Europeans frequently took Native people captive and either forced them to work as slaves or put them on display as curiosities. The Inuit woman and child shown in this woodcut were captured in 1566 on the Labrador coast by French sailors and taken to Europe. The image—the first known drawing from life of Inuit people—was published in 1567 on what was likely a handbill advertising an exhibition in Augsburg, Germany. The text reads (in part):

> In this year 1566 there arrived in Antwerp . . . a savage woman (a small person) together with her little daughter, and she is shaped and clothed as this picture shows, and was found in Nova Terra. . . . [T]his woman with her husband and little child were met by the French . . . and the husband was shot through his body with an arrow. However he would not surrender but took his stand bravely to defend himself. . . . Finally he was struck and wounded in his throat so severely that he fell to the ground and died from the wound. This man was 12 feet tall and had in twelve days killed eleven people with his own hand, French and Portuguese, in order to eat them. . . . [T]hen they took the woman with her child and brought her away; and none of the Frenchmen could understand a single word of hers or speak with her at all. But she was taught enough in 8 months that it was known she had eaten many men. Her clothing is made of seal skins.

. . . The paint marks she has on her face are entirely blue [and] . . . cannot be taken off again. . . . Her body is yellow-brown. . . . The woman was 20 years old when she was captured . . . the child 7 years. Let us thank God the Almighty that He has enlightened us with His word so that we are not such savage people and man-eaters as are in this district, that this woman was captured and brought out of there, since she knows nothing of the true God, but lives almost more wickedly than the beasts. God grant that she be converted to acknowledge Him. Amen.[9]

Conclusion

Every Aboriginal group in the Atlantic region would have had dramatic tales to tell once Europeans began to frequent their coasts in the early sixteenth century. In each case the encounter brought disease, death, and social and economic dislocation, even to those who, like the Mi'kmaq, had initially welcomed the Europeans and what they had to offer. The least affected were the most remote—the Inuit and northern Innu bands. Those who lived around the Gulf of St Lawrence bore the brunt of the first European efforts to explore, fish, trade, and spread the Christian faith.

Chapter Three

European Encounters: 1000–1598

When there were no people in this country but Indians, and before any others became known, a young woman had a singular dream. . . . A small island came floating in towards the land, with tall trees on it, and living beings. [The shaman] pondered the girl's dream but could make nothing of it. The next day an event occurred that explained all. What should they see but a singular little island, as they supposed, which had drifted near to the land and become stationary there. There were trees on it, and branches to the trees, on which a number of bears . . . were crawling about. . . . What was their surprise to find that these supposed bears were men.[1]

Josiah Jeremy's account of one Mi'kmaq community's first sighting of hirsute Europeans and their tall-masted sailing ships was recorded by Silas Rand, a nineteenth-century Baptist missionary. What encounter this story describes is impossible to determine, but one thing is clear: the meeting of two very different cultures marked the beginning of a new era for both.

The Norse

The first Europeans to reach Atlantic Canada were the Norse. Their arrival in Labrador and Newfoundland around 1,000 years ago marked the final stage in a process that had begun in Scandinavia several centuries earlier. Waves of migrants, often preceded by the raiders we know as Vikings, spread across northern Europe, and then westward over the North Atlantic. Unlike their successors 500 years later, they were looking not for Asia but for land that they could settle.

Eirik the Red colonized southeastern Greenland late in the tenth century. Shortly thereafter, in 986, a merchant-shipowner named Bjarni Herjolfsson was blown off-course while travelling to the new settlement. Finding himself sailing along an unknown coastline, he headed north and then east to Greenland without taking time to explore, but his voyage was remembered. A few years later, Leif Eiriksson retraced Bjarni's route in reverse. According to evidence from the Norse sagas, Leif found three lands. The first he called Helluland; consisting primarily of rock and ice, it was probably Baffin Island. The second, Markland, was flat, wooded, and almost certainly part of southern Labrador. Leif then reached

Timeline

c. 1000	Greenland Norse reach northeastern America.
1492	Columbus discovers the Caribbean.
1497	John Cabot reaches Newfoundland.
1498	Cabot disappears on his second voyage.
1500	Gaspar Corte Real reaches 'terra verde'.
1502	First known English fishing voyage to Newfoundland.
1504	First known French fishing voyage to Newfoundland.
1508–9	Sebastian Cabot looks for the northwest passage.
1520s	Basques enter the Newfoundland fishery.
1524	Giovanni da Verrazzano sails along the North American coast.
1525	Possible Portuguese colony on Cape Breton.
1534	Jacques Cartier's first voyage to the Gulf of St Lawrence.
1550s	French develop offshore bank fishery; Basques develop whaling industry in the Strait of Belle Isle.
1580s	English west country ports begin to enter Newfoundland fishery; decline of the Portuguese and Spanish fisheries.

a country he called Vinland, with grassy meadows and well-stocked rivers. The expedition over-wintered there before returning to Greenland.

Where was Vinland? This question has been debated for many years, and various locations along the northeastern American seaboard have been proposed. The only direct physical evidence that exists is the Norse habitation discovered in 1961 at L'Anse aux Meadows on Newfoundland's Northern Peninsula, yet in some ways it does not fit the saga descriptions of Vinland. The scholarly consensus today reconciles the literary and physical evidence by arguing that L'Anse aux Meadows was a base camp at the entrance to Vinland, a region that encompassed the Gulf of St Lawrence.

Leif Eiriksson made several later expeditions, and others followed. The—most ambitious of the known Norse ventures was that of Thorfinn Karslefni, who attempted to establish a settlement in Vinland and remained there for several years. Like at least one of its predecessors, Thorfinn's expedition found it impossible to co-exist with the people living in the region, whom the Norse called Skraelings—a highly derogatory term meaning 'wretches' or 'savages'. Largely as a result of conflicts with the Skraelings, Thorfinn retreated to Greenland. The Norse never created a permanent settlement in Vinland, and stopped travelling there. Whether their encounter with America had any impact in Europe is uncertain, but some scholars think that the story lingered on, and that later explorers such as John Cabot may well have heard rumours of lands to the west.

Reconstructed Norse dwellings at L'Anse aux Meadows, Newfoundland. The only authentic Norse site in North America was discovered in 1960 by Helge and Anne Stine Ingstad. Subsequent excavations revealed nine structures from the eleventh century—houses, workshops, and a forge—of the same kind as those built in Iceland and Greenland. The buildings were made of sods laid over a frame, with long, narrow fireplaces in the middle of the floor. These replicas were built a short distance from the actual ruins. Photo J. Steeves, Parks Canada, Department of Canadian Heritage.

Europeans on the Move

The possibility of other transatlantic voyages before the late fifteenth century has generated enormous interest and a large literature of uneven quality. Some think that St Brendan set sail in a curragh from Dingle Bay in Ireland with seventeen monks sometime in the sixth century and landed in Newfoundland or some other part of America. Others claim that the Welsh Prince Madoc reached Florida in 1170, or that the Scottish Prince Henry Sinclair landed in Chedabucto Bay on 2 June 1398 (an embellishment has Sinclair burying the holy grail at Oak Island, on the southern shore of what is now Nova Scotia). The more plausible theories limit themselves to suggesting that English vessels from Bristol, and Portuguese vessels from the Azores, may have reached North America sometime between 1450 and 1492.

The first to undertake the systematic exploration of the Atlantic were the Portuguese who probed south along the African coast and then began reaching farther west. Their goal was to develop new sea routes to India and other parts of Asia, in an effort to share in the lucrative spice trade monopolized by the Italians. By the end of the fifteenth century, the Portuguese had rounded the Cape of Good Hope and reached India, sparking increasing interest all along the European Atlantic seaboard in the possibility of reaching Asia by sailing west.

L'Anse aux Meadows

Although similar to other Norse sites of the eleventh century, the settlement at L'Anse aux Meadows differed in several important ways. First, the Norse usually sought sheltered places, but this site is very exposed. Second, there is no evidence of livestock or other animals, nor of barns or byres. Of the nine buildings that have been excavated at the site eight were sod dwellings; the other was a small forge.

The houses were designed for year-round habitation, and could accommodate between 70 and 90 people. The artifacts and debris that have survived suggest that women were present, but that most of the inhabitants were men. The main activities seem to have been carpentry, iron manufacture, and smithing—activities associated with boat repair and possibly boat building.

Most scholars now agree that L'Anse aux Meadows was a base for exploration and a transshipment point for goods collected elsewhere. It was not, and was not meant to be, a permanent colony. The archaeologist Birgitta Wallace thinks that the site is almost certainly the 'Straumfjord' mentioned in Eirik the Red's Saga, and that the Norse had a summer camp, which the saga calls 'Hóp', somewhere in northeastern New Brunswick. The cargoes sent back to Greenland would have consisted mainly of lumber and wild grapes.[2]

This base camp did not have a long life. While the Norse clashed with the local inhabitants, they were not driven out, and appear to have left in an orderly way. What Vinland had to offer was not vital to them, but the Norse continued for some time to visit Markland (Labrador).

Europeans had known for centuries that the earth was round, but for good reasons were reluctant to venture too far out to sea. With the development of more seaworthy vessels and improvements in navigational instruments in the fifteenth century, captains were better able to establish their positions, set their courses with reasonable accuracy, and sail for days without sighting land. These advances enabled Christopher Columbus, sailing in the name of the Spanish Crown in 1492, to reach what he (and everyone else in Europe) thought was Asia, but was in fact the Caribbean. Five years later another Italian mariner, Zuan Caboto (known to the English as John Cabot), also reached what was assumed to be Asia, where he raised a cross along with the banners of England and Venice.

Cabot had sailed from Bristol, England, on 2 May 1497, in a small vessel called the *Matthew*. Commissioned by King Henry VII to 'sail to all parts, regions, and coasts of the eastern, western, and northern sea' and authorized 'to conquer, occupy, and possess whatever towns, castles, cities, and islands, he discovered', Cabot returned to England in August bringing tales of 'new founde landes' whose adjacent waters swarmed 'with fish which can be taken not only with the net, but in baskets let down with a stone'.

Because the evidence is scanty, the location of Cabot's landfall has been the

subject of considerable debate. There are, roughly speaking, three groups of inter-
pretations: those that favour a landfall in the Strait of Belle Isle region; those that
argue for the east coast of Newfoundland; and those that champion Cape Breton
or points further south. Most Maritime historians used to support the claims of
Cape Breton, arguing that Cabot would have been carried south by storms and
ocean currents, and that cartographic evidence supports their case. Newfoundlanders have consistently dismissed these arguments, holding it as an article of faith
that Cabot's first landfall was Cape Bonavista. How, they ask, could he have missed
Newfoundland? And does not John Mason's 1617 map bear the legend 'Bona Vista
Caboto primum reperta'? Today most scholars lean towards a northern landfall,
somewhere either side of the Strait of Belle Isle. Cabot would have sailed north
along the Irish coast before turning west, and as a skilled navigator would have
been capable of holding that latitude.

Pleased by Cabot's apparent success, Henry VII authorized a larger expedition
in 1498, financed by Bristol merchants. Virtually nothing is known about this voyage, in the course of which Cabot himself disappeared. It seems likely that his ships
would have returned to the lands found in 1497 and then sailed south, looking in
vain for 'Cipango' (China). Information on early sixteenth-century maps suggests
that some of Cabot's ships returned to describe their findings. There were a few
more voyages from Bristol to the new lands, but the city's merchants were, for the
most part, more interested in trade than fishing. It was not until the second half of
the sixteenth century that England began to take a renewed interest in what North
America had to offer.

Meanwhile, Spain and Portugal had established that the Atlantic was the highway to the immense resource-base of the Americas. In 1494, by the Treaty of
Tordesillas, they divided the non-Christian world between them (with the blessing of the Pope). A north–south line was drawn west of the Cape Verde Islands:
territory west of the line was awarded to Spain, east of it to Portugal. Cabot may
have been trespassing.

In any event, his findings stimulated further exploration. Assuming that the
'new' lands in the North Atlantic lay within his sphere, King Manoel of Portugal
authorized a number of voyages by inhabitants of the Azores, sometimes in alliance
with Bristol merchants. In 1499 João Fernandes, a small landowner or 'labrador',
reached Greenland, which as a result was called 'Labrador' on some early maps. In
the sixteenth century the name was transferred to the coast of North America,
where it has since remained. In 1500 Gaspar Corte-Real reached 'Terra Verde'—
probably Newfoundland. There he captured 60 of the local people and delivered
them to Lisbon, where they attracted widespread interest. According to the
Venetian ambassador, the captives were 'tall, well-built' and 'will make the best
slaves I have ever seen'.[3] The family was awarded a 'captaincy' in eastern
Newfoundland, and Corte-Real returned to North America with three ships in
1501, but his vessel disappeared. A similar fate befell his brother Miguel in 1502.
A third brother made a futile attempt to find them both in 1503.

Although these voyages provided cartographers with important new information, it was not yet understood that the 'new founde landes' were part of a new

continent. Contemporary maps show the 'discoveries' of Columbus, Cabot, and the Portuguese either as islands in the ocean or as connected with Greenland and Asia. By the 1520s, though, the shape of the Americas was emerging. An important contribution to this process was made by Giovanni da Verrazzano. In 1524, on behalf of the French king, he explored the coast between the Carolinas and Cape Breton, and possibly part of Newfoundland as well. His purpose had been to find a passage to Asia, but instead he ascertained the existence of a continuous North American coastline and established the first formal link between France and North America. Similar voyages were made in 1524–5 on behalf of Spain by Estevão Gomes (who kidnapped a large number of Native people, probably on the Nova Scotian coast), and for England's Henry VIII by John Rut, who in 1527 sailed from Labrador to the Caribbean. It is probable but not certain that the Portuguese navigator João Alvarez Fagundes led an expedition in 1525 from the Azores to establish a colony, possibly on Cape Breton Island. Its failure has been attributed to the climate and the hostility of the local inhabitants.

In 1534 the king of France, François I, commissioned Jacques Cartier to sail beyond Newfoundland to 'discover certain islands and countries where it is said a great quantity of gold and other precious things are to be found'. From a landfall near Bonavista, Cartier sailed through the Strait of Belle Isle and circumnavigated the Gulf of St Lawrence, thinking that it was an inland sea. He found the north shore of the gulf uninviting, but on sighting Prince Edward Island on a warm summer day he proclaimed it 'the best-tempered region one can possibly see'. He spent little time exploring it, and seems not to have determined that it was an island. On his second voyage, in 1535, he found the entrance to the St Lawrence River. He and his men spent the winter of 1535–6 near present-day Québec City, and in 1541–2 he participated in an unsuccessful attempt to establish a permanent European settlement there.

With Cartier's voyages the first phase in the European discovery of North America came to an end. The coastline from Mexico to Greenland had been explored, described, and mapped. For most of the explorers, who had no intention of staying, their voyages ended in disappointment. They found neither gold nor spices, and the Native people were sometimes hostile. Even the northwest passage to Asia eluded them, although for many years English explorers, beginning with John Cabot's son Sebastian in 1508–9, tried to find it. Nevertheless, the first generation of explorers had located a region that some Europeans thought potentially rich and profitable. Cabot might not have found spices or precious metals, but he had located a rich new source of fish.

The Fishery

The northwest Atlantic fishery quickly emerged as a very profitable business. In this period fishing employed more Europeans than any other occupation except agriculture. Fish was an important source of protein, easy to preserve and transport, and often replaced meat on Roman Catholic fast days. Moreover, work in the fishery served to train mariners for service at sea in time of war. Thus the

A reconstructed Basque chalupa at Red Bay, Labrador. Crewed by six men and powered by either sails or oars, shallops such as this one were used for whaling in the Strait of Belle Isle. Photo Kevin Redmond, Parks Canada, 1998.

Atlantic region rapidly became 'a pole of European activity in every way comparable to that of the Caribbean and the Gulf of Mexico',[4] especially as there were opportunities to hunt whales and trade for furs. In the 1580s Spain was sending about a hundred ships and four or five thousand men to central America each year. Meanwhile, the Atlantic region attracted at least 400 European ships a year, possibly more, carrying approximately 10,000 men. They returned with some 200,000 metric tonnes of cod, and furs besides.

Although the English had sponsored Cabot, they were not the first to make significant use of the new fishing grounds. English markets were adequately supplied by local and Icelandic fisheries. Moreover, their major fishing ports were on the northeast coast—not the best starting point for transatlantic voyages. The ports of northern and eastern France were better positioned, and French markets for North Sea cod were already in place before the Cabot voyage. Vessels from Channel ports in Brittany and Normandy were therefore the first to fish regularly in Newfoundland waters, possibly as early as 1504. In their wake came fishermen from Atlantic ports such as Bordeaux and La Rochelle, who, after 1520, were joined by Basques from southern France and northern Spain. By the 1520s between 60 and 90 French vessels were crossing the Atlantic each year to the region known variously as 'the new found land', 'terre neuve', or 'terra de bacalhao'.

The role of Portugal in the north Atlantic fishery of the sixteenth century is a subject of some controversy. Certainly there was a Portuguese presence in the region, but whether it included a fishery of any significance is debatable. Given the current state of knowledge, the most that can be said is that the Portuguese sent over relatively few vessels and seem, on the whole, to have been more interested in the region's landward potential than in codfish. Nevertheless, Portuguese-derived place names line the shore south of St John's, among them Cape Spear (Cauo da espera), Ferryland (Farilham), and Cape Race (Capo raso).

The French ranged widely throughout the region. Bretons and Normans fished at Cape Breton and Gaspé. Later in the sixteenth century they moved along the coast of the Nova Scotia peninsula and into the Bay of Fundy. French and Spanish Basques often fished together off the Gaspé Peninsula, in the Gulf of St Lawrence, and in the Strait of Belle Isle (la Grande Baye). At Newfoundland, Bretons concentrated on the northeast coast between Cape St John and Cape Bauld (le Petit Nord). French and Basque vessels alike used the island's south coast, from Trepassey to Fortune Bay (la Côte du Chapeau Rouge), and Placentia emerged as the centre of the northwest Atlantic fishery. These were at first shore-based fisheries, but later in the century France also began to exploit the offshore banks—first the Grand Bank, then those off southern Newfoundland and in the Gulf.

Another form of mid-century diversification was the Basques' development of a whaling industry in the Strait of Belle Isle. They established stations on the Labrador coast between Cape Charles and the St Paul River, the most important at Red Bay (Butus, or Hable des Buttes), where archaeologists have recently excavated both the buildings and the wreck of the *San Juan*, a galleon that sank there in 1565. At the height of the industry, some 30 Basque ships hunted right and bowhead whales annually, employing about 2,500 men. Although whalers sometimes remained in Labrador for the winter, such sojourns were usually involuntary, the result of delaying departure so long that the ships became icebound. Perhaps it was during one such enforced stay that on Christmas Eve 1584, at Carrol's Cove (then known as Puerto Breton), Joanes de Echaniz dictated his will—one of the earliest in Canada.

In the late sixteenth century the Iberian fishery declined. The Spanish government imposed new taxes and restrictions on trade and shipping, and inflation increased costs. Moreover, the war with England, which culminated in the disaster of the Spanish Armada in 1588, caused serious disruptions and financial losses. Annexed by Spain in 1580, Portugal saw its fortunes decline as well. Having depleted the whale stocks off Labrador, Basque whalers moved elsewhere. Spanish Basques continued to fish in the Gulf and off southeastern Newfoundland throughout the seventeenth century, but in decreasing numbers. An important result of these developments was that Iberia now needed to import significant quantities of fish.

In response, the French fleet expanded to perhaps as many as 500 vessels in the 1580s, and French fishermen began using the Gulf much more extensively than they had before, steadily moving farther west into the St Lawrence River itself. The same market opportunity caught the attention of ports in southwestern England (the West Country) such as Poole, Plymouth, and Dartmouth. Anthony Parkhurst, a merchant who first came to Newfoundland in 1574, estimated in

This imaginative woodcut map of the Atlantic region was made by Jacoma di Gastaldi and published in Venice in 1556. Like other maps of this period it shows Newfoundland as a group of islands, and narrow off-shore banks; Gastaldi obviously had no knowledge of Cartier's exploration in the Atlantic region. CNS, MUN.

1578 that no more than 50 English vessels made the trip to the island each year; by the early seventeenth century that number had increased to at least 200.

At first, conflict between the English and French fisheries appears to have been relatively rare. The French, sailing from ports along the coast from Normandy to the Pyrenees, produced both a 'wet' (or 'green') cure, in which the fish was taken into the ship's hold and heavily salted or packed in brine, and a 'dry' cure, in which the fish was split, lightly salted, and then dried on shore. The French market, particularly in the north and east, generally preferred green fish, but in response to demand from Spain, Portugal, and the Mediterranean, French Basques in particular produced dry-cured fish, which kept better in hot climates. By contrast, the English, sailing almost exclusively from West Country ports, produced only a dry cure (known as saltfish) and ignored the domestic market in favour of Iberia and southern Europe. For the English, saltfish was above all an article of trade, a commodity to be exchanged for bullion, fruits, wines, and exotic Mediterranean goods.

The production of saltfish demanded the building of seasonal fishing stations where the catch could be cleaned, salted, and dried. Increasingly, the English began to establish themselves on the eastern shores of the Avalon Peninsula, gradually forcing out other nationalities, and in time extending as far north as

Bonavista. Newfoundland's 'English Shore' was the first English foothold in what is now Canada.

Native–European Trade

In the sixteenth century there were no permanent, year-round European settlements in the Atlantic region. The fisheries were seasonal extensions of a European industry, reliant on a European workforce and European markets, and there seemed little need for overseas colonies. One factor that eventually helped to change this attitude was the development of the fur trade. Native people were usually eager to barter with the newcomers, and casual trading was already commonplace well before the 1530s. By the time of Cartier's first voyage, the Mi'kmaq in the Gaspé region were certainly familiar with the rituals of the fur trade. In July 1534 Cartier met a group of Mi'kmaq near the Baie des Chaleurs:

> The next day some of these Indians came in nine canoes to the point at the mouth of the cove where we lay at anchor with our ships. . . . As soon as they saw us they began to run away, making signs that they had come to barter with us; and held up some furs of small value, with which they clothe themselves. We likewise made signs to them that we wished them no harm, and sent two men on shore, to offer them some knives and other iron goods, and a red cap to give to their chief. Seeing this, they sent on shore part of their people with some of their furs; and the two parties traded together.[5]

Basque whaling stations attracted Inuit, Innu, and St Lawrence Iroquoians, all of whom placed a high value on metal objects, especially knives and axes. Local people sometimes pilfered metal items when Europeans were absent, but by mid-century the practice of trading furs had become well-established. It was further stimulated after 1580 by the European demand for hats made of felted beaver fur.

Although the 'portage' trade—carried on by fishers, whalers, and sailors on their own behalf—continued, some French merchants began sending out vessels solely to buy furs along the coasts from Labrador to the Penobscot River in present-day Maine, as well as in the Gulf of St Lawrence. In 1583, for example, Étienne Bélanger of Rouen collected a valuable cargo that included moose, deer, and seal pelts as well as fine furs such as beaver, marten, and otter. Some outfitters had their vessels combine fishing and fur trading. There was little fur trading in Newfoundland largely because there were few Natives to trade with.

Seasonal though it was, the European presence had profound consequences for the region's Aboriginal people. European diseases eventually infected even people who had no direct contact with the newcomers, and Native populations diminished as a result, although the size of the decline is a matter of debate. At the same time, the fur trade upset traditional subsistence patterns and created dependence on Europeans for foodstuffs, alcohol, and metal implements, from copper cooking pots to guns. The Inuit showed considerable hostility to Europeans and the Beothuk avoided contact, but relations with other Native groups were generally good.

Document: The Voyage of the Grace from Bristol, 1594

In the 1590s, Bristol merchants became interested in the resources of the Gulf of St. Lawrence, particularly whales and walrus. Several expeditions were fitted out, among them the *Grace*, Sylvester Wyet master, carrying a Basque pilot. The voyage was not very successful; the *Grace* failed to find whales, and had to catch a cargo of fish instead.

We departed with the aforesaid Barke manned with twelve men . . . from Bristoll the 4 of Aprill 1594, and fell with Cape D'Espere [Spear] on the coast of Newefoundland the nineteenth of May . . . [*and sailed along the south coast of Newfoundland, and then north.*]

In this bay of Saint George, we found the wrackes of 2 great Biskayne [Basque] ships, which had bene cast away three yeeres before: where we had some seven or eight hundred Whale finnes, and some yron bolts and chaines. . . . Here we found the houses of the Savages, made of firre trees bound together in the top and set round like a Dovehouse, and covered with the barkes of firre trees, we found also some part of their victuals, which were Deeres flesh roasted upon wooden spits at the fire, & a dish made of a ryne of a tree, sowed together with the sinowes of the Deere, wherein the oile was of the Deere. There were also foules called Cormorants, which they had pluckt and made ready to have dressed, and there we found a wooden spoone of their making. And we discerned the tracks of the feete of some fortie or fiftie men, women and children.

.... [We then]shaped our course over to that lond Isle of Natiscotec [Anticosti]. . . . Here we . . . found wonderfull faire and great Cod fish. . . . And after wee had searched two dayes and a night for the Whales which were wounded which we had hoped to have found there, we returned backe to the Southwarde . . . and so came to the Bay of Placentia and arrived . . . among the fishermen of Saint John de Luz and of Sibiburo and of Biskay, which were to the number of three score and odd sayles . . . of whom we were very well used. . . . There the men of Saint John and Sibiburo men bestowed two pinnesses [pinaces] on us to make up our voyage with fish. Then wee departed over to the other side of the Bay . . . and fished so long, that in the ende the Savages came, and in the night, when our men were at rest, cut both our pinesse and our shippes boate away . . . yet it was our good fortune to . . . get them againe. Then for feare of a shrewder turne of the Savages, we departed . . . and arrived in Farrillon [Ferryland], and finding there two and twentie sayles of Englishmen, wee made up our fishing voyage to the full in that harborough . . . to our good content: and departing thence we arrived . . . in the river of Bristoll by the grace of God the 24 of September 1594.[7]

The Basques seem to have got on well with the Innu. In the last decade of the sixteenth century, the West Country sea captain Richard Whitbourne reported that the Innu were 'an ingenious and tractable people (being well used)', who worked in the whale fishery, helping to hunt and process the catch. The Mi'kmaq and Maliseet seem to have been eager to trade from the beginning, and gradually established close relations with the Europeans. Some Native people became middlemen, 'sailing in Basque shallops, wearing various items of European clothing . . . speaking a half-Basque, half-Indian trade jargon', and bartering furs from as far south as the coast of Maine with French or Basque traders in the Gulf of St Lawrence and at Tadoussac.[6]

Conclusion

The European discovery of North America in the late fifteenth century opened a period of encounter and exploration that gradually changed the way the world was perceived and experienced by Native North Americans and Europeans alike. Fishing, fur-trading, and whaling ensured that the European presence would be permanent, even if it was in this period largely seasonal. Aboriginal peoples adapted in differing ways to the new arrivals, developing relationships that at first were not grossly imbalanced. This fluid, maritime world was the beginning of the modern Atlantic region, and set in motion forces that would, over time, create a very different environment.

Chapter Four

Colonial Experiments, 1598–1632

The success of Europeans in colonizing the Americas and Australasia is one of the most significant developments in modern history. Until recently, historians assumed that the outcome was predetermined by the superiority of the Europeans—moral, technological, and institutional. Now it is recognized that, although their advanced technology and complex governance structures may have been advantages, they could not colonize a strange new environment until they had learned how to survive in it. This knowledge was obtained partly through experience, but largely from the local inhabitants. Sixteenth-century colonization efforts in the Atlantic region failed, and the small settlements established in the seventeenth century were vulnerable because they depended on the tolerance of both the Aboriginal inhabitants and other Europeans. This situation changed little until the eighteenth century, by which time Europeans, along with their animals, plants, and diseases, had become familiar features of the North American landscape.

Early Colonizers

Early colonization efforts reflected the weakness of the European powers competing for ascendancy in the region—primarily France, England, and Scotland. Because the rulers of these emerging nation-states had neither the financial nor the institutional resources required to undertake empire-building directly, they delegated colonization and governance to private individuals and companies. This approach, coupled with persistent international conflict, made the region vulnerable to economic, political, and religious rivalries defined in Europe. With the Atlantic serving as much to link them to Europe as to distance them from it, the eastern margins of North America became a stage on which imperial characters acted out their competing roles.

Colonization efforts between 1578 and 1632 yielded bold characters, high drama, and meagre results. In 1578 Elizabeth I of England gave Sir Humphrey Gilbert, an early enthusiast for overseas ventures, a patent to explore and occupy those parts of eastern North America not already taken by the Spanish. Gilbert's dream was a colony in some part of what is now Massachusetts. In 1583 a reconnaissance expedition sailed from Southampton. Arriving off Newfoundland, the four ships made for St John's harbour to obtain food and other necessities. After convincing the captains of the forty or so fishing vessels there that he was not a pirate, Gilbert was allowed to pass through the Narrows, where one of his ships

Timeline

1583	Sir Humphrey Gilbert claims Newfoundland for Elizabeth I.
1598	Marquis de la Roche attempts to establish a colony on Sable Island.
1604	Sieur de Monts attempts to establish a base at Ste-Croix.
1605	De Monts and Samuel de Champlain establish Port-Royal.
1606	Champlain founds the Ordre de Bon Temps.
1610	London and Bristol Company founds colony at Cupids.
1613	Destruction of Saint-Sauveur and Port-Royal by Samuel Argall.
1621	Sir George Calvert founds the Colony of Avalon at Ferryland; James I of England grants 'Nova Scotia' to Sir William Alexander.
1629	Alexander establishes colonies on Cape Breton and at Port-Royal.
1632	England recognizes French claim to Acadia in the Treaty of Saint-Germain-en-Laye.

ran anticlimactically aground. On 5 August he went ashore and formally claimed the land for the English Crown. He later erected a pillar with the arms of England fixed to it, issued licences to non-English ships, and appropriated shore premises that he then leased back to those who were using them. Before he reached the mainland of North America, the expedition began to fall apart. Gilbert eventually had to admit failure and decided to return home without reaching his destination. He drowned during the voyage, having last been seen sitting on board his vessel with a book in his hand, shouting, 'We are as neare to Heaven by sea as by land.'[1] Nineteenth-century historians tended to see Gilbert's performance in St John's harbour as a significant event in the evolution of the first British empire, but since neither Gilbert's successors nor the English Crown followed up his assertion of sovereignty, it meant little in practical terms.

It was not the English but the French who began the European settlement of the Atlantic region. In 1598 Henri IV ascended to the throne following a bloody civil war between Roman Catholics and Protestants (Huguenots) in France that had raged since 1562. Emulating the model established by other monarchs, he tried to restore his own treasury and the glory of his country through overseas ventures financed by private interests. Entrepreneurs were offered a monopoly of the fur trade in territories claimed by France if they would agree to transport settlers and support Christian missions among the local Native people. The first settlement attempt was made on Sable Island where, in 1598, the Marquis de la Roche shipped 40 settlers from Rouen and ten soldiers. Only 11 were left by the spring of 1603, when the settlement was abandoned.

The next, ultimately more successful, initiative was led by Pierre Du Gua, Sieur de Monts, a Huguenot who in 1603 was appointed by Henri IV as his viceroy in 'la Cadie', Canada, and 'autres terres de la Nouvelle France'. In return for a ten-year fur-trade monopoly, de Monts agreed to take out at least sixty settlers annually, and support efforts to convert Native peoples in the area to Christianity. The next year de Monts set out to establish a colony in 'la Cadie'. His entourage included two Roman Catholic priests, a Protestant minister, several noblemen, masons, carpenters, a miner, a surgeon, and an apothecary, as well as sheep and hens. It also included seasoned explorers, among them Samuel de Champlain, a veteran of the religious wars and an enthusiastic proponent of European colonization.

After exploring the south coast of Nova Scotia and the Bay of Fundy (named 'la Baie Française' by de Monts), they finally chose Dochet Island, at the mouth of the Ste-Croix River, as the site for a settlement. The choice seems to have been dictated by a concern for military protection, but it proved disastrous. The harsh climate, lack of firewood, and inadequate provisions brought singular hardship. By the spring 35 of the 79 men who had wintered on the island had died of scurvy.

Port-Royal

All but three of those who survived the ordeal returned to France. One of the few determined to remain was Champlain, who spent the summer of 1605 helping de Monts to find a more suitable location for a settlement. After exploring the coast as far as Cape Cod, they finally fixed on a sheltered basin on the south shore of the Baie Française. The previous year, Champlain had described Port-Royal, today the Annapolis Basin, as 'the most suitable and pleasant for a settlement that we had seen'.[2] While the natural military protection, agricultural potential of the soil, and temperate climate were all good reasons for choosing Port-Royal, it had another advantage as well. The Mi'kmaq in the area under their chief Membertou were prepared to tolerate the intruders. Having experienced a hostile reception from Natives in the Cape Cod region, the French recognized that friendship with the local inhabitants was a decided asset in any effort to establish a colony.

The would-be colonists established a new base on the north shore of the sheltered basin. More tightly constructed than the one at Ste-Croix, their 'habitation' included a 'very fine cellar, some five to six feet high', so that the cider and other supplies would not freeze as they had done on the Ste-Croix. Most importantly, the French planted gardens and made friends with the Mi'kmaq in the area, with whom they continued to trade over the winter. The Natives were particularly fond of fresh bread, which the colonists made from corn flour that they ground with hand mills. Only 12 of the 45 men who wintered at Port-Royal in 1605–6 succumbed to scurvy. At least the odds of survival were getting better.

In the spring of 1606 the new governor, Jean de Poutrincourt et de Saint-Just, brought skilled workmen to Port-Royal along with several aristocratic relatives and friends who would play important roles in the development of New France. These included his son, Charles de Biencourt; a cousin from Paris, Louis Hébert, who was an apothecary and horticulturalist; a cousin from Champagne, Claude de Saint-Etienne de La Tour and his 14-year-old-son, Charles; and Marc

Champlain's map of the first Port-Royal. The habitation is flanked by a trout brook (X) and Champlain's garden (B). The wheat fields (H) would become the site of Fort Anne, and the mill is located on the Allain River (I). LAC, NL 15325.

Lescarbot, a lawyer from Paris who would later publish an account of the activities of this charmed circle under the title *Histoire de la Nouvelle France* (1618). Determined to succeed in their venture, they planted wheat and built a gristmill so that they would be less dependent on supplies from France. Delighted by the relatively warm winters at Port-Royal, they developed innovative responses to the challenges of survival. In 1606 Champlain founded the Ordre de Bon Temps, which obliged each gentleman to take turns providing game and fish for the table, and Lescarbot wrote and produced a masque, *Le Théâtre de Neptune en la Nouvelle France*, which the colonists performed to welcome Poutrincourt back to Port-Royal. Only four people died of scurvy that winter.

Notwithstanding his success in planting the colony, de Monts faced insurmountable challenges. His fur-trade monopoly was impossible to enforce against the attacks of rivals, and in 1607 it was revoked. Financial losses soon obliged him to order the abandonment of Port-Royal. De Monts and Champlain concentrated their efforts on the St Lawrence while Poutrincourt—to whom de Monts had given the Port-Royal area—remained interested in Acadia. In 1610 he returned there with his son, Charles de Biencourt, and some 20 colonists, including a priest, Jessé Fléché. The Mi'kmaq had looked after the habitation while the French were sorting out their difficulties. In short order Poutrincourt collected a shipload of

The Theatre of Neptune, 1606

The early European explorers, traders, and colonizers were above all else intrepid sailors who braved the difficult Atlantic crossing to pursue their dreams of fame and fortune. Whatever their country of origin, they were men of the Renaissance who shared a cultural background centred on classical literature. Thus they all would have been familiar with the gods of Greece and Rome, among them Neptune, the god of the sea. Indeed, sea-sickness was politely described as 'yielding up the tribute to Neptune'.[3]

One of the more delightful moments at Port-Royal occurred on a mid-November day in 1606 when Poutrincourt, Champlain, and their crew returned from two months of exploration along the Atlantic coast. As they anchored in the waters adjacent to the habitation, they were approached by Father Neptune, complete with silvery locks and flowing beard, in a boat drawn by six Tritons. The sea god, brandishing his trident, drew alongside Poutrincourt's longboat and addressed him in Alexandrine verse:

> Halt mighty Sagamo, no further fare!
> Look on a god who holds thee in his care.
> Thou knows't me not? I am of Saturn's line
> Brother to Pluto dark and Jove divine.

After outlining what had been achieved through his command of the oceans—adventure, trade, exotic goods—the explorers were reminded:

> If Man would taste the spice of fortune's savour
> He needs must seek the aid of Neptune's favour.
> For stay-at-homes who doze on kitchen settles
> Earn no more glory than their pots and kettles.[4]

Believed to have been the first play written by a European in North America, *Le Théâtre de Neptune* may not be exceptional as poetry, but its existence underlines the rich cultural life that the French brought with them to the 'New World'.

furs, Fléché baptized Membertou and a number of other Mi'kmaq, and Biencourt set off for France to obtain support for his enterprise by demonstrating that it could be both financially and spiritually profitable. He managed to find a patron in the Marquise de Guercheville, but her support was tied to the condition that the Jesuits, who had become influential at the French court, would control missionary work in Acadia and become partners in the fur trade. In May 1611 Biencourt returned to Port-Royal with 36 colonists and two Jesuit priests, Pierre Biard and Énemond Massé.

This proved to be the start of the colony's troubles. While Poutrincourt was absent in Paris, serious quarrels broke out between young Biencourt and the Jesuits. The Marquise de Guercheville, who was determined to see the Jesuits pre-

Acadian settlements in the seventeenth century. Adapted from Reid, *Acadia, Maine and New Scotland*, 191–4.

vail, obtained control over territories in Acadia outside of Poutrincourt's jurisdiction and financed an expedition to move the Jesuits from Port-Royal to Saint-Sauveur, a new colony established on a site opposite what is now known as Mount Desert Island on the Penobscot River in Maine. Alarmed by developments to the north, the governor of the English colony of Virginia, established in 1607, instructed Samuel Argall to attack the French settlements. In the fall of 1613 he took the Jesuits prisoner, destroyed Saint-Sauveur, and put Port-Royal to the torch. Returning the following year to find complete devastation, Poutrincourt and most of the colonists returned to France. Only Biencourt, his cousin Charles de Saint-Étienne de La Tour, and a few others stayed on.

Backed by La Rochelle merchants, Biencourt and his partners built a successful business in fur and fish. They developed good relations with the Mi'kmaq and extended their activities into the harbours of Cap Nègre, Cap de Sable, Port Lomeron, and La Hève on the south shore of Acadia. Following the death of Biencourt in 1623, the direction of the colony was entrusted to Charles La Tour, who with his father Claude continued to make Acadia his home. Charles married a Mi'kmaq woman, likely a chief's daughter, and their union, later blessed by a

Récollet priest, produced three daughters, all of whom were baptized; one eventually entered a convent in Paris.

French claims to Acadia were directly challenged by English and Scottish patents issued in 1620 and 1621. The latter constituted a grant from King James I of England to Sir William Alexander, a Scottish nobleman, of 'New Scotland', defined as extending from the Ste-Croix to the St Lawrence. After his first attempt to found a colony failed, Alexander persuaded the king in 1624 to create 150 knights-baronet who, in return for payment, would each receive a title and a land grant of 30,000 acres (12,150 ha). There were few takers, but after many vicissitudes a fleet finally set sail for America in the spring of 1629, just as Charles I's short, disastrous war with France was coming to an end. Small colonies were established at Port-aux-Baleines on Cape Breton Island under the command of Lord Ochiltree and at Port-Royal under Sir William Alexander's son (also named William). Both efforts failed. Ochiltree's settlement was destroyed in September by a French force under Captain Charles Daniel, which had arrived too late to prevent David Kirke and his brothers—a family of English adventurers—from taking Québec. Alexander's colony survived by making accommodations both with the Mi'kmaq and with Claude de la Tour, whom Kirke had captured at sea and taken to England. Willing to switch allegiances, Claude became one of Alexander's knights-baronet and married a Scottish lady-in-waiting to the Queen. Charles I would probably have liked to retain 'New Scotland', but under the terms of the Treaty of Saint-Germain-en-Laye (1632) he was required to return it to France. Port-Royal was abandoned, and France's title to Acadia was left unchallenged for the time being. As for Alexander, his legacies are a name, a flag, and a coat of arms still used by the province of Nova Scotia.

The Newfoundland Plantations

The other, equally precarious, node of European settlement in the region was Newfoundland's Avalon Peninsula. In 1610 the London and Bristol Company decided to establish a plantation at Cupids Cove, Conception Bay. The investors hoped to develop a fur trade with the Beothuk and create a series of permanent settlements that would enable the company to control a substantial proportion of the Newfoundland fishery and trade. On behalf of the company, John Guy, a merchant from Bristol, brought out 39 men in 1610, followed by 16 women in 1612. The son born to the wife of Nicholas Guy in March 1613 was probably the first English child born in what is now Canada.

Although the colony's early years were quite promising, problems soon developed. The settlement was harassed by the pirate Peter Easton; the soil and climate proved to be less favourable to agriculture than expected; there was friction with the migratory fishermen; and since the settlers had virtually no contact with the Beothuk, the fur-trade did not develop. These factors, adding to internal dissension, led to the plantation's break-up. A few colonists remained in Cupids, and some moved to Bristol's Hope (now Harbour Grace), but others left Newfoundland behind them.

The John Mason Map, 1617. When Mason was appointed governor of the English colony at Cupids Cove, Conception Bay in 1616, he was already familiar with Newfoundland. His map—the first English depiction of the island—constitutes an important piece of evidence for those who believe that John Cabot made his landfall at Cape Bonavista. On the left, just below the peninsula named 'North Falkland' (now the Bonavista Peninsula), is the legend *C. Bona Vista a Cabato primum Reperta*. LAC, NMC-21046.

Although Cupids may have been a business failure, it marks the beginning of permanent English settlement on the Avalon Peninsula. To recoup some of its investment, the company began to sell tracts of land to other potential colonizers. The first of these was Sir William Vaughan, a Welsh lawyer and scholar who saw in overseas colonization a solution to social and economic problems at home. In 1616 he purchased the Avalon Peninsula south of a line from Caplin Bay (now Calvert) across to Placentia Bay, and called his land 'New Cambriol'. A flimsy settlement was established at Aquaforte, which Richard Whitbourne later moved to Renews. By 1621 the colony was finished. Vaughan sold off sections of his property to Sir George Calvert and Lord Falkland, and retired to his library to write *The Golden Fleece* (1626), a fanciful book promoting the colonization of Newfoundland.

Falkland did nothing with his holdings, but the wealthy and influential Calvert established a plantation at Ferryland in 1621. Known as the Colony of Avalon, it became one of the earliest permanent European settlements in northeastern America and was among the best capitalized, with stone houses, a cobbled street, a quay, warehouses, and defences. Lord Baltimore (as he was from 1625) viewed the colony as a business enterprise, but he also wanted Ferryland to be a haven of religious freedom. Himself a convert to Roman Catholicism, Baltimore allowed both Protestant and Catholic clergy to serve the colonists.

Still the colony failed to meet expectations. Baltimore was disheartened not

Document: Planting a Colony in Ferryland

On 26 August 1621, Edward Wynne wrote to his employer, Sir George Calvert, outlining his activities in planting a colony at Ferryland on the east coast of the Avalon Peninsula:

> The place whereon I have made choice to plant and build upon is . . . the fittest, the warmest, the most commodious of all about the harbour. As soon as the [Mansion] house and fortification is fitted and finished, I shall (God willing) prepare and fence in a proportion of seed ground and a garden, close by the house. It may please your Honour not to send out any cattle next year, because I cannot fodder for them so soon, before there be some quantity of corn [grain] growing, but it may please your honour to send some goats, a few tame conies [rabbits] for breed, as also pigs, geese, ducks and hens. I have some hens already. Some spades from London were necessary, if of the best making, also some good pick-axes, iron crows [crowbars], and a smith, and also such as can brew and bake.[5]

The Ferryland cross. This ornate iron cross was excavated at Lord Baltimore's Ferryland settlement. It was once gilded and embedded with gems. James Tuck, MUN.

A North Devon bowl decorated with intricate *scgraffito* designs. Also excavated at Ferryland, it probably dates from about 1673. James Tuck, MUN.

Like other European colonizers, Wynne was attempting to recreate the old world in the new, a project that proved more challenging than this optimistic letter implied. Baltimore himself spent part of 1627 and the winter of 1628–9 in Ferryland, before deciding 'to shift to some other warmer climate of this new worlde'. As he complained to King Charles I:

> . . . from the middest of October, to the middest of May there is a sad face of wynter upon all this land, both sea and land so frozen for the greatest part of the tyme as they are not penetrable, no plant or vegetable thing appearing out of the earth untill it be about the beginning of May nor fish in the sea besides the ayre is so intolerable cold as it is hardly to be endured.[6]

only by the inhospitable climate, but by a slump in the fishery and the high cost of dealing with French privateers. After an interval in England, he departed for Maryland in 1632, leaving his Ferryland property (in which he had invested more than £20,000—$4 million today) in the hands of agents, and a village of some 30 people. At this time the total European winter population on the English Shore was probably not more than 200.

Despite valiant efforts, the European presence in the Atlantic region in the early seventeenth century remained largely seasonal and migratory. Settlement was not necessary for catching fish and trading furs; indeed, much of the good agricultural land was far removed from the best harbours for trading and fishing. If formal colonization schemes in Newfoundland and Acadia were to be successful, they had to generate profits that would satisfy investors, and at the same time provide enough resources to support year-round habitation. There also had to be compelling reasons, whether ideological or self-interested, for Europeans to leave their homelands for an unknown and potentially dangerous 'new world'. Religious persecution unleashed in the wake of the Protestant Reformation and population pressures in Europe served as powerful stimuli for overseas migration, but other regions of North America were more easily adapted to European settlement.

After more than a century of contact, it was clear that unfavourable agricultural conditions made Newfoundland unsuitable for extensive colonization, even in the absence of a large Aboriginal population. The emergence of a permanent population on the island was the result of informal settlement, and its viability depended on the ability to import foodstuffs, though locally grown potatoes became an important dietary staple by the middle of the eighteenth century. Even so, in the seventeenth century 'plantations' linked to West Country ports were growing up in Conception Bay and at St John's, which was one of the most important centres of the migratory fishery. A resident fishery was made possible when 'sack' or cargo vessels (at first Dutch) entered the trade and began purchasing the planters' catch. In Labrador there were no European settlers at all. Barren and forbidding, with a subarctic climate and a seemingly hostile Native population, it attracted only migratory fishermen and traders.

Acadia

The story in Acadia, the present-day Maritimes, was quite different. On the periphery of the rapidly developing North Atlantic trading system, Acadia was bypassed by Puritans from England, who fetched up further south in the Massachusetts Bay area, and even by the French, many of them Huguenots, who moved to the West Indies. But Acadia had potential. Although its climate was more extreme than Europe's, with hotter summers and colder winters, Europeans could survive there, particularly with the help of the Mi'kmaq. The sheer abundance of resources—fish, fowl, and fur in profusion, trees growing down to the shoreline, and pockets of potentially productive agricultural land—and relative proximity to Europe commended the region to prospective immigrants.

The French were the first to explore Acadia's agricultural potential. As

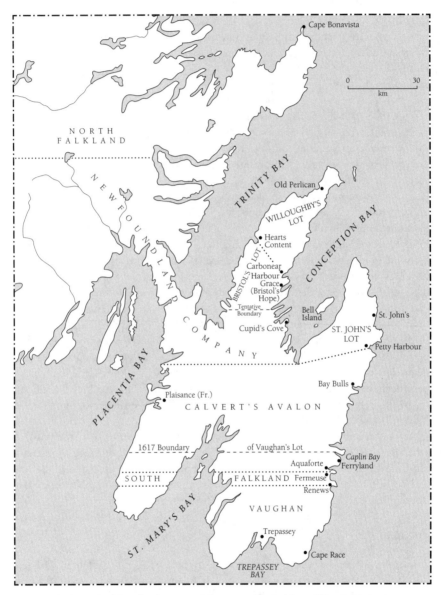

The English Shore of Newfoundland, seventeenth century. Adapted from Gillian Cell, ed., *Newfoundland Discovered: English Attempts at Colonisation, 1610–1630* (London: Hakluyt Society, 1982), 21.

Ramsay Cook has pointed out, French colonizers in Acadia were determined to cultivate the North American wilderness. Lescarbot, for example, was clearly pleased with his efforts at Port-Royal: 'I can say with truth that I have never done so much bodily work through the pleasure which I took in digging and tilling my gardens, fencing them in against the gluttony of the swine, making terraces, preparing straight alleys, building storehouses, sowing wheat, rye, barley, oats, beans, peas, garden plants, and watering them. . . '.[7] In creating his European oasis, Lescarbot was participating in a crucial part of the colonization process: the introduction of European animals, plants, and—through their very presence—diseases.

By Lescarbot's time, European ecological imperialism was already well underway. Plant seeds (including dandelion) were among the early passengers on fishing vessels; and European diseases were already taking their toll among the Aboriginal population. Père Biard noted in 1612 that the Native people 'are astonished and often complain that since the French mingle with and carry on trade with them, they are dying fast and the population is thinning out. . . . One by one the different coasts according as they have begun to traffic with us, have been more reduced by disease.'[8] Within another century, European rats, cats, rabbits, cattle, sheep, pigs and deer would be competing with bears, caribou, moose, and mice for the region's resources.

Europeans were notoriously careless of the abundance they found around them. When Sir Humphrey Gilbert arrived in Newfoundland in 1583, Stephen Parmenius, a young Hungarian poet who accompanied the admiral, noted that they considered burning down the forests 'so as to clear an open space for surveying the area'. This ill-conceived plan was apparently abandoned only after 'some reliable person asserted that, when this had occurred by accident at some other settlement post, no fish had been seen for seven whole years, because the sea-water had been turned bitter by the turpentine that flowed down from the trees burning along the rivers.'[9] Whether by accident or by design, Europeans were gradually making their mark on the North Atlantic landscape.

Conclusion

Although Europeans had difficulty forming stable colonies in the Atlantic region in this period, they had staked out the Avalon Peninsula and the Bay of Fundy area as potential sites for settlement. They had learned by hard experience what was required to survive through the long winter months and knew that there was wealth to be made in the fisheries and the fur trade. By 1632 the region had also become a pawn in imperial rivalries. As Native populations declined, retreated, or made accommodations with the intruders, the way was paved for settler societies that would gradually transform the Atlantic region into a satellite of western Europe.

Chapter Five

Colonial Communities, 1632–1713

Following the Treaty of Saint-Germain-en-Laye in 1632, the French government returned to the task of rebuilding its North American colonies. Most of its attention was focused on the St Lawrence, but efforts in Acadia and Newfoundland bore fruit as well. By contrast, the English government showed little interest in sponsoring colonial endeavours of any kind in the Atlantic region, and some even began to wonder whether the English Shore in Newfoundland should support any permanent settlers at all. Nevertheless, the Atlantic colonies figured prominently in England's negotiating strategies during its periodic wars with France—testimony not only to the significance of the fisheries but also to the Atlantic region's strategic location at the junction of competing territorial claims for imperial control in North America.

The Emergence of Acadia

France's new attitude towards Acadia became apparent when Louis XIII's chief minister, Cardinal Richelieu, appointed Isaac de Razilly to take the surrender of Port-Royal in 1632 and commissioned him as the royal lieutenant-general in New France. He arrived with three ships and roughly 300 men, three Capuchin fathers, and a few women and children. Most of the prospective settlers are thought to have come from Brittany and Anjou. Over the next three years Razilly, with his lieutenants Charles de Menou d'Aulnay and Nicholas Denys, laid the groundwork for a lasting Acadian colony to serve as a French bulwark against New England.

Razilly established his main base at Le Hève on the south shore, which was better suited to his military and commercial interests than Port-Royal. Meanwhile, Denys engaged in fishing, lumbering, and fur-trading, eventually concentrating his efforts at Canso, Saint-Pierre (St Peters), and Nepisiquit on the Baie des Chaleurs. Razilly managed to maintain harmonious relations with Charles La Tour, who claimed title to Acadia himself and conducted major trading operations from his bases at Cape Sable and the mouth of the Saint John River. Essentially dividing the territory between them, Razilly and La Tour dealt separately with the Compagnie des Cent-Associés, the Paris-based seigneurs of New France.

Razilly's sudden death early in 1636 seems to have prompted many of those who had accompanied him to return to France. Fortunately for the colony, his successor, Charles de Menou d'Aulnay, was equally committed to the development

Timeline

1632	Isaac de Razilly appointed Governor of Acadia.
1634	The English government issues the Western Charter to regulate the Newfoundland fishery.
1637	Commercial monopoly of the Newfoundland fish trade granted to Sir David Kirke and his business associates.
1640	Hostilities begin between Charles de Menou d'Aulnay and Charles La Tour.
1645	D'Aulnay takes la Tour's fort on the Saint John River.
1650	Emmanuel Le Borgne seizes Port-Royal and attacks other settlements.
1654	English force led by Robert Sedgwick attacks Acadia and imprisons La Tour.
1662	France establishes a colony and military base at Plaisance.
1667	Acadia returned to France by the Treaty of Breda.
1670	Acadia declared a royal colony.
1689–97	War of the League of Augsburg.
1690	Sir William Phips plunders Port-Royal.
1696–7	Pierre Le Moyne d'Iberville attempts to drive the English out of Newfoundland.
1697	Treaty of Ryswick.
1699	'King William's Act' passed to govern the fishery and settlement at Newfoundland.
1702–13	War of the Spanish Succession.
1704, 1707	New Englanders attack Acadia.
1705, 1709	French attack English Newfoundland.
1710	English force captures Port-Royal.
1713	Treaty of Utrecht; France recognizes British sovereignty over mainland Acadia and Newfoundland.

of Acadia, and arranged for the migration of settlers from his seigneury near Loudon in Poitou. Because he believed that agriculture should be the colony's mainstay, he moved most of the French settlers remaining at La Hève to the potentially more productive Port-Royal area. Families formed by marriages between the French and Mi'kmaq apparently remained at La Hève. By 1650, when d'Aulnay died, there were about 400 Europeans living in Acadia. Some returned to France, but most of them stayed to become the founding families of the French Acadie.

D'Aulnay's death marked the end of official French efforts to encourage immigration to the colony. It also brought to a close what has been described as 'a miniscule civil war between rival fur-trading seigneurs'.[1] Unlike Razilly, d'Aulnay was not prepared to accommodate La Tour's territorial claims, wanting to control all of Acadia and its trade. In 1640 commercial and political rivalry erupted into armed hostilities that culminated five years later in d'Aulnay's attack on La Tour's Saint John River fort, which was defended in La Tour's absence by his spirited and resourceful second wife, Françoise-Marie Jaquelin. She eventually surrendered and, so the story goes, was forced to watch the hanging of those of her men who had survived the battle. She died soon after, and La Tour went into exile in Québec.

The dispute with La Tour had driven d'Aulnay deeply into debt, and on his death his chief creditor, Emmanuel Le Borgne, seized Port-Royal and attacked other settlements in the region. Meanwhile, the equally debt-ridden La Tour attempted to consolidate his interests and get his property back. To this end, he married d'Aulnay's widow, Jeanne Motin, and resumed his position as governor— this time of all Acadia. The La Tours were joined in opposition to Le Borgne by Nicolas Denys, who by this time had substantial interests in the fishery and the fur trade between Canso and the Gaspé. Another civil war was averted in 1654 when an English force led by Robert Sedgwick plundered Port-Royal and other settlements. La Tour, taken prisoner, swore allegiance to England, sold his rights in Acadia, paid off his debts, and retired to Cape Sable.

The government of Oliver Cromwell in England took the view that Acadia had reverted to its former identity as New Scotland, and in 1662 appointed as its governor Sir Thomas Temple, who had bought out La Tour's claims. The French government, taking a different view of the situation, appointed Le Borgne governor of Acadia, and he continued to attack English settlements. In any event, the new arrangements were short-lived. In 1667 the Treaty of Breda returned Acadia to France, and three years later a reluctant Temple was finally persuaded to let the French assume control.

King Louis XIV of France (1643–1715) began to intervene directly in matters relating to overseas colonization following his decision in 1661 to take the reins of government into his own hands. As a result, most French colonies were put under the control of a powerful bureaucratic regime with a governor supported by a standing army; a legal system based on the Custom of Paris; a seigneurial system of land distribution that concentrated wealth in the hands of an aristocratic élite; a Roman Catholic church closely allied to the state; and a closed mercantile trading system designed to advance France's economic interests. Distance, administrative inefficiencies, and the king's preoccupation with European affairs meant that North American colonies could often avoid some of the strict regulations imposed upon them by officials based in France, but these factors were not enough to prevent the colonies from becoming pawns in the struggle for ascendancy in Europe that Louis XIV's ambitions unleashed.

In 1670 Acadia was declared a royal colony like the others, with an administration subordinate to officials in Québec. The St Lawrence-based colony of

Canada had received most of Louis XIV's attention and he had few resources, either financial or military, to spare for Acadia. Governor Hector d'Andigné de Grandfontaine established royal authority in the colony with only a handful of soldiers, and the 60 settlers he brought with him were joined by just 66 more (of whom only five were women) over the next 40 years. Without support from France, the 55 seigneuries failed to sustain social organization, and regulations forbidding trade with New England were openly flouted. The few priests in the area sometimes took on legal duties in the absence of judicial officers. Meanwhile, the settlers, especially those who moved beyond the confines of Port-Royal, learned to fend for themselves.

Despite the lack of imperial interest, a small colonial society managed to take root in Acadia. Colonial officials tried between 1670 and 1683 to establish their administrative base on the north side of the Bay of Fundy, first at Pentagouet, then at Jemseg and Beaubassin, but finally settled back in Port-Royal. With about 600 people in 1686, Port-Royal was the heart of French settlement. Other communities were developing in what is now Nova Scotia at Pubnico (Pobomcoup), Cape Negro (Cap Nègre), Musquodoboit Harbour (Mouscoudabouet), and St Peter's (Saint-Pierre). In the 1670s and 1680s, young families moved up the Bay of Fundy to Beaubassin and around the Minas Basin.

Geographical expansion reflected the spectacular population growth that characterized early French settlements. Well-adapted to their environment, people in Acadia were better nourished than most peasants in France and mercifully free of the plagues that periodically ravaged old-world communities. They married young and few remained single. Although agriculture was central to their survival, fishing and fur trading supplemented their well-rounded economy.

Roman Catholic clergy were present from the earliest days of French settlement

Document: Building Dykes in Acadia, 1699

One of the most enduring features of colonial Acadia was dykeland agriculture. Instead of clearing the forests, the settlers reclaimed the rich alluvial soils flooded by the high tides of the Bay of Fundy. The practice began in the Port-Royal area in the 1630s, introduced by *saulniers* (salt marsh workers) from Poitou who knew how to drain and cultivate marshlands. As settlement spread so did the construction of dykes, creating a landscape that still distinguishes the Bay of Fundy region. The marshland farms were highly productive, allowing the settlers to grow wheat and barley, as well as fodder for livestock, and the salt produced in the drainage process was used to cure fish.

Dyke-building represented a major engineering achievement. The Sieur de Dièreville, a French surgeon and writer who visited the colony in 1699, was clearly impressed by the labour-intensive process through which the marshland soil was reclaimed from the sea:

To grow Wheat, the Marshes which are inundated by the Sea at high Tide, must be drained; these are called Lowlands & they are quite good, but what labour is needed to make them fit for cultivation! The ebb & flow of the Sea cannot easily be stopped, but the Acadians succeed in doing so by means of great Dykes called Aboteaux, & it is done in this way; five or six rows of large logs are driven whole into the ground at the points where the Tide enters the Marsh, & between each row other logs are laid, one on top of the other, & all the spaces between them are so carefully filled with well-pounded clay, that the water can no longer get through. In the centre of this construction, a Sluice is contrived in such a manner that the water on the Marshes flows out of its own accord, while that of the Sea is prevented from coming in. An undertaking of this nature, which can only be carried on at certain Seasons when the Tides do not rise so high, costs a great deal, & takes many days, but the abundant crop that is harvested in the second year, after the soil has been washed [of the salt] by Rain water compensates for all the expense. As these lands are owned by several Men, the work upon them is done in common.[2]

The size of this work crew, photographed at the turn of the twentieth century at Boyd Creek, New Brunswick, suggests how much labour was required to maintain the dykes originally built by Acadians in the seventeenth and eighteenth centuries. PANB, P-61-439.

and remained a significant force even after the British conquest of 1713. In the first half of the seventeenth century, Acadia was an open field for competing clerical orders. Récollet, Jesuit, and Capuchin priests conducted missions among the Native people, ministered to French settlers and sojourners, and clashed both with each other and with the secular authorities. The Capuchins were particularly active, sending at

These ink drawings of missionaries teaching Christianity to the Mi'kmaq were used to illustrate Chrestien LeClercq's *New Relation of Gaspésia*, published in Paris in 1691.

least 40 priests and 20 lay brothers to Acadia between 1632 and 1656. Most priests spent only a few years in Acadia, but they achieved their goals. French settlers remained committed to Roman Catholicism, and many Mi'kmaq and Maliseet gradually reconciled their beliefs with those of the persistent Christians in their midst.

In 1676 Father Louis Petit was appointed vicar-general of Acadia, under the jurisdiction of the Bishop of Québec. Bishop Saint-Vallier visited his Acadian province in the spring of 1686, and resident priests were subsequently appointed to communities outside Port-Royal. From 1701 to 1710, a sister of the Congregation of the Holy Cross conducted a school for young girls at Port-Royal. Legal and clerical records show that most people followed clerical injunctions relating to marriage and sexual conduct. In a highly controversial case at Beaubassin in 1688, the local priest responded to a paternity suit by insisting that not only the reputed father but also 19 members of his family be expelled from the community and their confiscated goods given to the girl's father.

Because Acadians generally did not settle on Native hunting and fishing grounds, and provided valued opportunities to trade, their relations with the Mi'kmaq and Maliseet were amicable. On occasion, marriages between Native women and French immigrants played a significant role in cementing military alliances. In 1670, for example, Bernard-Anselme d'Abbadie de Saint-Castin accompanied Governor Grandfontaine to Pentagouet (in present-day Maine) and married the daughter of a Pentagouet chief. He then devoted himself to extending French influence among the Abenaki in that area. Faced with the expansion of New England settlers up the Atlantic seaboard, the Abenaki welcomed the support provided by Saint-Castin and valued his advice. As war engulfed the region in the closing decades of the seventeenth century, the Abenaki, Penobscot, and Passamaquoddy joined the Maliseet and Mi'kmaq in an alliance—later known as the Wabanaki ('Dawnland') Confederacy—to confront the aggressive New Englanders and their British and Iroquois allies.

Cultural exchange between Natives and French immigrants, initiated by trade and military alliances, was extensive and long-lasting. Acadians adopted those elements of local cultures that they found most useful, including canoes, moccasins, and knowledge of local herbs and vegetables, while European metal products, foods, clothing, religious rituals, and military support became standard features of Aboriginal society. According to Naomi Griffiths, Natives in the eyes of Acadians 'were permanent neighbours, neither the middlemen in commercial enterprise nor a hostile force'.[3] This symbiotic relationship was highly unusual in the story of European settlement in North America.

A more ambiguous relationship developed between the Acadians and the English colonists in Massachusetts. Regarding Acadia as within their sphere of influence, the New Englanders were hostile to the French presence and periodically attacked Acadian settlements. At the same time they fished along the Acadian coastline and traded with Acadian settlers, who exchanged furs and surplus agricultural produce for a variety of manufactured goods and foodstuffs. Both La Tour and d'Aulnay had conducted extensive business in Boston, and this axis of trade continued after 1670, despite royal injunctions against it. Since few French merchants were interested in Acadia—there had been some heavy losses in the past—and because administrators lacked the resources even to control the trade, the colony emerged as an economic satellite of New England. In the Acadian phrase, the English became 'our friends the enemy'.

By the turn of the eighteenth century the settled population of Acadia was approaching 1,500 and—with a balanced population of men and women—was doubling every generation. Most of the inhabitants were related to each other, giving a society of varied origins the close-knit character of an extended family. A common language and religion further cemented an interdependence that was also encouraged by the political vacuum in the region. With a government that was always distant, often ineffectual, sometimes English, sometimes French, the Acadians became singularly self-reliant and pragmatic. Periodic attacks on their communities—mostly conducted by the English, but also by the Dutch in 1674— drove home the reality of their precarious political situation. Learning to live both with their neighbours and with whatever regime was in power, the Acadians kept their own counsel. Frustrated French administrators thought them 'republican,' lacking in deference and respect.

The English Shore

Acadia was a permanent French colony, and viewed as such in Paris. The British attitude towards Newfoundland was not as clear-cut. Officials in London were not opposed to settlement, but were preoccupied by the economic and naval value of the migratory fishery and provided neither local administration nor a military presence. As a means of formalizing the rules and customs governing the English inshore fishery, Parliament issued a Western Charter in 1634. It detailed how masters could claim fishing rooms, and empowered the fishing admirals—masters of migratory vessels who acquired authority by being the first to arrive in a given harbour—to settle disputes; it banned taverns, the dumping of ballast in harbours, 'rinding' trees, stealing, Sabbath-breaking, and the destruction of fishing stages and cookrooms. In the absence of penalty clauses—except for capital offences, which were to be tried in England—it proved to be a weak legal document, and its provisions were often ignored.

In 1637 Charles I made a 'Grant of Newfoundland' to Sir David Kirke and some aristocratic associates, and acquiesced in Kirke's appropriation of the Ferryland plantation the following year. Known as the Company of Adventurers to Newfoundland, the patentees had not been granted property, but a commercial monopoly: the right to 'the sole trade of Newfoundland, the Fishing excepted', with the power to tax French and Dutch vessels. The goal was to give English West Country merchants a monopoly of the fishery, while the patentees would monopolize the sack trade in association with a London business run by Kirke's brothers. David Kirke set himself up as a fish merchant in Ferryland, and developed a profitable transatlantic trade in fish and wine. As governor, he held courts, and administered the southern Avalon Peninsula in a rough-and-ready way.

Kirke's career in Newfoundland ended with the victory of Parliament in the English civil war. Since he was a royalist, his estates were sequestrated in 1651.

B. *The cod-fishers' stage*

A Newfoundland fishing room, *c.* 1663, sketched by the surgeon James Yonge at either Renews or Fermeuse. The key reads: 'A The Stage Roofe. B ye Stage head. C A fishing boat. D A cooke room. E A flake to dry fish over'. From F.N.L. Poynter, ed., *The Journal of James Yonge, 1647–1721*, Plymouth Surgeon (London: Green and Co., 1963).

Biography: David and Sara Kirke

David Kirke was the tough, adventurous son of an English wine merchant. When war broke out between England and France in 1627, Kirke led a privateering expedition against the French in Canada. Largely a family affair, this effort was partly financed by his father and included David's four brothers. With the help of Innu allies, the Kirkes eventually managed to take Québec from Champlain in 1629 and stayed there until 1632, when the Treaty of Saint-Germain-en-Laye obliged them to return it to France. Knighted for his achievements, David Kirke turned his attention to Newfoundland.

Kirke and his partners were interested in the 'sack' trade—the term derived from *vina de sacca*, wine for export—in which fish was collected at Newfoundland, freighted to southern Europe, and exchanged for wines and other Mediterranean commodities that were then sold in England. The need for a steady and adequate supply of fish persuaded Kirke and his wife Sara to take over the Ferryland plantation, where in 1650, they were joined by Lady Kirke's sister, Lady Frances Hopkins, and her children. Because the Hopkins family had sheltered Charles I while he was under house arrest in 1648, they were suspect to Cromwell's new parliamentary regime.

By 1654 the sisters were both widows, and despite their royalist affiliations, they survived the civil war and interregnum with their properties intact. They did not go back to England, but remained in Newfoundland to manage their substantial plantations—independent, and in local terms, wealthy. Although Frances had a short-lived second marriage to an Acadian merchant, Alexandre Le Borgne de Belle-Isle, Sara did not remarry. Peter Pope suggests that, as heirs to large plantations, these women 'had the least to gain and the most to lose from a new alliance' that would give control of the family wealth to a new husband.[4] Both women died in Newfoundland in the early 1680s.

Moreover, it seems that he had manipulated his operations to benefit his brothers rather than the other patentees. Recalled to face a suit brought by the Calverts, Kirke died in prison in 1654. The Ferryland plantation survived under the management of his widow, Lady Sara Kirke, while her sons developed their own plantations at Ferryland and Renews. In effect, the Kirkes functioned as a provincial gentry under the new governor, a merchant from Maine named John Treworgie.

The West Country merchants who controlled the migratory fishery were concerned about the activities of Kirke and Treworgie, but they faced other challenges as well. Among them was an extensive bye-boat fishery, carried on by independent fishermen who bought passage to and from England annually and leased fishing rooms. Bye-boat keepers worked closely with planters, whose presence also concerned some of the merchants. In the mid seventeenth century, there were between one and two thousand people who had some sort of permanent attachment to Newfoundland, living in about 30 settlements along the English Shore, all linked to West Country ports. Around this core group of planters moved a much larger, shifting, seasonal, overwhelmingly male population that during the summer helped to produce saltfish and cod oil for export.

After the restoration of the monarchy in 1660, a West Country lobby argued that the growth of a settled population on the island, small as it was, threatened the viability of the migratory fishery because planters pre-empted the best fishing places and destroyed fishing stages. In addition, it was argued, settlement was not desirable since Newfoundland was 'productive of no commodities as other Plantations, [n]or affords anything of food to keep men alive'. The government responded with an addition to the Western Charter in 1661 purporting to forbid bye-boat fishing, and, concerned by a decline in the migratory fishery, adopted an anti-settlement policy that was enshrined in a new charter issued in 1671. The naval commodore was instructed to encourage planters to leave the island.

By contrast, France placed a far higher value on the Newfoundland fisheries than on Acadia or even Canada. Determined to protect their interests in Newfoundland, the French established a colony and fort at Plaisance, on the island's southeast coast, in 1662. Theoretically subordinate (like Acadia) to Québec, Plaisance was designed to act as a base for the French fishing fleet, to monitor English activity on the Avalon Peninsula, and to protect the approaches to the Gulf. The community became home to a governor and other administrators, a military force, Roman Catholic priests, and, on its beach properties, bona fide settlers. By the end of the seventeenth century Plaisance boasted 52 resident fishing families and served a fleet of over 400 vessels, employing more than 1,000 men. As in Acadia, there was a flourishing clandestine trade with New England.

Delayed by the Anglo-Dutch war of 1672–4—during which the Dutch attacked both Ferryland and St John's—the English government did not try to enforce its anti-settler policy until 1675. The naval commodore sent to implement the order reported that the policy was both impractical and mistaken: 'if the habitants are taken off and the French left solely in possession. . . . they will in a short time invest themselves of the whole at least of Ferryland and St John's, where harbours are almost naturally fortified, to the disadvantage of the trade, if not the loss of all' in 1525.'[5] Moreover, the planters were in reality an asset to the migratory fleet; they protected equipment, cut lumber, made oars and boats, and also provided hospitality. The government sensibly reconsidered its position, cancelled its instructions, and adopted a compromise: Settlement in Newfoundland would be accepted and tolerated, but not encouraged. Eventually enshrined in the 1699 statute known as King William's Act, this policy was to remain on the books until 1824. There is an old and hardy myth that the British government opposed settlement in Newfoundland and made it illegal. In fact, until the 1660s the government supported settlement. Thereafter, British policy reflected the assumption that Newfoundland was an industry, not a colony.

The Impact of War, 1689–1713

When war was declared between England and France in 1689, Acadia and Newfoundland were seriously affected. The origins of the conflict (King William's

War, or the War of the League of Augsburg) were European, but North Americans—both Native and newcomer—could not avoid involvement. The Comte de Frontenac, Governor of New France, organized mid-winter raids along the New England frontier, while French privateers attacked English shipping. Alarmed by the prospect of a hostile alliance between the Aboriginal peoples and the French, the New Englanders struck back. In 1690 a force commanded by Sir William Phips attacked French posts along the coast and then plundered Port-Royal, taking the governor prisoner. Some inhabitants fled. The remaining men were ordered to assemble in the damaged church, where they were forced to swear allegiance to English Crown. Phips also appointed a council of residents to act as a local government. Once Phips was gone, the residents publicly reaffirmed their allegiance to Louis XIV, but the French administration thought it prudent to leave the Phips-appointed council in place, and itself moved north of the Bay of Fundy, locating at Jemseg, then Nashwaak, and finally at the mouth of the Saint John River. For ordinary Acadians, Maurice Basque argues, the imperative was to survive amidst ambiguity, and to that end the best strategy was 'a form of neutrality in which they could continue to trade with the English while avoiding conflicts with their Native neighbours and maintaining communication with the French administration of the colony'.[6]

Neutrality was no longer an option for the region's Aboriginal residents. During King William's War, the Mi'kmaq, Maliseet, Penobscot, Passamoquoddy, and Abenaki—the so-called Wabanaki Confederacy—threw in their lot with the French, attacking New England settlers and forts on Abenaki land. The historian William Wicken points out that their motivation was twofold. Not only did they want to defend their territory against New England expansionism, but they had a long-standing conflict with the Iroquois (Houdenosaunee) who were now allied with the British.[7] In retaliation for the damaging attacks on New England by the French and their Native allies, Benjamin Church and a force of New Englanders burned and pillaged the Beaubassin settlements in 1696 and extracted yet another pointless oath of allegiance from the Acadians.

The Massachusetts General Court forbade trade with Acadia, but there was no way to enforce the prohibition. As a result trade between New England and Acadia continued throughout the war. Wheat, fur, and feathers (the latter essential for mattresses) were traded for Indian corn, tobacco, molasses, sugar, spices, lace, ribbon, and fabrics. This was not the first time that economic and political policies were at odds in the Atlantic region; nor would it be the last.

In Newfoundland there were French raids on Ferryland and St John's, and repeated English raids on Plaisance. The main French campaign, intended to drive the English out of Newfoundland, began in November 1696, when Pierre Le Moyne d'Iberville and a force of Canadiens, Acadians, Mi'kmaq, and Abenaki marched overland from Plaisance to meet a force of French regular troops at Renews. The French rapidly moved north, burning houses and boats, and by the end of the month had occupied St John's, which they then destroyed, along with 80 fishing ships. In January 1697 d'Iberville and Testard de Montigny moved against the English settlements in Conception and Trinity bays. The French terrorized the scattered settlements, driving all before them except a group of defenders on Carbonear Island. Only Bonavista remained beyond their reach. In all, the French destroyed 36 settlements, killed 200 people, took 700 prisoners, and captured 300 fishing vessels. Sir David Kirke's three surviving sons died as prisoners of war at Plaisance, and the planter gentry of the southern Avalon was effectively eliminated.

If the French had capitalized on this exercise in brutality, Newfoundland would have become a wholly French island, with important strategic consequences, but France lacked the resources necessary to follow up its victory. D'Iberville retreated to Plaisance and was then dispatched to campaign against the English in Hudson Bay. While Newfoundland's English population had suffered a severe blow, the survivors were able to reoccupy their territory without difficulty and a garrison was established at St John's.

The Treaty of Ryswick officially ended the war in 1697, but in effect it only called a truce. In North America each side was awarded what it had held in 1689 and began preparing for the next round, which came in 1702 with the War of the Spanish Succession. Again Canada and Acadia became bases for attacks on New England, which led to a trade embargo and retaliatory raids. In the summer of 1704 Benjamin Church led an attack against Acadia in response to the 'Deerfield Massacre' of the previous year, in which 50 New Englanders had been killed and 112 taken prisoner to Montréal, many of them women and children. Church and his men decimated all the major Acadian settlements except Port-Royal, which was defended by its fort and garrison. Leaving a trail of broken dykes, burned homes, slaughtered cattle, and devastated crops at Chignecto, Cobequid, Pisiquid, and Minas, the New Englanders also took some 50 Acadian captives to Boston. They were returned in 1706.

New England mobilized a force of 1,600 men to attack Port-Royal again the next year, but the new governor, Daniel d'Auger de Subercase, repulsed the attackers with the help of a hastily assembled Acadian militia. Although his situation was precarious, both militarily and economically, Subercase managed to hang on. Port-Royal became the base for privateers from the French West Indies, who attacked trading vessels from Massachusetts, securing much-needed foodstuffs and manufactured goods. In 1709 the privateers seized 35 vessels and took over nearly 300 prisoners, fuelling the New Englanders' resolve to rid themselves of their French tormentors.

The following year proved to be a decisive one in the history of Acadia. Supported by a detachment of British marines and a company of grenadiers, General Francis Nicholson led a force of 1,500 colonial troops and Iroquois allies in a bruising campaign against Port-Royal. After holding out for a week, Subercase and his small, demoralized garrison of fewer than 300 soldiers were forced to surrender. Articles of capitulation were signed on 2 October 1710 and Port-Royal, which had been passed back and forth between England and France several times over the previous century, was handed over for what turned out to be the last time.

In Newfoundland, settlers along the English Shore again suffered raids from Plaisance, which also served as a base for privateers. In 1705 Subercase and

Acadian settlements, 1755. Adapted from Daigle, ed., *Acadia of the Maritimes*, 33; *Historical Atlas of Canada*, I (Toronto: University of Toronto Press, 1987), plate 30.

Montigny led a repeat performance of the 1697 raid, taking 1,200 prisoners and wreaking destruction as far north as Bonavista. In 1709 French forces took the fort at St John's, burned most of the town, and forced the inhabitants to pay a huge ransom. Again, the French found it impossible to secure their advantage: they withdrew to Plaisance, where they were blockaded by British naval vessels and suffered severe privation.

In the negotiations leading up to the Treaty of Utrecht, which ended the War of the Spanish Succession in 1713, the British demanded that France abandon its claims to both Acadia and Newfoundland. After long and intense bargaining, France recognized British sovereignty over Newfoundland and ceded mainland Acadia, but retained Île Royale (Cape Breton Island) and Île Saint-Jean (Prince Edward Island) in the hope that they would protect the route to Canada and serve as footholds from which to regain control over the region. As for the Newfoundland fisheries, France extracted a valuable and clever concession: the right to fish in season on the Petit Nord, defined as extending from Cape Bonavista to Pointe Riche on the northwest coast.

The treaty contained some serious loose ends. The precise nature of French fishing rights in Newfoundland was unclear, and the definition of boundary lines between French and English possessions—Acadia was ceded according to its ill-defined 'ancient boundaries'—was left for future discussion. Although France now accepted British sovereignty over Hudson Bay, that territory was also left undefined, the parties agreeing only that sometime in the future a boundary line should be drawn in the Labrador peninsula.

The Treaty of Utrecht was severely criticized in both England and France—'an indication,' writes John Reid, 'of the virtually irreconcilable interests at stake'.[8] The rivalry between Britain and France was unresolved, and the two powers were left uneasily and resentfully to share northeastern America. For the residents of the Atlantic region, who had received a severe mauling during the wars, the future was uncertain. French settlers in Acadia and Plaisance had the choice of swearing allegiance to a Protestant monarch hostile to France or moving to French-controlled territory. For English settlers in Newfoundland and New England, the prospect of the French re-establishing themselves on Île Royale and Île St Jean was troubling because it would leave them vulnerable to attack in any future war between Great Britain and France. Meanwhile, the Aboriginal people found that their land had been given away to their enemies without their knowledge, let alone their consent. The Treaty of Utrecht, in short, left much to be contested.

Chapter Six

Renegotiating the Atlantic Region, 1713–63

Fifty years separated the treaties of Utrecht (1713) and Paris (1763). The first confirmed Great Britain's acquisition of territory in the Atlantic region; the second confirmed Britain's ascendancy. In the interim, the British and French continued to jockey for control, encouraged by ambitious colonial officials in Québec and Boston. Caught between the two powers, Aboriginal people and Acadians suffered severely. As the equilibrium in the region gradually tipped toward the British, Mi'kma'ki/Acadia/Nova Scotia took on global significance, becoming 'a virtual laboratory for cultural and political realignments in the Atlantic world'.[1]

Administrative Challenges

The acquisition of Acadia/Nova Scotia in 1713 presented the British with an imperial dilemma. How were they to deal with a colony with disputed borders, settlers who were primarily French and Roman Catholic, and Native peoples allied with the enemy? These difficulties were compounded by the continued French presence on Île Royale, where an imposing military base at Louisbourg was soon under construction. Designed to contain British power in North America, safeguard the approaches to the St Lawrence, and support the migratory fishery, Louisbourg made a major statement about French intentions in the region.

France also asserted its position in the region through diplomacy. Nova Scotia's boundaries were ill-defined, and France insisted that the area north of the Bay of Fundy (present-day New Brunswick) and even Canso, on the eastern end of the Nova Scotia peninsula, were still its possessions. In Newfoundland, France claimed that its fishing rights on the French (or Treaty) Shore were exclusive, rejecting the British government's argument that its nationals had every right to fish there so long as they did not interfere with French operations.

British officials, with a small garrison, established their capital at the former Port-Royal. Renamed Annapolis Royal, it was a small enclave within a territory inhabited by 2,000 Acadians and 3,500 Mi'kmaq. Since both groups were unwilling to sever their ties with France, negotiations to secure an unqualified oath of allegiance to the British Crown failed. Meanwhile, with the British hold on the territory apparently tenuous, few immigrants—British or otherwise—were interested in settling there. Nor was any thought given to introducing an elected assembly of the kind that was by now common in Britain's other North American

Timeline

1713	Treaty of Utrecht signed.
1720	French begin construction of Fortress Louisbourg; Saint-Pierre establishes a colony on Île Saint-Jean.
1722–5	Wabanaki–New England War.
1726	British sign treaties with Mi'kmaq, Maliseet, and Passamaquoddy; French send a military detachment to Île Saint-Jean.
1729	Captain Henry Osborne appointed naval governor of Newfoundland.
1744–8	War of the Austrian Succession.
1745	Louisbourg captured.
1746	D'Anville Expedition.
1747	Battle of Grand Pré.
1748	Treaty of Aix-la-Chapelle.
1749	Founding of Halifax by the British.
1750	Construction of Fort Beauséjour and Fort Lawrence.
1752	Treaty of Peace and Friendship with the Mi'kmaq.
1755	Fort Beauséjour falls to the British.
1755–62	Expulsion of the Acadians.
1756–63	Seven Years' War.
1760–1	Mi'kmaq, Maliseet, and Passamaquoddy sign peace treaties with the British.
1762	French attack on St John's.
1763	Treaty of Paris; Royal Proclamation.

colonies. Instead, a governor (or, more often, his delegate) and an appointed council were charged with responding to legal and administrative issues as they arose.

In Newfoundland, despite a growing resident population, the British had no intention of establishing a regular colonial administration of any kind. Local problems were sufficiently serious, however, to warrant something more than the often-ignored provisions of King William's Act, which empowered the fishing admirals to decide local disputes, with commanders of the naval warships sent out each summer acting as appeal judges. This administrative structure, such as it was, disappeared altogether in winter. In 1718 a known murderer in Torbay remained free because no one had the legal authority to arrest him. Clearly something had to be done to ensure law and order.

Eventually it was decided that the commodore of the annual naval squadron would double as governor and commander-in-chief. The first migratory naval governor was Captain Henry Osborne, who in 1729 appointed magistrates and constables along the coast from Bonavista to Placentia. In summer these new authorities were supplemented by naval officers acting as surrogate magistrates, and the fishing admirals in time disappeared as an independent force. Thus was born what has been called a 'naval state'.[2] If the island did not fit the usual model of colonial development, neither was it—as sometimes has been assumed—a violent, anarchic frontier.

French Designs

Determined to challenge British ascendancy in the region, the French established their headquarters at the ice-free port of Havre L'Anglois, renamed Louisbourg, on the south shore of Île Royale. Construction of the fortified town began in 1720. Louisbourg cost a fortune, fell both times it was attacked, and proved ineffective in protecting the St Lawrence; but in other respects it succeeded admirably. Louisbourg quickly became a major fishing port and commercial entrepôt, with a thriving trade that soon equalled Canada's in value. At the same time, French officials used Louisbourg to maintain communication with the Acadians and the Mi'kmaq, in the hope of undermining the British position in Nova Scotia.

By 1744, with a population approaching 3,000, Louisbourg was the largest and most cosmopolitan community in the Atlantic region. Its residents included evacuees from Plaisance, French and Basque fishermen, German and Swiss soldiers, a few Irish, Scots, and Spanish sojourners, and both Native and Black servants and slaves. The latter catered to the town's administrative and commercial élite, most of them from France, who lived in comfort if not opulence. Eager to maintain their standard of living when they returned home, many of them bilked the colonial treasury and traded discreetly with the English colonies. The troops, required to work long hours maintaining the fortifications, were only too aware that they were being cheated: tensions reached such a pitch in the winter of 1744–5 that they took over the town, demanding better food, more firewood, and adequate uniforms.

The Treaty of Utrecht had given Acadians a choice: stay where they were and accept British rule, or move away. French authorities hoped that they would settle on Île Royale and produce foodstuffs for the residents of Louisbourg. Most Acadians, however, preferred to remain in British territory. Having established highly productive agricultural communities by 1713, they were reluctant to leave them. Pragmatic as ever, the majority saw little advantage in trying to farm on the thin soils of Île Royale. Only 60 Acadian families moved to Île Royale in the two decades following the conquest.[3] Most of them settled in outlying communities, such as St-Pierre (St Peter's), Rivière de Miré (Mira), and Baie-des-Espagnols (Sydney), where they farmed, fished, built boats, and mined coal.

Because Île Royale failed to develop a significant agricultural base and depended on imported foodstuffs, its security was threatened. Cod fishing, both sedentary and migratory, remained the chief economic activity, producing most of the island's exports to France and, importantly, to the West Indies, where slave plantations were becoming significant markets for saltfish.

Slavery in Louisbourg

Europeans did not introduce slavery to the Americas: many Aboriginal societies used enslaved labour. Nevertheless, by the eighteenth century whole economies in the Americas had been built on the African slave trade. By 1750 over 3,800,000 African slaves had been shipped to the Americas. Enslavement became equated with skin colour and racial stereotyping quickly followed.

Slavery existed in both the British and French colonies. Male slaves worked as common labourers in the fishery, military, and trade, and in artisan and service occupations; female slaves were employed primarily as domestic servants. Kenneth Donovan has determined that at least 216 slaves lived on Île Royale between 1713 and 1760. Over 90 per cent were Black, reflecting the close trading ties with the West Indies, where sugar, tobacco, indigo, and coffee plantations relied on African slave labour. The other slaves were Aboriginal people, called *Panis* or *sauvages*. Most Panis came from the colony of Canada, where they outnumbered those of African origin.

In the French empire slavery was regulated, in theory, by the Code Noir. It obliged slave owners to house, feed, and clothe their slaves properly, to care for the aged and infirm, to encourage marriage, and to provide instruction in the Roman Catholic religion. Masters could whip their slaves, but not imprison or execute them without recourse to the courts. Women—about one-third of the enslaved population on Île Royale—were not to be sexually exploited, and children were not to be sold separately from a parent before reaching adolescence. The Code Noir was not registered in Île Royale, and it is unlikely that its provisions were widely known. Only six slaves in the colony were freed in this period, and they had little recourse for help when subjected to physical, psychological, or sexual abuse.

Nevertheless, a few slaves at Louisbourg triumphed over their difficult circumstances. Marie Marguerite Rose, for example, obtained her freedom after nearly two decades in the service of the family of a Louisbourg officer, Jean Chrysostome Loppinot. On 27 November 1755 she married a man of Aboriginal descent, Jean Baptiste Laurent. They lived next door to Marguerite's former owners and set up a tavern. That 'Madam Rose negress' was able to open a business and secure credit in her own name for supplies of meat and rum suggests that there was a degree of 'limited opportunity' available to slaves in Louisbourg.

Although Île Saint-Jean offered plenty of agricultural potential, it attracted little interest. Its forest-covered soils proved far less attractive to Acadians than their dykeland farms, and French authorities initially left development there to private interests. In 1719 the Comte de Saint-Pierre was granted the right to the cod fishery on Saint-Jean, Miscou, and the Îles de la Madeleine in return for sponsoring settlement. The following year his Compagnie de l'Île Saint-Jean sent out more than 250 colonists, who established themselves at coastal locations such as Port LaJoie (near present-day Charlottetown) and Havre Saint-Pierre.

The venture was well-conceived and designed to be permanent. Twenty married couples arrived in 1720 and the company recruited potential brides for their unmarried workers and even a midwife. To encourage family formation indentured servants were promised that they would be released from their contracts if they married on Île Saint-Jean. Despite this careful planning the company failed, its efforts dogged by competition from interlopers, crop failures, and ultimately bankruptcy. The settlers moved away, some of them to Île Royal.

To maintain its sovereignty, in 1726 France installed a detachment of 30 naval fusiliers in the dilapidated buildings at Port LaJoie formerly occupied by Saint-Pierre's company. During the 1730s Jean-Pierre Roma, an energetic Parisian merchant, established fishing operations on the island. Building roads to connect his base at Trois-Rivières with Havre Saint-Pierre and Port LaJoie, he hoped to develop the colony into an important trading centre. He might well have succeeded if the War of the Austrian Succession had not intervened.

Imperial Rivalries and Local Strategies

French officials viewed the Acadian and Aboriginal residents of Nova Scotia as their main bulwark against the British. Using Roman Catholic priests (who under the Treaty of Utrecht were permitted to minister to both groups) as agents, French authorities kept a watchful eye on these potential sources of support in time of war.

Most Acadians would have preferred to live under a French Roman Catholic sovereign, but they were not prepared to jeopardize their security by challenging the new regime. A few ambitious families married their daughters to British officers, but most Acadians were wary of aligning themselves too closely with the British. Culture and tradition might predispose them to support the French, but their historical experience seemed to demonstrate that neutrality was the best option. Who could tell which power would win the imperial struggle and gain permanent sovereignty over Acadian lands?

For thirty years, the Acadian strategy of playing both sides paid off. The expansion of North Atlantic trade, much of it focused on New England and Île Royale, offered unprecedented opportunities for the Acadians to increase their wealth and well-being. Indeed, Naomi Griffiths has described the years between 1713 and 1744 as a 'golden age' in Acadian life,[4] largely because it was a period of peace. Family life flourished and by the mid-eighteenth century, there were over 9,000 Acadians in Nova Scotia and 3,000 more on Île Saint-Jean and Île Royale.

It was French policy in North America to nurture alliances with Native peoples through subsidized trade, annual gift-giving, and missionary influence. In the Atlantic region, two priests in particular were effective as missionaries and *agents-provocateurs*: Pierre-Antoine-Simon Maillard and Jean-Louis Le Loutre. By the 1750s Abbé Maillard's base at Chapel Island on Île Royale had become the site for an annual Mi'kmaq celebration combining worship, gift-giving, and trade. Le Loutre ministered to mainland Mi'kmaq from his base at Shubenacadie (some fifty kilometres north of Halifax) until 1750, when his political activities forced him to move to the Isthmus of Chignecto.

Map of Île Royale by Louis Franquet, 1751. This carefully labelled plan shows French settlement on the island before its final capture by the British in 1758. LAC, NMC-148.

After more than a century of French presence, the Mi'kmaq and Maliseet (now closely aligned with the Passamaquoddy) were not interested in an alliance with the British, whose language and religion were foreign. With New England settlement moving up the coast, France offering better terms of trade, and British authorities demanding an oath of allegiance, the Aboriginal people in the region soon made their position clear. During the summer of 1715, Mi'kmaq mariners seized Massachusetts fishing vessels off Cape Sable, declaring that 'the Lands are theirs and they can make War and peace when they please.'[5] Governor Richard Philipps, who arrived in 1720, managed to extract a promise of friendship from the Maliseet, but the Mi'kmaq remained hostile, driving New England fishermen out of Canso in 1720 and, in 1722, capturing 36 trading vessels off Nova Scotia.

The New Englanders were quick to retaliate, setting off an 'Indian War' along the New England–Nova Scotia frontier. In the summer of 1724, Mi'kmaq and Maliseet warriors attacked Annapolis Royal, burning part of the town and killing several British soldiers. A treaty concluded in Boston in December 1725 and ratified at Annapolis Royal in June 1726 finally ended hostilities. The text indicated that the Natives were obliged to recognize British sovereignty. For their part, the British promised that the Natives would not 'be molested in their Persons, Hunting [,] Fishing and Shooting & planting. . . nor in any other [of]their Lawfull

Document: The Treaties of 1725–1726

In the summer of 1725, delegates from New England and the Wabanaki Confederacy met in Boston to negotiate an end to the war that had started three years earlier. The Mi'kmaq and Maliseet were represented by four Penobscot Abenaki. On 15 December 1725 an agreement was reached, with the stipulation that each group would be required to ratify the treaty. Mi'kmaq, Maliseet, and Passamaquoddy did so at Annapolis Royal on 4 June 1726. The first part of the treaty consisted of the articles of peace and agreement that the Native peoples would be obliged to follow in their relations with the British colonies of Massachusetts, New Hampshire, and Nova Scotia. The second part of the treaty outlined Britain's obligations, and was signed by Captain John Doucett, Lieutenant Governor of Annapolis Royal. The treaties read in part:

Article of Peace and Agreement: Annapolis Royal, 1726

Whereas His Majesty King George by the Concession of the Most Christian King made att the Treaty of Utrecht is become ye Rightfull Possessor of the Province of Nova Scotia or Acadia According to its ancient Boundaries, wee the Said Chiefs & Representatives of ye Penobscott, Norridgewalk, St. Johns, Cape Sables, & of the Other Indian Tribes Belonging to & Inhabiting within This His Majesties Province of Nova Scotia Or Acadia & New England do for our Selves & the said Tribes Wee represent acknowledge His Said Majesty King George's Jurisdiction & Dominion Over The Territories of the Said Province of Nova Scotia or Acadia & make our Submission to His said Majesty in as Ample a Manner as wee have formerly done to the Most Christian King.

That the Indians shall not molest any of His Majesty's Subjects or their Dependants in their Settlements already made or now fully to be made or in their carrying on their Trade or any other affairs within the said Province.

That if there Happens any Robbery or outrage Committed by any of our Indians the Tribe or Tribes they belong to shall Cause satisfaction to be made to ye partys Injured.

That the Indians shall not help to convey away any Soldiers belonging to His Majesty's forts, but on the contrary shall bring back any soldier they shall find endeavouring to run away.

That in case of any misunderstanding, Quarrel or Injury between the English and the Indians no private revenge shall be taken, but Application shall be made for redress according to His Majesty's Laws.

That if there [be] any Prisoners amongst any of our aforesaid Tribes, wee faithfully promise that the said prisoners shall be releas'd & Carefully Conducted & delivered up to this Government or that of New England.[6]

Reciprocal Promises Made by Captain John Doucett, 1726

Whereas the Chiefs of the Penobscott, Norridgewalk, St. Johns, Cape Sable Indians and of the other Indian Tribes & their Representatives Belonging to and Inhabiting within this his Majesty's Province of Nova Scotia Conforme to the Articles Stipulated by their Delegates . . . at Boston in New England The Fifteenth day of December one thousand Seven hundred & twenty five have come to this His Majesty's Fort of Annapolis Royal and Ratifyed said Articles and made their submission to his Majesty King George . . . and Acknowledged his said Majesty's Just title to this his said province of Nova Scotia or Acadia & promised to Live peaceably with all his Majestys Subjects & their Dependants & to performe what Further is Contained in the Severall articles of their Instruments. I do therefore in His Majesty's name for and in Behalf of this His said Government of Nova Scotia or Acadia Promise the Said Chiefs & their Respective Tribes all marks of Favour, Protection & Friendship.

And I do Further promise & in the absence of the honabl the Lt Govr of the Province in behalf of the this said Government, That the Said Indians shall not be Molested in their Persons, Hunting Fishing and Shooting & planting on their planting Ground nor in any other their Lawfull occasions, By his Majesty's Subjects or Their Descendants in the Exercise of their Religion Provided the Missionarys Residing amongst them have Leave from the Government for So Doing.

That if any Indians are Injured By any of his Majesty's Subjects or their Dependants They shall have Satisfaction and Reparation made to them According to His Majesty's Laws whereof the Indians shall have Benefit Equall with his Majesty's other Subjects.

That upon the Indians Bringing back any Soldier Endeavouring to run away from any of His Majesty's Forts or Garrisons, the Said Indians for this good Office Shall be handsomely rewarded.

That as a Mark and token of a true Observation & Faithfull Performance of all and Every Article promised on his Majesty's part by the Government I have by and with the Advice of the Council for the said Government Releas'd and Sett att Liberty the Said Indian Prisoners.[7]

occasions. . .'. Since formal treaties were a British innovation, only time would tell whether they were worth the paper on which they were written.

The War of the Austrian Succession, 1744–48

The test of Acadian neutrality and Aboriginal alliances came in 1744, with the outbreak of the War of the Austrian Succession. News that war had been declared reached Louisbourg three weeks before it arrived in Annapolis Royal and Boston. Taking advantage of this intelligence, Governor Jean Baptiste-Louis Le Prévost Duquesnel authorized privateers to attack New England shipping and dispatched a force against Canso. The 87 soldiers stationed there were caught off guard and surrendered almost immediately in May 1744.

Duquesnel then moved against Annapolis Royal, sending an advance force of some 300 Mi'kmaq and a few Acadians, mobilized by Le Loutre, to lay siege to the poorly defended capital. Fortunately for the British, a Massachusetts force intervened. Le Loutre's army took flight, believing that the New Englanders were accompanied by a contingent of Mohawks, reputed to be formidable enemies. Later in the summer, Captain François Du Pont Duvivier attacked Annapolis Royal with the help of 160 Mi'kmaq and 70 Maliseet. Commander Paul Mascarene might well have been forced to surrender, but once again reinforcements arrived from Boston and assistance from France failed to materialize.

Alarmed by developments on their northeastern frontier, the New Englanders moved quickly against Louisbourg. In the spring of 1745 a volunteer militia of 4,300 men, led by William Pepperrell and supported by a British naval squadron, landed at Gabarus Bay, about three kilometres from the fortress. Dragging their cannon over difficult terrain, the New Englanders pounded their objective for seven weeks. Governor Louis Du Pont Duchambon, his town in ruins and its inhabitants facing extreme deprivation, surrendered on 17 June. New Englanders also destroyed French installations on Île Saint-Jean, including Roma's base at Trois-Rivières. In June 1746 the French tried to recapture Louisbourg, but the large expedition led by the Duc d'Anville—54 ships carrying 7,000 men—was dogged by bad weather, poor management, and debilitating diseases. D'Anville died and his successor tried to commit suicide. By October the tattered remnants of the squadron had retreated to France without firing a shot against the enemy.

Its navy devastated, France could not support military campaigns in North America. Thus a force of 680 men under the Sieur de Ramezay, sent from Québec to support the hapless Louisbourg expedition, was left to its own devices. Learning that Governor Shirley of Massachusetts had sent 500 colonial militiamen to keep the Acadians under surveillance, de Ramezay dispatched Captain Louis Coulon de Villiers and 300 Canadiens on a classic winter guerrilla campaign. They made their way through heavy snow to Grand Pré, where the New Englanders were quartered in Acadian homes. Using information provided by sympathetic Acadians, the French surrounded the houses where the New Englanders were sleeping, killed 70, and forced the rest to surrender.

The 'Massacre of Grand Pré', as the English called it, made the Acadian strategy of neutrality irrelevant. The British would remember the few 'treacherous informers' and 'traitors' who had helped de Villiers, not the majority who had tried to maintain a desperate neutrality. British administrators were now convinced that Acadians could be pressed into supplying both French and Natives with billets, intelligence, and provisions. Whether their compliance was voluntary or extracted under duress was immaterial.

An Uneasy Peace, 1749–55

The Treaty of Aix-la-Chapelle in 1748 temporarily averted reprisals. Britain and France agreed to return what each had captured from the other. The New Englanders were outraged when they learned that Louisbourg was included in the deal. Nevertheless, each side understood that the treaty represented a truce rather than a final settlement.

To counter the threat posed by Louisbourg, the British government decided to build a fortified base on the south shore of the Nova Scotia peninsula. In June 1749 Edward Cornwallis led an expedition of more than 2,500 British soldiers, settlers, and labourers to the shores of Chebucto Bay. The founding of Halifax was Britain's first serious attempt to colonize the territories acquired under the Treaty of Utrecht. As such it marked a turning point in the history of the Atlantic region, signalling a new determination on the part of the British to control Nova Scotia.

This initiative posed a threat not only to the French but also to the Native people in the region. The British insisted that all First Nations that had fought on the French side must sign separate peace treaties. The Maliseet and Passamaquoddy seemed prepared to reconfirm the treaty of 1726, but the Mi'kmaq remained defiant. They attacked the British at sea and harassed the settlers at Halifax, which had been established on a favourite Mi'kmaq summer encampment site. Cornwallis responded not by declaring war—to do that, he reasoned, 'would be . . . to own them a free and Independent people'—but by ordering British subjects to 'take or destroy the savages commonly called Micmacks wherever they are found', offering a reward 'to be paid upon producing such savage taken or his scalp (as is the custom of America)'. Not surprisingly, the Mi'kmaq resistance continued, encouraged by Le Loutre and Maillard, who had been instructed to do everything possible to impede British expansion.[8] Authorities at Louisbourg and Québec strengthened their military presence and, not to be outdone by Cornwallis, offered bounties for British prisoners and scalps.

As tensions mounted, the Acadians were caught in the middle, pressed by both British and French to take sides. Shortly after his arrival, Cornwallis summoned Acadian representatives to Halifax and demanded that their people take an unqualified oath of allegiance. They refused, fearing reprisals from either the French or the Mi'kmaq, if not both. It was becoming impossible to remain neutral. In 1750 the French built Fort Beauséjour north of the Missaguash River on the Chignecto Isthmus, and urged Acadians to move to French-controlled territory, where they could establish farms to supply food to Île Royale, augment the colonial militia, and bolster French territorial claims. Acadians who refused to relocate were instructed on pain of death not to sell their produce to the British, or to assist them in any way. The golden age of Acadia had come to an abrupt end.

In response to France's audacity in occupying disputed territory, inciting the Mi'kmaq to war, and mobilizing the Acadians into a fifth column, Cornwallis ordered the construction of Fort Edward at Pisiquid (Windsor) to keep an eye on the populous Minas settlements, and dispatched Lieutenant-Colonel Charles

Lawrence to build a fort across the river from Beauséjour. Despite stiff opposition from French forces, Fort Lawrence was completed in 1750, but the French still had the upper hand. Acadians and Le Loutre's Mi'kmaq allies began to move in significant numbers to the Chignecto area and to nearby Île Saint-Jean. In 1752 Cornwallis's successor, Peregrine Thompson Hopson, concluded a treaty of peace and friendship with the Mi'kmaq to the east of Halifax, but raids, skirmishes, and reprisals continued both in Nova Scotia and elsewhere.

Following clashes on the Ohio frontier in 1754, the British and aggrieved New Englanders decided to launch a four-pronged attack against the outer defences of New France: Fort Duquesne in the Ohio Valley, Fort Niagara in the Great Lakes region, Fort Frédéric on Lake Champlain, and Fort Beauséjour in Nova Scotia. The offensive proved ineffective on all fronts save one. A colonial militia force of 2,500 men commanded by Colonel Robert Monckton captured Beauséjour on 12 June 1755 after a brief siege. With only 160 regular soldiers and 300 militia, the French commander's position was hopeless.

For the British, the discovery that many of the French militiamen were Acadians marked a turning point. They had already made plans to remove Acadians from the Chignecto region. Now the fate of the entire Acadian population hung in the balance.

Le Grand Dérangement

In July 1755 Governor Charles Lawrence offered Acadian delegates one last chance to take an unqualified oath of allegiance. When they refused, Lawrence and his council decided to solve the problem of the 'neutral French' once and for all. Military commanders at Chignecto, Pisiquid, and Annapolis Royal were instructed to seize Acadian men and boys, along with their boats, so that they could not escape. The Acadians were to be deported to the other British colonies in North America, taking only what they could carry.

Awaiting the arrival of transports from Boston, Acadians watched in horror as soldiers burned their homes, barns, churches, and crops, and seized their cattle to pay the costs of what was by any measure an expensive operation. The sorrows of the deportation did not end there. Since authorities in the receiving colonies had not been informed in advance, they offered little assistance, and some even refused to accept their quotas of deportees. By the time the expulsions ended, in 1762, nearly 11,000 Acadians out of a total of about 14,000 had been deported. Others managed to hide out until hostilities ended. Some 2,000 made their way to Québec. Many deportees died of disease and misadventure. Of the 3,100 Acadians shipped from Île St-Jean in 1758, for example, 679 drowned at sea and another 970 died from various causes before reaching their destinations.[9]

Even the French in Newfoundland were not spared. In August 1755 a British naval expedition had appeared off the southwestern coast. Commanded by Captain John Rous, who later played a role in the main deportation, it captured several French Basque ships and sent their crews north to Port au Choix to find passage home. The shore facilities and houses at five harbours between St George's

Letter from Charles Lawrence concerning the expulsion of the Acadians, 11 August 1755. LAC, MG 53, No. 71 2–4.

Bay and Port aux Basques were burned and their 67 residents dumped on Île Royale, where they faced a second deportation.

The Acadian diaspora had a remarkable reach. It took some to Louisiana, where their descendants, the Cajuns, still live; to Canada, where they quickly integrated into the colonial population; to the Îles de la Madeleine, St-Pierre-et-Miquelon, the West Indies, Great Britain, France, and even the Falkland Islands. Those who went to France felt like strangers and asked to be returned to North America. When the war ended, some of them got their wish. In 1764 Acadians who agreed to take an oath of allegiance were permitted to settle in their former homeland—but not, for the most part, in the areas where they had lived. New immigrants had already taken up their farms.

Cruel as it was, the expulsion of the Acadians had the military effect that Lawrence had intended. The food-supply problem reached crisis proportions in Louisbourg, where the authorities were besieged by destitute Aboriginal allies and Acadian refugees. Even before warfare formally resumed in 1756, the French had

Table 6.1   Acadian Population in 1763 (approximate)

Massachusetts	1,050
Connecticut	650
New York	250
Maryland	810
Pennsylvania	400
South Carolina	300
Georgia	200
Nova Scotia	1,250
Saint John River	100
Louisiana	300
England	850
France	3,500
Québec	2,000
St John's Island	300
Baie des Chaleurs	700
Total	12,600

Source: Adapted from R. Cole Harris, ed., *Historical Atlas of Canada*, vol. 1 (Toronto: University of Toronto Press, 1987), Plate 30.

lost the first round. 'Maybe more than any other single factor,' the historian Stephen E. Patterson suggests, 'the supply problem spelled doom to French power in the region'.[10]

Newfoundland, 1713–55

Newfoundland escaped much of the drama that engulfed the Maritime region between the Treaty of Utrecht and the Seven Years' War. No military campaigns were conducted on the island, and as a result a settler society began to develop once again, untroubled by the kind of devastation wrought during earlier wars.

Until the late 1720s, the fisheries were generally poor, prompting the English to enter the offshore bank fishery for the first time. Thereafter the banks became an increasingly important part of the overall fishery. The inshore failures may explain the fairly slow movement of the English fishery along the south coast, now abandoned by the French. Expansion on the northeast coast, into Bonavista and Notre Dame bays, was more vigorous, possibly because of the opportunities to diversify into furring, sealing, and salmon fishing.

Economic activity picked up in all the bays as fish catches improved from the 1730s onward. The number of winter inhabitants reached over 7,000 in the 1750s (the summer population was more than twice as large). Of these, just under half were immigrants from southeast Ireland. Before the 1720s Newfoundland's inhabitants had come almost exclusively from the hinterlands of the English West Country ports involved in the fishery. The arrival of the Irish reflected not only domestic economic problems, but also the fact that West Country vessels habitually stopped at Waterford for provisions and fishing crews.

This change in the population was noted with some concern by the British authorities, but there was little they could do about it. Indeed, it was in this period that the views held by the authorities and the merchants began to diverge. While the government still saw Newfoundland as a fishery and a nursery for mariners, merchants increasingly saw it as a place to make money—not just by fishing on their own account, but by supplying residents and bye-boatmen and purchasing their catches. A quasi-colonial society began to emerge, without any encouragement from the British government. Largely male—women made up less than a third of the population—and transient, it was composed of British merchants at the apex, planters in the middle, and servants at the bottom, and lacked a middle class in the usual sense of the term.

The Seven Years' War, 1756–63

The Seven Years' War had important consequences for the whole Atlantic region. Even before hostilities officially opened in 1756, it was clear that the Atlantic colonies would become a major theatre of war. Louisbourg and Halifax, as well as the fisheries, were important prizes and the instability of the border between British and French territory invited a military resolution.

Although the British were slow to mobilize their forces in North America, once in action they proved effective. They launched a massive attack on the fortress of Louisbourg in 1758. Governor Drucour surrendered after a seven-week siege, his army of 4,000 regular troops, colonial militia, and Aboriginal warriors overwhelmed by a force twice that size led by General Jeffery Amherst and supported by the British navy.

Amherst consolidated his victory by sending troops to Île Saint-Jean, the Gaspé, the Miramichi, and the Saint John River valley to round up Acadians for deportation and destroy both their settlements and those of their Native allies. To assist in these mopping-up operations, the British employed detachments of Rangers—special forces of colonial militia known for their ruthlessness. Even Amherst blanched when he learned of the bloody campaign conducted along the Saint John River by Rangers under Moses Hazen. 'I gave a Commission of Captain to Lieutenant Hazen as I thought he deserved it,' he wrote. 'I am sorry to say what I have since heard of that affair has sullied his merit with me, as I shall always disapprove of killing women and helpless children.'[11] A similarly brutal policy was carried out by General James Wolfe in the Baie des Chaleurs and Gaspésie.

As French power collapsed, the Mi'kmaq, Maliseet, and Passamaquoddy made their accommodation with the British. During 1760 and 1761, all bands sent delegates to Halifax to sign formal treaties of 'peace and friendship' with the governor and council, acknowledging 'the jurisdiction and Dominion of His Majesty George the Second over the Territories of Nova Scotia or Accadia' and agreeing to submit 'to His Majesty in the most perfect, ample, and solemn manner'. These treaties promised government-operated trading posts, but did not reserve lands for hunting and fishing. Governor Jonathan Belcher was instructed by the British government to draw up a proclamation forbidding encroachment on Aboriginal lands, which he obediently did, but he refused to publicize it because, as he told his superiors, 'If the proclamation had been issued at large, the Indians might have been incited . . . to have extravagant and unwarranted demands, to the disquiet and perplexity of the New Settlements in the province.'[12]

The final chapter in the Seven Years' War took place in Newfoundland. Following the surrender of Montréal in 1760, the French devised a bizarre plan to

The church of Saint Paul and the Parade are shown in a view of Halifax drawn by Richard Short in 1759. By this time the town was basking in the glow of wartime prosperity—a glow that would dim after New France surrendered in 1760. LAC, C-4293.

disrupt the English bank fisheries by capturing St John's and impressing French and Irish fishermen to help them retake Île Royale. In 1762 six vessels bearing 750 soldiers under the command of Charles-Henry d'Arsac de Ternay set sail from France. They occupied St John's, Harbour Grace, Carbonear, and Trinity, and destroyed fishing premises and fishing vessels along the coast. A hastily assembled British force, recruited from New York and Nova Scotia and led by Colonel William Amherst, recaptured St John's. It was the last Anglo–French battle to occur in the Atlantic region.

Peace and Reconstruction

In the Treaty of Paris, which formally ended the war, France gave up its North American empire to Great Britain. A major sticking point in the negotiations was the Newfoundland fisheries. The final agreement renewed the French right to fish on the Treaty Shore and ceded St-Pierre-and-Miquelon to France. The islands would serve as an unfortified shelter for French migratory fishermen and a minimal replacement for Île Royale, which French negotiators had fought hard to keep.

On 7 October 1763 the British government issued a proclamation outlining, in broad strokes, what it intended to do with its newly-acquired territories. In the Atlantic region, Île Royale (renamed Cape Breton) and Île Saint-Jean (anglicized to the Island of St John) became part of Nova Scotia, while the coast of Labrador,

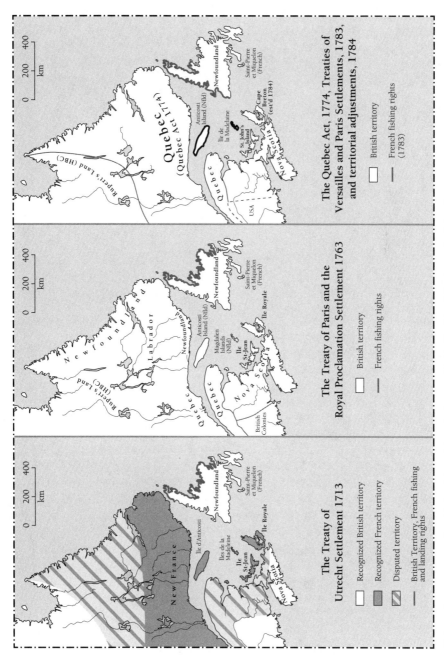

The Quebec Act, 1774, Treaties of
Versailles and Paris Settlements, 1783,
and territorial adjustments, 1784

British territory

French fishing rights
(1783)

The Treaty of Paris and the
Royal Proclamation Settlement 1763

British territory

French fishing rights

The Treaty of
Utrecht Settlement 1713

Recognized British territory

Recognized French territory

Disputed territory

British Territory, French fishing
and landing rights

Eighteenth-century treaty boundaries. Adapted from Buchner and Reid, *The Atlantic Region to Confederation*, 143.

Anticosti Island, and the Îles de la Madeleine were placed 'under the care and inspection' of the governor of Newfoundland.

The proclamation also set out the Crown's policy regarding Aboriginal peoples. No European settlement would be permitted west of the Appalachian Mountains. Elsewhere, Native people were not to be 'molested or disturbed' in the areas set aside for their hunting. All lands in the settled colonies not 'ceded or purchased by Us' were to be 'reserved to the said Indians', and no 'private person' was authorized to buy Native land. Conceived with the western frontier in mind, these policies were deliberately ignored by administrators in Nova Scotia, who were slow to establish reserves and only minimally involved in Native land transactions. Whether the Royal Proclamation even applied in Newfoundland and Labrador is still a matter of contention today.

Conclusion

Fifty years of rivalry ended in 1763 when, for the first time, all of what is now Atlantic Canada came under a single jurisdiction, to which the Aboriginal people and returning Acadians had no option but to submit. The French presence was reduced to a seasonal fishery on the Newfoundland Treaty Shore and a base at St-Pierre-et-Miquelon. In this situation, the British government was eager to see the region—apart from Newfoundland and Labrador—settled, preferably by English-speaking Protestants.

Chapter Seven

Community Formation, 1749–1815

Between the founding of Halifax in 1749 and the end of the Napoleonic wars in 1815, the Atlantic region was reorganized and essentially remade.[1] The expulsion of the Acadians, the destruction of their farms and communities, and the razing to the ground of the great fortress of Louisbourg struck major blows to the region's economy. At the same time, these policies made it easier for British culture to prevail during post-war reconstruction. Many communities in the region trace their origins to the period from 1749 to 1815, when nearly 75,000 people, mostly of British origin, arrived in the Atlantic colonies.

Immigration and Settlement

In this period a great wave of immigration transformed Atlantic Canada. The early immigrants were recruited by the British authorities, but in time others began to arrive independently. Some were refugees from the political and economic revolutions sweeping the North Atlantic world; others were attracted by the region's potential to profit from resource development and warfare. Many of the new settlers came from other parts of North America, but they shared with immigrants from Great Britain and Europe a determination to improve their lot in an unstable and rapidly changing world.

Between 1750 and 1753 nearly 2,500 German- and French-speaking Protestants, recruited by the British in Europe, arrived in Nova Scotia. Some of these 'foreign Protestants' stayed in Halifax, but the majority helped to found the town of Lunenburg in 1753. With the threats posed by hostile French and Aboriginal forces uppermost in their minds, British authorities designed Lunenburg as a compact community that would be more easily defended in the event of attack than scattered farm settlements. The rigid grid of streets marching up the steep slope from the harbour still testifies to the classic principles that governed town planning in the eighteenth century. Despite several difficult years, the Lunenburg settlers soon became productive farmers and eventually began fishing and shipbuilding as well.

Many of the disbanded soldiers and sailors who helped to build Halifax quickly escaped to Boston, but merchants and artisans, eager to profit from the money being invested in the colony, stayed—at least for a time. The Jersey-born merchant Joshua Mauger emerged as the most powerful figure in the capital, making his fortune from the West Indies trade, smuggling with Louisbourg, and the

Timeline

1749	Halifax founded.
1750–3	Foreign Protestants arrive in Halifax.
1756–63	Seven Years' War.
1758–9	Governor Lawrence's Proclamations.
1759	New England Planters begin moving to Nova Scotia.
1763	Treaty of Paris; Royal Proclamation.
1764–8	Hugh Palliser serves as governor of Newfoundland.
1764	Samuel Holland surveys St John's Island; Acadians permitted to resettle in the Maritimes.
1767	St John's Island granted to British proprietors.
1769	St John's Island granted colonial status.
1770	George Cartwright builds a trading and fishing base in Labrador.
1771	Moravians establish mission station at Nain, Labrador.
1772–4	Yorkshire settlers arrive in Nova Scotia.
1772	The *Hector* arrives in Pictou.
1774–1809	Labrador under the jurisdiction of Québec/Lower Canada.
1775–83	American Revolutionary War.
1783	Treaty of Paris.
1784	New Brunswick and Cape Breton Island established as separate colonies.
1789	French Revolution begins.
1791	Supreme Court established in Newfoundland.
1792	More than 1,200 Black Loyalists depart for Sierra Leone.
1793–1815	French Revolutionary and Napoleonic Wars.
1799	St John's Island renamed Prince Edward Island.
1812	War of 1812 begins.
1814	End of the War of 1812
1815	End of the Napoleonic wars

sale of rum. In the early 1760s he returned to Great Britain, where, as a member of Parliament, he played an important role in determining colonial policy.

Although its proximity and rapidly growing population made New England a promising source of immigrants, people there were reluctant to move to a colony where their 'rights as Englishmen' were in question. This obstacle was overcome when the Board of Trade, which was responsible for colonial policy, obliged a reluctant Governor Charles Lawrence to call Nova Scotia's first elected assembly in 1758

Mapping the Region

To support their imperial objectives, the British engaged in extensive exploration and mapping. During the Seven Years' War, James Cook charted part of the Gulf of St Lawrence and helped to prepare the map that enabled Wolfe to reach Québec in 1759. After the war, Cook became the naval surveyor for Newfoundland, charting the island's south and west coasts and the Strait of Belle Isle. A century later Cook's charts were still in use, as were those of his assistant Michael Lane, who completed his work.

Cook's equivalent in Nova Scotia was Joseph F.W. DesBarres, who painstakingly charted the waters around the Nova Scotia peninsula, Cape Breton, and St John's Island between 1764 and 1773. His drawings were published in several volumes as *The Atlantic Neptune* (1774–84). A major achievement in Canadian cartographic history, DesBarres's charts also remained in use for many years.

Beginning in 1764 an army officer named Samuel Holland carried out extensive surveys in the Atlantic region. His report on St John's Island laid out counties, parishes, and townships; fixed the site of the projected capital, which he named Charlottetown in honour of George III's Queen; and gave a detailed account of the island's resources and climate. Holland then moved on to the Îles de la Madeleine and Cape Breton, where he drew attention to the island's deposits of coal, building stone, and gypsum. In the early 1770s he helped to map the coast from the Saint John River to New York, and conducted hydraulic surveys in Nova Scotia.

Northern Labrador became better known in the second half of the eighteenth century, largely through the activities of the Moravian missionaries who began investigating the coast in 1765. The interior of Labrador remained largely unknown to

Samuel Holland's map of St John's Island. LAC, NMC-23350

Europeans. The same was true of Newfoundland until concern about the dwindling numbers of Beothuk led to exploration of the Exploits River and Red Indian Lake, beginning in 1768 with an expedition led by Lieutenant John Cartwright. Local Mi'kmaq, who began moving to the island in increasing numbers after 1763, also ranged throughout the interior. It was the Mi'kmaq who informed Cook about the island's river systems, which he included on his 1770 general map.

and issue a proclamation, widely circulated in New England, inviting prospective immigrants to Nova Scotia. A second proclamation issued early in 1759 outlined the rights that settlers would enjoy: two elected assembly representatives for each settled township, a judicial system similar to the one in 'Massachusetts, Connecticut, and the other Northern Colonies', and freedom of worship for Protestant dissenters. Bona fide settlers were to receive land grants—100 free acres (40 hectares) for each head of household, with an additional 50 for each family member and servant—that would be exempt from taxes for ten years. Assistance was even provided to help some of the immigrants move to their new homes.

Their concerns thus addressed, nearly 8,000 New Englanders settled in Nova Scotia between 1759 and 1767. Known as 'Planters', they created a new New England on the south shore of Nova Scotia, in the Annapolis Valley, and in parts of the north shore of the Bay of Fundy. In 1762 James Simonds, James White, and William Hazen—New England merchants associated with Joshua Mauger—established trading operations in the region, eventually locating their headquarters at Portland Point, near the mouth of the Saint John River. They developed a flourishing trade with the local Native people, and brought in labour to exploit the area's resources of fish, timber, and limestone. When, farther up the river, a group of farmers from Essex County, Massachusetts, squatted on land occupied by Acadians and Maliseet, Mauger intervened to ensure that the newcomers prevailed. In 1765 twenty pacifist German Protestant families from Pennsylvania settled on the Petitcodiac River, where they became the founders of Hopewell, Hillsborough, and Moncton.

The largest group yet to settle in the Maritimes, the New England Planters added a distinctly 'Yankee' flavour to the region. They drew freely on the resources of their homeland, recruiting ministers for their Congregational churches in New England, trading fish and farm produce in Boston, and returning 'home' periodically to visit family and friends. Although most Planters came with little capital, they were among the most fortunate of immigrants, making impressive progress in standards of living and institutional development in only one generation.

After the Seven Years' War, Acadians were again permitted to settle in the Atlantic region. They carved out communities in a number of locations, especially Argyle and Clare in southwestern Nova Scotia, Île Madame and Cheticamp in Cape Breton, the northeastern shore of what would later become New Brunswick, and the western end of St John's Island. The Îles de la Madeleine, though settled by Acadians, were administered by Québec after 1774 and granted in 1787 as a seigneury to Captain Isaac Coffin. Scratching a hardscrabble existence from the inferior soil typical of the lands granted them, the Acadians soon turned to fishing and became an indispensable labour force for the Jersey-based fishing companies that set up operations in the Gaspé and Cape Breton following the British conquest. By 1800 the Atlantic region counted at least 8,000 francophones and their numbers would continue to grow impressively with each generation.

In an attempt to populate the region on the cheap and at the same time promote a land-based social hierarchy, British authorities made large land grants to 'proprietors' on condition that they recruit Protestant settlers, improve their properties, and pay quitrents (taxes) to sustain the colonial administration. In a single 17-day period in 1765, more than one million hectares of mainland Nova Scotia were handed over to speculators. Two years later, in an even more spectacular display of largesse, 64 of the 67 lots on St John's Island that Samuel Holland had surveyed in 1764 were granted to favourites of the king and court.

Most of the proprietors failed to meet the conditions of their grants, but a few tried. Alexander McNutt, who had planned to settle thousands of Ulster Protestants, from Ireland and from New Hampshire, on his enormous grants, managed to bring a few hundred to communities such as Londonderry (Colchester County) and New Dublin (Lunenburg County). Near Windsor, Nova Scotia, two would-be aristocrats, Henry Denny Denson and J.F.W. DesBarres, employed tenant and slave labour to work their estates. Located on the Minas Basin, Windsor was fast becoming not only the country seat of the Halifax élite but also a commercial centre of some importance, and in 1767 it hosted the region's first agricultural fair.

The Philadelphia plantation, granted in 1765 to 14 proprietors in what is now Pictou County, attracted a few settlers from Pennsylvania, but the majority of its inhabitants arrived on board the *Hector* in 1773—the beginning of what was to become a substantial wave of immigration from Scotland. Always alert to lucrative trading opportunities, Scottish merchants were drawn to the region specifically for its timber and fish. In 1765 William Davidson and his associates received a grant of 100,000 acres (40,500 hectares) on the Miramichi, where they developed a salmon fishery and eventually diversified into timber and shipbuilding.

Between 1772 and 1776 roughly 1,000 people from Yorkshire, many of them Methodists, settled in the Chignecto area and elsewhere in Nova Scotia. Pushed out of England by high rents, land enclosure, and their own ambitions, they arrived with commercial and farming skills of a high order. Many of them had sufficient capital to purchase their farms outright, and they quickly brought them into efficient production.

Most of the unsettled proprietorial grants in Nova Scotia eventually reverted to the Crown, but this was not the case on St John's Island (renamed after Prince Edward in 1799). By having the island proclaimed a separate colony in 1769 and controlling its administration, the proprietors succeeded in frustrating all attempts to settle 'the land question'. In this way the colony became saddled with an absentee landlord system that was increasingly out of step with the tendency to grant land in freehold tenure throughout most of North America.

Biography: Mikak

Born in Labrador around 1740, Mikak was a member of an Inuit band that frequented the south Labrador coast, trading with Europeans and often scavenging from their establishments. Conflict and violence were commonplace.

In 1767 trouble developed between Mikak's band and Europeans at Cape Charles. Marines from the blockhouse in Chateau Bay retaliated, and at least 24 men were killed in the ensuing skirmish, among them Mikak's husband. Taken captive—along with two other women and six children, including her son, Tutauk—Mikak spent the winter at Chateau Bay, where she and the second in command, Francis Lucas, each learned some words of the other's language.

In the summer of 1768 Lucas took his captives to St John's. Governor Palliser, impressed by Mikak, arranged for Lucas to escort her to England with Tutauk and a boy named Karpik. In London Mikak was visited by the Moravian Jens Haven, whom she had met in 1765, and was lionized at court. The Dowager Princess of Wales gave her presents, including a fine dress, and John Russell, a fashionable artist, painted her portrait. She returned to Labrador in 1769.

Mikak was now a person of status among her own people, and this, together with her knowledge of English, made her a potentially important intermediary for Europeans. In 1770, for example, both Lucas and the Moravians wanted her assistance, but the Moravians reached her first. With her new husband, Tuglavina, Mikak agreed to help them find a suitable site for their mission. Lucas looked for Mikak in vain, and was lost at sea later that year.

The Moravians established Nain in 1771. Deciding not to live there, Mikak and Tuglavina drifted away from the mission and its influence. They separated in 1776, and she had a succession of other husbands. At one time she showed an interest in baptism, but in 1783 she left for south Labrador. In 1795 she became ill and returned to Nain, where she spent the last ten days of her life. Tuglavina, now a convert, died there three years later.

Mikak's son Tutauk, who called himself Jonathan Palliser, moved back south. When a Methodist missionary met him in Hamilton Inlet, in 1824, one of his wives was wearing Mikak's English dress. His descendants still live in Labrador.[2]

John Russell, 'Esquimaux Lady', oil on canvas, 1769. Mikak is clothed in a dress given to her by the Dowager Princess of Wales. Mikak was returned to Labrador in 1769, and later helped the Moravian mission become established there. Völkerkundliche Sammlung der Universität Göttingen, Germany.

Despite this handicap, the island managed to attract settlers. Many of the early immigrants were Scots, whose homeland was suffering such severe political and economic upheaval that emigration seemed an attractive option even if it meant leasing rather than owning land outright. The first settlers, some 80 Scots recruited by Captain Robert Stewart for Lot 18, arrived on the *Arabella* in 1770. They were soon followed by a group of indentured servants under contract to grow flax on the estates of Sir James Montgomery, Roman Catholic Highlanders under the direction of John MacDonald of Genaladale, Protestants from Ulster, and Quakers from London. By 1775 the 300 Acadian and Mi'kmaq residents of the island were outnumbered four to one by the 1,200 immigrants from Great Britain.

The year-round population of Newfoundland grew as well, to about 10,000 in the 1770s, but in the same way as earlier in the century: slowly, informally, and without official encouragement. The reactionary Sir Hugh Palliser, governor from 1764 to 1768, did what he could to discourage permanent settlement and to support the migratory fishery. He focused his attention on southern Labrador, where a state of warfare existed between fishermen and the Inuit who travelled south to the Strait of Belle Isle to trade whalebone and to scavenge from fishing camps.

Eager to pacify the area, Palliser welcomed a proposal from the highly disciplined Protestant sect commonly called the Moravians—officially the Unitas Fratrum (United Brethren)—to establish a mission in Labrador. In 1771 the first Moravian mission station, complete with a trading store, was built at Nain. Its presence eventually helped to persuade the Inuit to stay in the north—as did the growing number of Europeans in the south and the increasing mortality from European diseases among the Inuit living there.

British entrepreneurs also had their eyes on Labrador. In 1770 George Cartwright established a fishing and trading base at Cape Charles and later moved to Sandwich Bay. A man of great energy, Cartwright published an account of his experiences in 1792. Although Labrador was placed under the jurisdiction of Québec in 1774, the governor of Newfoundland continued to supervise the mission stations and the fisheries in the area, which was formally restored to the jurisdiction of Newfoundland in 1809.

The American Revolution

The Seven Years' War turned out to be only an interlude in the warfare that engulfed North America in the eighteenth century. By the early 1770s growing tensions over British taxation, trade, and military policies were moving the New England colonies towards armed conflict. Colonial defiance led the British, in 1774, to curtail the trade conducted by Massachusetts, close the port of Boston, and send in troops. In September of that year, delegates from all but five of Britain's North American colonies (Newfoundland, St John's Island, Nova Scotia, Québec, and Georgia) met in Philadelphia to coordinate a response. The First Continental Congress demanded the repeal of what came to be known as the Coercive Acts. When Britain refused to back down, the colonial militia was placed on alert. The first shots were fired at Lexington, Massachusetts, in April 1775.

Within weeks a second Continental Congress had commissioned George Washington to raise an army for the defence of 'American liberty'. After driving the British out of Boston, they planned to march on Québec. The invasion of Québec failed, but the colonial resolve remained strong. On 4 July 1776, the rebellious colonies declared their independence from Great Britain.

Historians have spent considerable energy exploring why the North Atlantic colonies failed to join the rebellion. In the case of Newfoundland, the reasons are fairly clear. Without formal political institutions, Newfoundlanders had no way of entering into an alliance. Moreover, any sympathy that individuals might have had for the American cause was quickly blunted when, in retaliation against British regulations forbidding New Englanders from fishing in Newfoundland waters, the Americans put a ban on trade with the island. This move caused widespread hardship for Newfoundlanders, who had come to depend on New England for foodstuffs and shipping in the West Indies trade. Throughout the Revolutionary War, American predators made all fishing hazardous, especially offshore. Migratory activity decreased, the resident population fell, and food shortages were frequent. In the winter of 1779–80 James Balfour, a Church of England missionary in Conception Bay, reported 'raging Famine, Nakedness & Sickness in these Parts. None can express the heart felt woe of Women & Children mourning for want of Food.'[3]

In Nova Scotia and Saint John's Island, as in Newfoundland, political and economic development was not sufficiently advanced to make independence an appealing option. Many people who had received land from the Crown on exceptionally favourable terms were reluctant to support the rebellious colonies for fear that, as seemed likely at the outset of the war, the British would prevail. Even if there was sympathy for the rebel cause in certain areas, the British military presence in colonial capitals and coastal waters was a powerful deterrent to armed resistance.

The reach of Halifax was clearly demonstrated in the fall of 1776, when Jonathan Eddy and John Allen, both from the Cumberland area, led a force of 180 men, including a few Maliseet and Acadians, against the garrison at Fort Cumberland (formerly Fort Beauséjour). The attack was easily repulsed, but British authorities were obliged to remain vigilant. In July 1776 Mi'kmaq and Maliseet chiefs had attended a meeting in Massachusetts at which they agreed to support the American cause. Mi'kmaq attacks on settlers in the Miramichi area and, in 1778, a Maliseet threat to Fort Howe, at the mouth of the Saint John River, underscored the continuing vulnerability of the British in the region. Michael Francklin, Superintendent for Indian Affairs for Nova Scotia, tried to address Native grievances by bringing in a French-speaking priest and agreeing to issue grants for lands promised in 1768, but some chiefs continued to side with the Americans. The British finally decided to seek assistance from their Aboriginal allies outside of the region. In June 1780 'three hundred fighting men besides six hundred women and children' were assembled to meet with delegates from 'the Ottawas, Hurons, Algonkins, Abenakis and other nations from Canada', who promised to wage war against any Mi'kmaq or Maliseet aligned with the Americans.[4]

Notwithstanding the presence of the British fleet, raids by New England privateers were a fact of life even as far north as Labrador, where George Cartwright's trading posts in Sandwich Bay were plundered in 1778. Most raids were selective, leaving all but the targeted victims unmolested, but they did little to endear the rebels to the pioneer settlers. In November 1775 Yankees even attacked Charlottetown, seizing provisions and carrying away the colony's acting governor, Phillips Callbeck.

After the British defeat at Saratoga in 1777, the fighting moved away from the region and Nova Scotians settled down to profiting from the increased military presence and the influx of Loyalist refugees. Meanwhile, a religious revival, led by the charismatic itinerant preacher Henry Alline, gained momentum in the colony. Many New England Planters, who had more difficulty than other settlers in deciding where their loyalties lay, responded enthusiastically to Alline's message that good Christians should pursue spiritual salvation rather than fight military battles. Alline's ministry was short—he died in 1784—but he laid the foundations of an evangelical tradition that is still strong in Nova Scotia and New Brunswick.

In 1778 France joined the war on the side of the United States, and the British were eventually forced to concede defeat. In the Treaty of Paris (1783) Britain recognized the independence of the United States of America, leaving the Atlantic colonies, Québec, and the Hudson's Bay Company territory—all originally claimed by the French—to form what was left of 'British' North America. In a significant concession, Americans were allowed to continue fishing in the Gulf of St Lawrence, on the banks, and along the Newfoundland coast outside the French Treaty Shore; they also had the 'liberty' to dry fish on the unsettled coasts of Nova Scotia, the Îles de la Madeleine, and Labrador.

In a separate treaty with Britain, France obtained concessions in Newfoundland. The boundaries of the Treaty Shore were moved to Cape St John and Cape Ray, away from the areas where the English usually fished, and an appended declaration, while avoiding the word 'exclusive', in effect defined the Shore as a French fishing zone. In addition, St-Pierre-et-Miquelon were returned to France without the deeply resented conditions of 1763; however, a vaguely worded declaration that the islands would never become 'an object of jealousy' between Britain and France invited continuing dispute.

The Loyalists and Post-war Reconstruction

The American Revolution was a defining moment in the history of the Atlantic region. Not only did it create a new boundary separating the colonies from New England; it also more than doubled their population. The first of at least 35,000 'Loyalists' began moving to Nova Scotia even before hostilities were officially declared, but most of them arrived between 1782 and 1784 on ships from New York, where they had gathered under British protection in the final stages of the war. Although they had few good words for 'Nova Scarcity', the Loyalists were luckier than many refugees. The British government supplied provisions and temporary shelter, compensated some of them for their losses, and provided most with

'View of Saint John, New Brunswick', 1814 by Joseph Brown Comingo (1784–1821, Canadian School). Fuelled by a vibrant timber industry during the French and Napoleonic Wars, Saint John quickly developed into the commercial capital of the Bay of Fundy region. Born in Nova Scotia, Comingo painted this watercolour in 1814. Courtesy of the New Brunswick Museum, Saint John, NB. 1966.100A.

free land. In response to intensive lobbying by the Loyalists, it also created two new colonies to accommodate them in 1784: Cape Breton and New Brunswick.

Nearly 15,000 Loyalists landed at the mouth of the Saint John River, engulfing the tiny population already living there and founding the city of Saint John. Maliseet and Acadians were pushed off their land farther up the river, the former into reserves, most of the latter to Madawaska. Even more Loyalists—approximately 19,000—went to peninsular Nova Scotia. Half of them settled in Shelburne, which for a time became the largest city in British North America. When it failed to develop into the prosperous trading centre they had expected, most of the Loyalists drifted away. Some moved back to the United States when they judged it safe. Others went to Québec; still others to Halifax, Saint John, and the dozens of smaller communities, including Aylesford, Digby, Gagetown, Guysborough, Rawden, Ship Harbour, St Andrew's, and Sussex Vale, established by Loyalists.

Relatively few of them settled on Cape Breton, even though Sydney was founded as a Loyalist town. In 1784 the island was made a separate colony, largely on the strength of Abraham Cuyler's abortive scheme to attract 5,000 Loyalists from Québec. Interest in St John's Island was low as well: only some 800 Loyalists were prepared to begin new lives as tenant farmers on land granted to absentee proprietors. And no one was interested in what Newfoundland had to offer.

New Brunswick attracted a significant number of élite Loyalists. Determined to rebuild their fortunes in the frontier colony, which they expected to dominate, they hoped to make New Brunswick 'the envy of the American states', a model of order and hierarchy in contrast to the democratic anarchy that they felt would surely engulf their neighbours to the south. Concluding that the busy mercantile town of Saint John was both too crass and too close to the American border, they chose Fredericton as the capital of what they hoped would become 'a stable agricultural society led by a landholding gentry'.[5] Not surprisingly, the pretensions of the Loyalist élite were not well received by the mass of the refugees. When 55 prominent Loyalists, 'of the most respectable Characters', as they themselves declared, petitioned for estates of 5,000 acres—nearly ten times the average grant—the wishes of the majority prevailed and the request was denied. In the 1785 election the inhabitants of Saint John violently protested the condescension of the government based in Fredericton.

Loyalists were also politically active in Nova Scotia, where the New Hampshire-born Sir John Wentworth was appointed lieutenant-governor in 1792.

Document: Edward Winslow's Plan for a 'Gentlemanlike' Colony, 1783

When the American Revolution began in 1775, 29-year-old Edward Winslow was a young man with great prospects. He was a Harvard graduate, descendant of one of the founders of Massachusetts Bay colony, and the only son of a prominent New England family with valuable estates in the Plymouth area. In the tensions leading to the war, Edward supported the British cause and during the war he was based in New York as muster master general of the colonial troops that fought with the British. The success of the patriots left Edward and his family nearly destitute. Without the resources to establish themselves in England, Edward, his mistress Mary Simmonds, their three children, and servants moved to Nova Scotia early in 1783.

Winslow wrote the following letter to his friend Ward Chipman, in New York, from the Saint John River on 7 July 1783. The letter reveals much about the attitudes of élite Loyalists faced with beginning life over again on the colonial frontier. Not surprisingly, Winslow and Chipman were strong advocates of a separate colony north of the Bay of Fundy where they might seek the government positions denied them in Halifax.

> We have just begun our operations in the land way—the people who have arrived here are prodigiously pleased with the country—& I shall certainly soon be possess.ᵈ of a good farm, and if we've our half pay I will be more than comfortable.—I have left those sweet little ones in as comfortable a place, as is in this province made so by my own exertions—I found a house & hired it for £6 a year & I've taken a lease for two years— I added two rooms—& a chimney & have now a spare bed-room at your

service 'tis just on the bank of a most beautiful river immediately opposite the town of Annapolis.—I have left Thomson's William (now Q.ʳ M.ʳ)
to superintend & Mother Silk & little George, we have plenty of poultry a
good garden & such a variety of fish as you never saw & I have built a tol-
erable boat. So much for the family.

. . . I am determined at all events to distinguish myself by proposing
a plan which affords the grandest field for speculation that ever offered.—
take the general map of this province (even as it's now bounded) observe
how detached this part is from the rest—how vastly extensive it is—
notice the rivers—harbours &c. consider the numberless inconveniences
that must arise—from [its] remoteness from the metropolis [Halifax] &
the difficulty of communication.—Think what multitudes have & will come
here—and then judge whether it must not from the nature of things—
immediately become a separate government, & if it does it shall be the
most Gentlemanlike one on earth. Suppose you & he go to England after
being provided with the necessary facts—can you be better employed
than in a solicitation of this kind—properly authorized. You know how
Industrious I can be if I please—& you may rest assured that I will pursue this project with unremitted attention.—the people on the other side
are already jealous—even the Gov.ʳ fears it evidently—we have therefore
[been] perfectly snug. . . .[6]

Revelling in the court-like atmosphere of Halifax social life, the Loyalist élite were
enchanted by the presence of the king's son, Prince Edward Augustus, and his
beautiful mistress, Madame de St Laurent, who resided in the city between 1794
and 1799. Outside provincial capitals the pioneer experience had a levelling effect,
and Loyalist roots counted for little in a region where, after 1783, nearly everyone
claimed to have supported the British cause.

The Loyalists represented a thick slice of North American society and greatly
increased the region's cultural diversity. As well as élites with aristocratic ideals, the
mix included military veterans of all ranks, farmers and tradesmen, and a wide range
of ethnic groups, including African Americans, many of them former slaves who
had been encouraged to leave their masters by promises of freedom if they fought
in British regiments. Over 3,000 Black Loyalists moved to Nova Scotia, but they
soon realized that freedom did not bring equality. Given smaller and less fertile
grants than white Loyalists, they were often targets for hostility and violence during the tension-ridden early years of settlement. Nearly 1,200 Black Loyalists left
the region in 1792 for the new colony of Sierra Leone—though the 2,000 slaves
in the Loyalist migration, were denied that option. Following the abolition of the
slave trade in 1807, slave-holding gradually disappeared in the Atlantic region, and
in 1833 it was abolished throughout the British Empire by an act of Parliament.

In the wake of the American Revolution the British government was eager to strengthen the authority of the Crown and to create a rigid class system in the colonies. The Church of England, the established church in Great Britain, was selected to play an important role in achieving these goals. In 1787 Charles Inglis, the Loyalist former rector of Trinity Church in New York, was consecrated the first bishop of Nova Scotia, with jurisdiction over all the British North American colonies, including Newfoundland and Bermuda. The Society for the Propagation of the Gospel, the Church of England's missionary arm, helped to pay the salaries of clergymen and the cost of building churches. To help sustain the class structure, Inglis supported the founding of King's College in Windsor in 1788 as an exclusive institution for the sons of the Church of England élite, as well as the Provincial Academy of Arts and Sciences in Fredericton, which received its charter as the College of New Brunswick in 1800. Inglis and his clergy strenuously opposed evangelical enthusiasm and the 'levelling' tendencies it seemed to encourage. Despite all its efforts, the Church of England in the Maritimes steadily lost adherents to the Baptists and Methodists, whose ministers promised ordinary people personal salvation and spiritual equality.

In Newfoundland the American Revolution forced changes in customary trade patterns. Merchants began to send their own ships to the West Indies, sometimes using Bermuda shipowners as middlemen. Although it was still possible to import food from the United States after the war, so long as it was transported in British ships, Newfoundland importers increasingly looked to other sources of supply, especially in the Maritimes and the Canadas. A shipbuilding industry grew on the island, and a Newfoundland-based fleet, managed largely by merchants newly arrived from Greenock, Scotland, traded to the mainland and Caribbean. The winter population soon recovered to pre-war levels and began to grow steadily, with residents taking an increasing proportion of the total cod catch as migratory activity declined.

The naval state remained in place on the island, with the court system becoming more elaborate over time. A government house was built in the early 1780s, a supreme court was established in 1791, and civilians began to join naval officers as surrogate magistrates. It was a practical and reasonably effective system of government. The navy even contributed to religious life, since its chaplains were active on shore as well as on board their vessels, at least among Protestants. A proclamation of 1784 established religious freedom in Newfoundland. In the same year Father James O'Donnell arrived as prefect apostolic (he would become bishop in 1796) to organize the few Roman Catholic priests available to minister to the increasing numbers of Irish. As in the Maritimes, the Church of England clergy in Newfoundland were supported by the Society for the Propagation of the Gospel. Most immigrants from England belonged to the established church, but Protestant dissenters were gaining ground. From 1766 the Reverend Laurence Coughlan preached Methodism on the north shore of Conception Bay with considerable success, and in St John's dissenters attended John Jones's Congregational 'Dissenting Church of Christ'.

Between 1783 and 1803 nearly 17,000 Highland Scots immigrated to the Maritimes, most of them settling on St John's Island, on Cape Breton, and in east-

The Maritime colonies, c. 1800. Adapted from *Historical Atlas of Canada*, I (Toronto: University of Toronto Press, 1987), plates 25 and 32.

ern Nova Scotia. One of the most ambitious settlement schemes was sponsored by the Earl of Selkirk, who in 1803 brought 800 Highlanders to the Orwell–Point Prim area of Prince Edward Island. On the Miramichi, Fraser and Thom, a Scottish timber and shipbuilding company, recruited Scottish labourers. Scottish Highlanders tended to be Gaelic-speaking Roman Catholics, whereas Lowland Scots were more likely to be English-speaking Presbyterians, and to place strong emphasis on education; it was two immigrant Presbyterian ministers, James Mac-Gregor and Thomas McCulloch, who helped to make Pictou, Nova Scotia, a religious and educational centre.

Like Scotland, Ireland was experiencing major social and economic upheavals, including periodic famines, that contributed significantly to the stream of immigrants to the Atlantic region. While Protestant Irish quickly assimilated into the dominant culture, Roman Catholics remained distinct, separated by religion, history, and in many cases their Gaelic language. Irish Catholics swelled the population of southeastern Newfoundland outports, became tenant farmers on Prince Edward Island estates, harvested New Brunswick forests, and worked as domestic servants. In the major port cities such as St John's, Halifax, and Saint John, the Irish quickly came to constitute a significant portion of the population, and the desperate condition of many among them inspired their philanthropic compatriots to found a Charitable Irish Society in Halifax in 1776 and similar organizations in Saint John and St John's in 1806.

For the Mi'kmaq and Maliseet these migrations represented yet another threat to their survival as more territory fell into private hands and competition for fish and game increased. Recognizing their vulnerability, Aboriginal leaders petitioned for land and sometimes received it, but much of it was stolen back by squatters who knew that the authorities would not take action against them. In 1783 the Mi'kmaq chief John Julien obtained a licence of occupation for 20,000 acres (8,100 hectares) on the Miramichi River, but half of it was gone by 1807, when the government finally got around to establishing the Eel Ground Reserve. In Prince Edward Island the Mi'kmaq eventually received permission from proprietor James Montgomery to live on the barren and rocky Lennox Island, but no formal reserves were established.

The French and Napoleonic Wars

Following the outbreak of the French Revolution in 1789, Britain became engaged in the prolonged French and Napoleonic Wars that inevitably spilled over into North America. The final round of the Anglo–French struggle began in 1793 and would not end until 1815. Like its predecessors this lengthy conflict between Great Britain and France had a profound and lasting impact on the Atlantic region. British demand for fish, foodstuffs, and timber skyrocketed and, with alternative sources of supply cut off, the Atlantic colonies found ready markets for their resources. The Navigation Acts and the whole framework of mercantilist regulation that gave colonial producers preference in British markets over their foreign competitors further stimulated production. With the demand high and money pouring in to pay for defence against a possible French attack, colonials found themselves in a privileged and profitable position.

The most critical resource for an empire at war in the eighteenth century was wood, and for many years the British had reserved great stands of timber in North America to supply the Royal Navy. After 1800 these forest reserves came under intense development. Between 1805 and 1812 the exports of fir and pine timber from New Brunswick, Britain's pre-eminent 'timber colony',[7] increased more than twenty-fold. Businessmen, many of them based in Greenock, brought their capital, labour, and technology to the shores of the Miramichi and Saint John rivers, and shipbuilding soon emerged as a sideline of the timber trade. By 1815 New Brunswick's economy was dominated by forest-based industries.

Attempts by the United States to remain neutral and trade with both sides were met by Great Britain's insistence on a strict definition of the rights of neutral countries, one that could be backed up with sea power. President Thomas Jefferson responded in 1807 with an embargo on British trade. While this hurt American exporters, it also wrought havoc with the British war effort. Britain retaliated by declaring Halifax, Shelburne, Saint John, and St Andrews to be 'free ports'—a clever manoeuvre that effectively undermined the embargo.

Annoyed by the restrictions, New England shippers took advantage of the free ports to sell their cargos and buy colonial produce and manufactured goods from Britain. Thus the policy not only served its purpose of keeping the British army and navy supplied, but also helped to make the designated ports important commercial centres in the expanding regional economy. During the war vessels from the Maritimes also began competing successfully with New Englanders in the carrying trade to the West Indies, where the sugar plantations worked by vast numbers of slaves represented a lucrative market. Halifax in particular emerged as a significant entrepôt for produce shipped under convoy to the Caribbean.

If the trade war between Great Britain and the United States benefited the Maritimes, the official conflict known as the War of 1812 brought more economic blessings. Buffered by New England, whose leaders refused to participate in the war, the Atlantic region was spared military invasion and became the centre of a vigorous clandestine trade between the two belligerents. In addition, the British naval and military presence generated unprecedented market opportunities and increased the supply of hard currency. The war also inspired moments of great excitement. In June 1813 Haligonians were treated to the spectacle of HMS *Shannon* arriving with the USS *Chesapeake* in tow following a brief engagement off Boston harbour. The following year, a British army under Sir John Sherbrooke occupied part of the coast of present-day Maine, providing more opportunities for commercial profit.

The War of 1812 expanded the potential for privateering, an activity that had a long history in the region. During the conflict with the Americans, 37 vessels from the Atlantic colonies captured 207 of the enemy's merchant ships. Privateers from Liverpool, Nova Scotia, were particularly successful in their escapades on the high seas. While historians still debate the military significance of privateering, there can be no doubt that it helped to line the pockets of ambitious merchants who bought the captured vessels in 'prize courts' and sold their contents at immense profit. The *Liverpool Packet*, the most successful of the privateer vessels, is reputed to have captured enemy prizes worth $1.5 million, and greatly advanced the fortunes of its owner, Enos Collins. The communities where captures were auctioned, such as Halifax and St John's, also reaped financial rewards. On one memorable occasion, residents of St John's witnessed the spectacle of 30 American prize ships roped together in the harbour.

By 1815 St John's had emerged as the capital of Newfoundland, which had become a colony in all but name and constitutional status, and whose government had recovered control of Labrador in 1809. The long period of warfare all but killed the English migratory fishery, and the bye-boatmen completely disappeared. As a result, the resident fishery expanded and the permanent population increased to more than 20,000. The settlers were not prosperous, but they survived by growing potatoes and fishing along an expanding stretch of the coastline. In the 1790s, for the first time, schooners from Conception Bay and other areas began to exploit the spring seal fishery; it rapidly became an important feature of the local economy, and in good years a lucrative one. During the War of 1812, Newfoundland fish producers enjoyed a monopoly in Spain and Portugal, while continuing to supply the Italian and West Indian markets. Fish prices climbed to unprecedented levels, producing a few fortunes and attracting a wave of migrants from Ireland.

Conclusion

As the French and Napoleonic wars came to a weary end, the demand for colonial products declined and prices fell, but the contours of the Atlantic regional economy had been set. Newfoundland had found its niche in the rich fisheries off its shores; New Brunswick in the timber trade and shipbuilding; Prince Edward Island in wheat, root crops, and cattle. Nova Scotia had not only developed the most diversified economy (based on farm, fish, and forest resources) but was carving a place for itself in the carrying trade to the West Indies and beyond. Meanwhile, in every colony, British settlers and culture prevailed.

Chapter Eight

Maturing Colonial Societies, 1815–60

Let the Frenchman delight in his vine-covered vales,
   Let the Greek toast his old classic ground;
Here's the land where the bracing Northwester prevails,
   And where jolly Blue Noses abound.[1]

As Joseph Howe's ode to 'The Blue Noses' suggests, colonials in the Atlantic region in the first half of the nineteenth century were beginning to express a new confidence in themselves. Expansion in farming, fishing, forestry, and shipbuilding nurtured a prosperous mercantile sector, while communities large and small sprouted newspapers, churches, schools, and even colleges. When Great Britain dismantled the mercantile system in the 1840s, the Atlantic colonies quickly adjusted to an era of free trade. They were also among the first in the British Empire to embrace a limited form of political autonomy, known as 'responsible government'. For some at least, this period would appear in retrospect as a golden age, when opportunities beckoned and anything seemed possible.

People and Place

The international boundary between New Brunswick and the United States remained a source of tension in this period. Although the Ste-Croix River and 'highlands' south of the St Lawrence River were established as the border following the American Revolution, no one was certain which river was the Ste-Croix and the highlands proved difficult to find. A boundary commission eventually agreed on the location of the Ste-Croix River in 1798, when the site of Champlain's ill-fated settlement on an island in the river's mouth was discovered, but the territory on the upper St John River remained in dispute. By the late 1830s tensions in the Aroostook–Madawaska region reached a fever pitch, prompting Great Britain and the United States to seek a diplomatic resolution. The boundary question was finally resolved in 1842 by the Webster–Ashburton Treaty, named after the principal negotiators. Although the treaty ended the uncertainty over the boundary, it disappointed New Brunswickers because it left a hump of American-controlled territory between their colony and the Eastern Townships in the United Canadas.

   The flood tide of largely British immigration, most of it to the Maritimes,

Timeline

1814–15	African-American refugees arrive in Nova Scotia and New Brunswick.
1818	John Young writes *Letters to Agricola*.
1820	Cape Breton re-annexed to Nova Scotia; Bank of New Brunswick founded.
1821–3	Thomas McCulloch writes *The Stepsure Letters*.
1822	William Cormack walks across Newfoundland.
1824	Newfoundland is granted colonial status; Julia Catherine Beckwith publishes *St Ursula's Convent*.
1825	Great Miramichi fire.
1826	General Mining Association receives a monopoly of Nova Scotia's mineral wealth.
1829	Death of Shawnadithit; Catholic emancipation.
1832	Representative government adopted in Newfoundland.
1833	British parliament passes the Act to Abolish Slavery in the British Empire.
1839	The region's first railway line opens between Albion Mines and Pictou.
1840	Samuel Cunard inaugurates the first transatlantic steamship service.
1841	Webster–Ashburton Treaty.
1845	Great Irish famine begins.
1846	Great Britain adopts free trade.
1848	Nova Scotia is granted responsible government.
1849	Telegraph service comes to Nova Scotia and New Brunswick.
1852	Public schools established in Prince Edward Island.
1854	African United Baptist Association founded in Nova Scotia.
1854–66	Reciprocity Treaty with the United States.
1855	New Brunswick briefly adopts prohibition.
1858	General Mining Association's monopoly abolished.

continued from 1815 until the 1840s. Thereafter population growth depended on natural increase, which in the 1850s and 1860s reached impressive levels. By 1861 there were nearly 800,000 people living in the Atlantic region, up from 200,000 in 1815. Census figures record a mature and relatively stable pre-industrial society: the ratio of men to women was nearly equal, more than half the inhabitants were under the age of 18, and in all of the four colonies 80 per cent or more of the population was native-born. Families were large, averaging seven children, although this statistic masked great differences in family size across class and culture. Like other areas of the Western world, the Atlantic region in the second half of the nineteenth century began to reflect the impact of new values that favoured later marriages and smaller families, especially among members of the urban middle class.[2]

As in the eighteenth century, economic and political pressures in Great Britain encouraged emigration in this period. Irish (both Protestant and Catholic), Scots, English, and a few Welsh immigrants filled up unsettled areas in the Maritimes. Emigrants from southeast Ireland moved in large numbers to Newfoundland's Avalon Peninsula, and the population began to spread along the south and northeast coasts. Following the War of 1812, 2,000 African-Americans, offered their freedom if they deserted their owners to join the British cause, also moved to the Maritimes, most of them settling in Preston and Hammonds Plains in Nova Scotia and Loch Lomond, New Brunswick.

Settlers came to the region seeking land and opportunity. Some found one or both, but others had a more difficult time. The African American refugees, like the Black Loyalists before them, faced bureaucratic delays in securing land, and their grants were invariably small and located in less desirable areas. Although no strangers to hard work, many settlers from Great Britain were ill-equipped to survive on what was at best marginal land. In many remoter settlements only an overgrown graveyard testifies to the hardship and heartbreak that characterized the immigrant experience.

The most tragic episode by far was the arrival of thousands of destitute Irish fleeing the 'great famine' that began with the failure of the potato crop in 1845. The Atlantic region received only a small percentage of the more than 300,000 Irish who came to British North America between 1846 and 1851, and many of them quickly moved on, but they nevertheless represented a challenge to the port authorities whose job it was to process them. As many as 30,000 destitute and often disease-ridden refugees entered through Partridge Island, the quarantine station at the mouth of the Saint John River, while others fetched up in Chatham, Charlottetown, Halifax, St Andrews, and other ports connected to the North Atlantic carrying trade. Most of the good agricultural land in the Maritimes had been long taken up and the destitute Irish had to be content to work as labourers or eke out a living in marginal and often remote farming frontiers.

Clearing the land was a daunting task for most immigrants. Slashing and burning their way through the forests that impeded their progress, they often set runaway fires that devastated huge areas. Walter Johnstone, a Scottish visitor to Prince Edward Island, remarked in 1820 that the burnt woods around the settlements formed 'a scene the most ruinous, confused and disgusting the eye can possibly look upon'.[3] In 1825 a fire on the Miramichi consumed more than two million hectares of forests and took the lives of 160 people. Animals also felt the impact of the immigrants and their profligate ways. In New Brunswick moose had virtually disappeared by the 1820s, and the great auk, a large flightless bird that

Cartier had observed in vast numbers on the Funk Islands off Newfoundland in the sixteenth century, had already become extinct by 1800.

A Dark Age for Aboriginal Peoples

With the increase of European settlement, Aboriginal people reached new levels of desperation. Their numbers declined dramatically in the first half of the nineteenth century as settler hostility, disease, and poor living conditions took their toll. By 1850 there were perhaps 3,000 Mi'kmaq, Maliseet, and Passamaquoddy living in Atlantic Canada outside of Labrador. Low in numbers and in morale, they often found it impossible to prevent encroachment on reserve lands.

In the 1830s the Colonial Office began delegating responsibility for Indian policy to the colonies. New Brunswick and Nova Scotia appointed men of considerable integrity—Joseph Howe and Abraham Gesner in Nova Scotia and Moses Perley in New Brunswick—as Indian Commissioners, but the story remained the same. In the late 1840s Gesner made a telling comment on the unjust exchange between Native and newcomer: 'in return for the lands for which they were the rightful owners, they have received loathsome diseases, alco-

Document: Chief Joseph Malli Goes to London, 1842

In 1842 Joseph Malli, Chief of the Mi'kmaq on the Restigouche River in New Brunswick, travelled to England in an effort to persuade the British government to stop incoming settlers from stealing Mi'kmaq property. His statement said in part:

> When the Superiority over the Territories in which we were born passed out of the hands of the French into those of the British, We—the Mic-Macs of the Restigouche River—were in possession of a Tract of Country, the quiet and undistinguished holding of which was secured to us by a written Deed.—The care of that Deed We entrusted to our Christian Priest.—He lost it. About 50 years ago a white man of the name of Mann came to us,—and asked our leave to build a Hut for him to sleep in when he came to fish—We said 'No! If we allow you to build the Hut, you will keep Pigs and Sheep—We Indians have many Dogs—the Dogs will worry the Pigs & Sheep and bad consequences will spring up'.—Mann did build his Hut, and we did not use force to expel him from our Reserve.—After some time Mann claimed a large Tract of our Reserve as his own.—We went and complained to the Governor.—The Governor sent three Commissioners [from Québec] to enquire into that Claim. I calculate that it must have been about eighteen years ago, in 1824, that these Commissioners were sent. . . .no portion of our own Lands have been restored to us, nor has any other land been allotted to us.—We remain without redress.[4]

holic drink, the destruction of their game, and threatened extermination.'[5]

Gesner's comment reflected a shift in attitude, at least at the official level, towards Aboriginal peoples. No longer a threat to European dominance, they became the subject of political, philanthropic, and ethnographic interest. In 1856 Prince Edward Island finally appointed an Indian commissioner, and with the assistance of the London-based Aborigines' Protection Society it would purchase Lennox Island as a reserve in 1870. Although his evangelizing efforts had little impact, the Baptist missionary Silas Rand helped to preserve Mi'kmaq culture by collecting oral history and compiling a Mi'kmaq dictionary. Native crafts—quill boxes, woven baskets, brooms, and birchbark canoes, in particular—were widely sought by collectors.

Despite predictions to the contrary, the resilient Mi'kmaq and Maliseet managed to survive the European presence. The fate of the Beothuk, in contrast, was tragic. Cut off from marine resources by the spread of European fishing and settlement along Newfoundland's northeast coast, they retreated to the interior, where their health declined along with their living conditions. Efforts to make contact with them, now that their survival was in doubt, sometimes led to disastrous consequences. In 1819, for example, a woman named Demasduit was captured at Red Indian Lake. Her husband was killed in the encounter, and her child was left behind to die. Two years later Demasduit (known to her captors as Mary March) died of tuberculosis. In 1829 Shawnadithit, the last known Beothuk, suffered the same fate. In the final year of her life she lived in St John's under the care of William Cormack, president of the recently established 'Boeothick Institution', helping him to develop a Beothuk vocabulary and drawing pictures depicting the culture of her people as she had known it.

The Labrador Middle Ground
Labrador's story was quite different in this period. There the Innu and Inuit outnumbered the resident European population, which was small and widely scattered. By the 1860s there was a British 'settler' population of some 1,600 living along the coast from Blanc Sablon to Hamilton Inlet. Most of these people were the children or grandchildren of Native women and British fur traders and fishers who had had arrived after 1830. In mid-century a clerical visitor remarked that 'all the females are either Esquimaux, or mountaineer Indians, or descended from them.' The settlers traded with Jersey and West Country firms established in south Labrador, with visiting traders, or with posts in Hamilton Inlet and Lake Melville operated by Québec merchants. In 1837 these posts were purchased by the Hudson's Bay Company and linked through a chain of posts in the interior to Ungava Bay to tap the Innu fur trade.

Continuing to lead a migratory life, the Innu came to the North Shore, Ungava Bay, or the Labrador coast to trade, and increasingly, to meet Roman Catholic priests. The Oblates of Mary Immaculate arrived in Canada in the 1840s, and established a mission to the Innu, initially based on the Québec North Shore.

North of Cape Harrison, the most significant European presence was that of the Moravians, with their mission stations and trading stores at Nain (1771), Okak

Newfoundland and Labrador, *c.* 1840

(1776), Hopedale (1782), and Hebron (1830). After a religious revival in 1804–5 many Inuit were baptised and reorganized their lives to spend much of the time between Christmas and Easter near the missionaries. Besides stores and religious observances, the mission provided schools—where children were taught in Inuktitut—and rudimentary medical care. The Hudson's Bay Company broke the Moravian trade monopoly after 1850, and the isolation of northern Labrador was further disturbed from the early 1860s by the arrival each summer of migratory fishing schooners ('floaters') from Newfoundland.

Courtney Bay, New Brunswick, *c.* 1860. Many of the region's sailing ships were launched from this port, near East Saint John. Among them was the *Marco Polo*, famed for the speed with which it delivered its passengers and cargo to the Australian gold fields in the early 1850s. PANB George Taylor fonds, P5-360.

Colonial Economies

In the first half of the nineteenth century European society in the Atlantic region was buoyed by an increasingly productive commercial economy. A post-war recession caused hardship for rich and poor alike, but by the 1820s conditions began to improve. The colonial staples—fish, foodstuffs, and timber—found markets in an expanding global economy, and shipbuilding, financed by British and colonial capitalists, emerged as a major industry.

The success of the shipping and shipbuilding industries in Atlantic Canada between 1850 and 1878 has become the stuff of legend and a source of local pride. In this period the Maritimes and Newfoundland accounted for as much as 72 per cent of the tonnage registered in British North America, which boasted the fourth largest merchant marine in the world, after Great Britain, the United States, and Norway. Ships such as the *Marco Polo*, built in Saint John in 1851, broke world speed records on the Australian run and made the region's shipbuilding skills famous.

Although Saint John was the largest shipbuilding centre, other communities, such as St Martins, Yarmouth, Windsor, and Pictou, became well-known for their output of wooden vessels. Saint John, Charlottetown, Halifax, and St. John's also emerged as major trade entrepôts. By the 1860s Maritime vessels, operated in large part by foreign crews, could be found in ports all over the world, carrying cargoes at competitive prices. In the 1880s, shipping barons in the Maritimes decided to invest their fortunes in railway and manufacturing ventures rather than in a steel and steam-driven merchant marine, a decision that led to a rapid decline in ship-building and the carrying trade.[6]

The region's mineral resources also came under more intense exploitation in this period. Under a monopoly granted by the British Crown in 1826, the General Mining Association began developing Nova Scotia's coal resources in Cape Breton and Pictou County. The company brought in skilled miners and introduced modern technology, including steam-driven machinery and vessels. In 1839 it opened a railway line to carry coal from Albion Mines (now Stellarton) to Pictou harbour. After its monopoly was abolished in 1858, investment in coal mining increased dramatically, stimulated by rising demand in the rapidly industrializing United States.

At the same time Newfoundland's resources attracted growing interest. In 1822 Cormack walked across the island—the first European known to have done so. In 1839–40 the government sponsored the first geological surveys, conducted by James Jukes. Copper was discovered in Notre Dame Bay in the late 1850s and copper mining commenced at Tilt Cove in 1864. In the same year, the government established a permanent Geological Survey that, under its first director, Alexander Murray, and his assistant, James P. Howley, undertook systematic exploration of the island. Their optimistic reports had an important influence on public policy, raising the possibility that Newfoundland might become something more than a producer of saltfish and seal oil.

In Albert County, New Brunswick, more than 230,000 tons of Albertite (a sort of solidified asphalt yielding oil and gas) were produced between 1850 and 1880. Gypsum and stone for building and grinding found markets both locally and in the United States. The discovery of gold on Nova Scotia's south and eastern shores stimulated a brief flurry of activity in the 1860s. By this time the iron works at Londonderry was turning out $40,000 of products annually. The founding of banking institutions, beginning with the Bank of New Brunswick in 1820, testified to the growth of the region's economy.

Although constrained by their colonial location, the region's mercantile élite were anything but narrow in their ambitions. Samuel Cunard, who invested in the New Brunswick timber trade and owned estates in Prince Edward Island, inaugurated transatlantic steamship service between Great Britain and North America in 1840. Beginning with a clock-making business in St John's, Benjamin Bowring became the head of a highly successful mercantile house with links to Liverpool. The most successful entrepreneur of all in this period was Enos Collins; having made a fortune in trade and privateering during the French and Napoleonic Wars, he went on to build a business empire based on trade and banking in Halifax.

Although the region's economic growth was tied to the fortunes of the Empire, there were no special privileges after the 1840s, when Great Britain aban-

The Farmer's Bank of Rustico. In the early 1860s, Father George-Antoine Belcourt helped his fellow Prince Edward Island Acadians to establish a school and a banking co-operative to meet the challenges of the new industrial order. PEIPARO, Acc. 2320/20.4

doned colonial preference in trade and shipping. The dismantling of the old mercantile system helped to make the 1840s a 'decade of tribulation',[7] but the transition proved less problematic than many had feared. Part of the reason was that Britain negotiated reciprocity (free trade) in primary products—fish, farm produce, minerals, and timber—with the United States in 1854. The Reciprocity Treaty remained in place until 1866 and, together with the high demand generated by the American Civil War (1861–5), stimulated colonial production and the carrying trade.

The Newfoundland economy was altogether more precarious. Nevertheless, merchants invested in larger wooden vessels—brigs and brigantines especially—mainly to exploit the seal fishery off the island's northeast coast more effectively. Although sealskins were taken, the main object of the hunt was the seal fat; rendered into oil, it was widely used during the nineteenth century for lighting and lubricants.

By mid-century the Industrial Revolution was beginning to transform production processes. The steam-driven machinery, the factory system, and the conflicts between capital and labour that were the hallmarks of the industrial age required difficult adjustments for people accustomed to artisan production, kinship loyalties, and noblesse oblige. Saint John emerged as the major industrial centre,

Sealing in Newfoundland

Seals were important to Native peoples, providing meat, oil, and skins for clothing and other purposes. Although European migratory fishers were not originally much interested in seals, migrating seals were caught in nets along the Strait of Belle Isle, the Québec North Shore, and the northeast coast of Newfoundland. A growing demand for seal oil in the eighteenth century gave rise to a sealing industry, which became concentrated in Newfoundland and to a lesser extent in the Îles de la Madelaine and Cape Breton.

In 1802 the magistrate at Bonavista reported that 'This adventurous and perilous pursuit' was now carried on it two ways: 'during the winter months by nets, and from March to June in ice-skiffs and decked boats, or schooners'. Netting seals was a northern practice that continued well into the twentieth century, and seals are still hunted from small boats close to shore. The use of sailing vessels to 'go to the ice' in the spring to find whelping seals started in 1793, allowing St. John's and other southerly ports to become involved in the industry. The spring sealing fleet reached a peak of nearly 400 vessels in the late 1850s, carrying about 14,000 men, and seal products—oil and skins—represented one-third of the value of Newfoundland's exports.

Over-exploitation of the seal herds led to a decline in the industry, from 546,000 skins in the early 1840s to 400,000 in the late 1850s. During the following decade, outfitters turned to steam-powered vessels—'wooden walls'—to increase both yields and profits, a process that centralized the industry in St John's and Conception Bay and also reduced the number of schooners and men involved.

Although sealing became steadily less important to the Newfoundland economy, it retained a considerable cultural significance. An outport man summed it up early in the twentieth century: 'Ye know, sir, that when we gets to be young men in this country they don't think much of a chap unless he's bin to de ice. It's a sort o' test of hardiness. . . . It's jest dog's work while it lasts, but somehow there's an excitement in it. . . . We sealers say, too, that man'll go for a swile where gold won't drag'un.'[8]

with foundry, footwear, and clothing industries all surpassing shipbuilding in value by the 1860s. Halifax also developed an industrial base, specializing in food-processing industries such brewing, distilling, and sugar-refining.

Most people lived at one remove from industrial discipline, their lives dominated by the seasonal rhythms of domestic production based on farming, fishing, and forestry—or in many cases all three. Most families continued to make their own cloth and clothing, to produce and preserve their own food, and to craft their own houses, barns, ploughs, carriages, horseshoes, furniture, soap, and candles. Milling was the most common industry in rural areas of the Maritimes. Prince Edward Island alone boasted 500 carding, fulling, grist, dressing, saw, and shingle

The Reverend Mr Richard Preston, ink drawing by Dr J.P. Gilpin, *c.* 1850. An African American who fled to Nova Scotia following the war of 1812, Preston studied for the ministry in Great Britain and helped to establish the African United Baptist Association in 1854. History Collection, Nova Scotia Museum, Halifax, NSM, p176.25 copy neg. N-4442

mills by 1871. Surplus produce was bartered for the imported items—flour, molasses, sugar, tea, cloth, metal utensils of various kinds—that stocked the shelves of local merchants. In turn, the merchants sold the products of farm and fishery in colonial towns and cities, to the men engaged in the region's fishing, shipping, and timber trades, or to markets in Europe, the United States, and the West Indies. In many communities, especially those centred on the fisheries, survival depended on a credit system in which merchants advanced supplies and paid for local products in goods rather than cash. This 'truck system' encouraged dependence, but it also enabled producers to participate, however minimally, in the market economy.

Despite the growing complexity of the region's economy, poverty and destitution were common. The demand for foodstuffs outstripped the supply, and even farming families often had difficulty making ends meet. When crops or fisheries failed, as they sometimes did in all areas of the Atlantic region, disaster threatened. The potato blight hit the colonies in the late 1840s, creating hardship almost as severe as in Ireland and prompting at least one group of settlers in St Ann's, Cape Breton, under their puritanical leader the Reverend Norman McLeod, to search for greener pastures in Waipu, New Zealand. Others shipped off to the United States, where jobs in the expanding industrial and service sectors, and free homesteads on the western frontier, offered hope for a better life.

By the 1830s most of the good farmland in the Maritimes had been taken up, and free land was largely a thing of the past. Not only recent immigrants but growing numbers of descendants of earlier settlers were therefore obliged to purchase property or take up marginal lands that yielded a meagre subsistence. Some of the poor squatted on Crown and Native reserves; others drifted to urban centres to find work.

Given the small size and poor quality of their original grants, it is hardly surprising that Blacks in Nova Scotia began moving to Halifax, where wage-paying jobs were more plentiful. They kept to themselves in an area on the Bedford Basin that soon became known as Africville. Shunned by their white neighbours, the residents of Africville found comfort in their own religious institutions. The spectacular growth of Baptist churches under the leadership of Richard Preston, led to the establishment in 1854 of the African United Baptist Association, which was to become a lynchpin in the Black community's struggle to seek justice in a society riddled with racial prejudice.

Societies in Transition

Christian churches became firmly rooted throughout the colonies in this period and played a major role in community life. At a time when the family economy was the main source of security, churches often stepped in when the family could no longer find the wherewithal for survival. Church leaders also offered spiritual counsel in an age when Providence was widely held to be the cause of human suffering.

Even before Roman Catholics were granted full civil rights in the British Empire in 1829, they had gained concessions in the Atlantic region. The laws that had prevented them from voting, acquiring land, and worshipping in public were abolished in the 1780s, and the ban on their holding public office was lifted first in Nova Scotia in 1823 for Lawrence Kavanagh, a Cape Breton merchant elected to the Assembly. Although Newfoundland had its own Roman Catholic bishop as early as 1796, Maritime Catholics remained under the jurisdiction of Québec until 1817, when Edmund Burke was appointed bishop of Nova Scotia. Twelve years later, his jurisdiction was divided and separate bishops were appointed for New Brunswick and Prince Edward Island. These administrative changes marked the beginning of a new era in which a reinvigorated Catholic church ministered to a growing constituency. By the mid-nineteenth century, over 40 per cent of the populations of Newfoundland and Prince Edward Island, a third of New Brunswickers, and a quarter of Nova Scotians were Roman Catholics.

Although the evangelical churches—especially the Baptists and Methodists—generally took the lead in seeking converts and promoting moral rectitude, all churches were swept up in the reforming spirit of the age. The temperance movement took root in the late 1820s and became so popular that New Brunswick briefly experimented with legislated prohibition in 1855. Most denominations supported initiatives to found academies, Sunday schools, charity schools, orphanages, hospitals, and shelters. Eager to spread the gospel to lost souls near and far, evangelicals became prominent in both home and foreign missions. The Maritime

Baptists sent Richard Burpee to India in 1845 and in the following year the Presbyterian Church of Nova Scotia sponsored John Geddie's mission to the New Hebrides. Major religious denominations either published or supported newspapers sympathetic to their views. In St John's, for instance, *The Public Ledger* represented a Protestant perspective, while *The Newfoundlander* and *The Patriot* reflected Roman Catholic viewpoints. The first French-language newspaper in the region, the *Moniteur Acadien*, founded by Israël J.-D. Landry in 1867 in Shediac, New Brunswick, was closely aligned with the Roman Catholic hierarchy.

Reformers argued that sectarian tensions could be alleviated by the creation of a system of public schools that were uniform, non-denominational and state-funded. In all the Atlantic colonies, their efforts were opposed not only by the Roman Catholic hierarchy but also by linguistic minorities such as the Acadians, who feared the homogenizing tendencies of a state-supported system. In 1852 Prince Edward Island became the first colony in the region to embrace a public school system, but controversy quickly erupted over Bible reading in the classroom. Protestants insisted that the practice was essential to instilling Christian values; Roman Catholics were staunchly opposed because independent Bible reading was associated particularly with Protestant denominations and could, it was feared, lead to proselytizing. They were ultimately placated by regulations that allowed students who found Bible-reading offensive to be excused from attendance. In Newfoundland, efforts to introduce non-denominational public education in the 1830s were just as strongly opposed by the Church of England hierarchy as by its Roman Catholic counterpart. As a result, in 1842 the education grant was split between Protestants and Catholics.

Denominationalism prevailed in higher education throughout the region. The Church of England's exclusive control of King's College in Windsor and the College of New Brunswick in Fredericton inspired other denominations to establish their own institutions. In the mid-nineteenth century the foundations were laid for seven denominational colleges in the Maritimes: Acadia (Baptist); Mount Allison (Methodist); St Mary's, St Dunstan's, St Francis Xavier, Collège St-Joseph, and Mount Saint Vincent (all Roman Catholic). Dalhousie College, founded in 1818 as a non-denominational institution, became effectively Presbyterian when it finally began to offer classes in the 1860s. Prince of Wales College, established in Charlottetown in 1860, served a primarily Protestant student population.

Although clerics preached spiritual equality, church practices perpetuated worldly notions of hierarchy and prejudice. Many churches rented their pews, permitting the rich to sit closer to the pulpit. In some churches women were relegated to separate sections. People of colour were almost always set apart. Protestants and Catholics each formed (or imported) their own organizations, of which the Protestant Orange Order was one of the most successful. Battles between Protestants and Catholics in the Maritimes became particularly violent during the late 1840s. On 12 July 1847, the 147th anniversary of the Battle of the Boyne, a confrontation between 300 Irish Catholics and an equal number of Protestants in Woodstock, New Brunswick, resulted in ten deaths. Two years later, another bloody confrontation rocked the Catholic enclave of York Point in Saint John.

Violence was not confined to religious rivalries: it punctuated all aspects of colonial life. At election time, voting was conducted orally, with the result that polling stations often became scenes of violence and intimidation. Political tensions in Newfoundland were such that the conservative St. John's newspaper editor Henry Winton had his ears cut off by masked opponents in 1835, and the Church of England archdeacon in the 1830s kept a pistol under his pillow. In Prince Edward Island, tensions between tenants and their landlords (or their agents) reached dangerous levels at the same time. Strikes by workers sometimes erupted in riots. Wife-beating was still legally sanctioned, and the foundation of

The Telegraph

The e-mail of the nineteenth century, the electric telegraph dramatically increased the speed of communication. The first telegraph lines in the Atlantic region reached Saint John and Halifax in 1849. In 1851, Frederick Newton Gisborne, one of the pioneers of telegraphy in Montréal, began to promote the extension of the telegraph to St John's, Newfoundland. He planned to have European news dropped off by steamer at St John's or Cape Race and then transmitted by land line to Cape Ray, where steamboats or carrier pigeons would pick it up and carry it across the Cabot Strait to the mainland telegraph system. This strategy was soon replaced by a proposal for a submarine cable, a new but proven technology.

With the blessing of the Newfoundland government, Gisborne completed a remarkable survey of a route along the island's south coast, travelling with Mi'kmaq and some white companions. The Nova Scotia government refused permission to land a cable at Cape North in Cape Breton. An alternative was to route the line via Prince Edward Island and New Brunswick. In 1852 Gisborne connected Cape Tormentine and Carleton Head by the first undersea cable in North America. The following year he started work on the line across Newfoundland. After 65 kilometres the money ran out, work ceased, and his Newfoundland Electric Telegraph Co. declared bankruptcy.

Looking for financial backing in New York in 1854, he met Cyrus W. Field, a wealthy businessman who became interested not only in Gisborne's project but also in a cable across the Atlantic. Field organized the New York, Newfoundland, and London Telegraph Company, which completed the line between St John's and Cape Ray in 1856. In the same year the company successfully laid a submarine cable under the Cabot Strait, the Nova Scotia government having changed its mind. Field moved on to complete the transatlantic cable. Although the first attempt, in 1858, failed, in 1866 a cable was successfully laid between Valencia, Ireland, and Heart's Content, Newfoundland, by the *Great Eastern*, an enormous iron vessel designed by I.K. Brunel. Thereafter the Associated Press no longer had to station a boat at Cape Race to intercept transatlantic steamers and pick up the watertight canisters of messages from Europe that they threw overboard. Communication between the two continents had become almost instantaneous—at least for those who could afford to pay for it.

discipline at home and at school was the adage 'spare the rod and spoil the child'. Cock fights and bear-baiting were popular pastimes. In Newfoundland, mummering—a folk tradition associated with Christmas—became so menacing that in 1861 legislation made it illegal in St John's to appear in public wearing a mask or other disguise.

Seaport towns were renowned for the violent and illegal activities that flourished along their waterfronts where an underworld of crimps (procurers of crewmen for sailing vessels), prostitutes, and unsavoury boardinghouse-keepers took advantage of the sailors in port. Like the British soldiers who were stationed in the region's major cities until mid-century, or the men confined throughout the long winters to remote lumber camps, sailors on board ship lived in an all-male environment, under repressive and often harsh conditions. Because colonial courts were likely to side with captains, sailors were notorious for various forms of resistance ranging from absence without leave to desertion, insubordination, and even mutiny.

Middle-class citizens were concerned about violence and made concerted efforts to control it. City councils (in unincorporated areas, magistrates) appointed marshals and constables to keep the peace, swore in special deputies, and in extreme cases called on the military for help. By mid-century, full-time police forces began to emerge in the larger urban areas. Legislation, backed by force, was imposed to control workers who dared to use strikes or intimidation to improve their wages and working conditions. By encouraging self-discipline, public schooling, and church attendance, reformers hoped to create a society in which the values of peaceful coexistence and civic virtue would be internalized, and force would no longer be required to maintain social control.

Colonial life was not all conflict and drudgery. In rural areas 'bees' and 'frolics' brought people together in communal bonhomie, and everywhere Sundays offered relief from weekday routines. Significant events on the Christian calendar, such as Christmas, Easter, and saints' days, provided opportunities for holidays and celebrations. In cities and towns, regimental bands, choral recitals, and singing schools flourished. Organized sport was still in its infancy, but racing, yachting, rowing, curling, and cricket clubs were becoming popular in urban centres. Hockey, also called 'hurley' or 'shinny', made inroads in Nova Scotia, though one commentator in 1864 argued that such a rowdy and dangerous game 'ought to be sternly forbidden'.[9] In St John's an annual regatta on Quidi Vidi Lake, begun in 1826, became a highlight of the summer season.

Educated people in the Atlantic region were full participants in the intellectual awakening of the nineteenth century. In a matter of weeks, ideas percolating in Boston, New York, Edinburgh, and London became topics of debate among colonial newspaper editors, college professors, and members of the urban élite. Ambitious colonials travelled to Great Britain and the United States for their education and returned home to practice or teach what they had learned. In the 1830s Mechanics' Institutes, founded in Scotland to disseminate scientific education among the artisan class, took root in the colonies, offering a broad range of literary, dramatic, and artistic activities.

Literacy was highly prized. Newspaper editors emerged as influential political figures, often because they championed progressive causes. Others too took up writing, whether for literary glory or simply to make a living. Thomas McCulloch, the Presbyterian minister who founded Pictou Academy, wrote the *Stepsure Letters* (1821–3), one of the first works of fiction produced in British North America. In 1824 Julia Catherine Beckwith of Fredericton became the first native-born British North American novelist, with the publication of the little-read *St Ursula's Convent*, written when she was 17 years old. The Reverend R.T.S. Lowell's novel *The New Priest in Conception Bay* (1858)—the first to be set in a Newfoundland outport—captured a distinctive lifestyle and dialect. No doubt the most successful colonial writer was Judge Thomas Chandler Haliburton, who made an international reputation with his series recounting the adventures of the clock-peddling Yankee salesman Sam Slick. Before turning his hand to satire, Haliburton had written a two-volume history of Nova Scotia, published in 1829. By that time, the Reverend Lewis Anspach's *History of the Island of Newfoundland* (1819) and Peter Fischer's *First History of New Brunswick* (1825) had already appeared.

These pioneering works reflected a cultural maturity that also expressed itself in practical ways. In 1818 John Young, a Scottish merchant in Halifax writing under the name 'Agricola', published a series of letters encouraging scientific methods in agriculture. His efforts, together with financial assistance from the government, led to the establishment of numerous agricultural societies in Nova Scotia. This fashion spread throughout the region, and by 1842 a society was founded in Newfoundland to encourage more effective use of the island's thin, acidic soils. Meanwhile, colonial inventors such as Charles Fenerty and Abraham Gesner were devising ways to make paper out of wood and kerosene from petroleum.

By mid-century developments in transportation and communication further reduced the time it took for ideas to penetrate the Atlantic region. Telegraphic communication developed quickly after it was successfully tested by the American inventor Samuel Morse in 1844, and railways, the wonder of the age, were promising not only to overcome the limits of land-based travel and bring prosperity to those communities fortunate enough to lie near them, but also to transform colonial politics.

Political Awakenings

In the wake of the American Revolution, the British government had deliberately imposed on its remaining North American colonies constitutions designed to limit the democratic tendencies of elected assemblies. Power was weighted towards appointed elements—the governor, his council, and the judiciary. Assemblies—where they existed—were relatively powerless talking-shops, although their consent was needed to pass legislation relating to money bills. As a result deadlocks were common.

Cape Breton and Newfoundland were still without elected assemblies in the early nineteenth century. Although considered the birthright of all self-respecting Britons, representative government was denied to Cape Breton until the island colony was united with the mainland in 1820. Thereafter, with two seats in the Nova Scotia assembly, Cape Breton had representative government, at least in theory, but little political clout. In Newfoundland the struggle for representative government was more protracted. After the end of the Napoleonic Wars business and professional élites in St John's, led by Dr William Carson and Patrick Morris, began to demand formal recognition as a colony with representative government, security of land tenure, and the full range of British civil rights. Naval government no longer made sense, now that the English migratory fishery had died out and Newfoundland's economic and strategic importance to Britain had faded. Nevertheless, it took time and effort to change attitudes in London. Arguing that the migratory fishery and naval government had stunted Newfoundland's development, the reformers drew attention to injustices such as the case of two Conception Bay fishermen who, in 1820, were flogged for contempt by order of the surrogate magistrates and had their premises seized for debt. Finally, in 1824–5 circuit courts were instituted, King William's Act was repealed, and Newfoundland was declared a Crown colony.

Sir Thomas Cochrane became the colony's first civil governor in 1825, and the naval state came to an end. After further agitation, representative government was established in 1832. Religious and ethnic divisions characterized Newfoundland politics in the early years of representative government, and electoral violence erupted in some districts. In an attempt to calm the situation and prevent legislative deadlocks, the Colonial Office instituted an experimental constitution that amalgamated the assembly and council, but it proved a temporary, lasting only until 1848.

Meanwhile, the Maritime colonies were beginning to demand not just representative but 'responsible' government, in which the executive would be composed of members of the majority party in the assembly, to which it would be directly responsible. The most eloquent advocate of this reform was Nova Scotia's Joseph Howe, who in his famous letters to the Colonial Secretary, Lord John Russell, in 1840 insisted that 'every poor boy in Nova Scotia' should have 'the same rights to honours and emoluments as he would have if he lived in Great Britain or the United States'.

In Prince Edward Island, William Cooper, the leader of the movement to escheat (take back) the lands granted to absentee proprietors, won an overwhelming election victory in 1838. He was refused even a hearing from Russell, who would have nothing to do undermining property rights. In New Brunswick, the central issue in political debates was the revenue from the sale, leasing, and licensing of Crown lands. Charles Simonds, a powerful Saint John timber baron and leader of the reform cause, managed to extract two important concessions from the Colonial Office in 1837: control over Crown land revenues (as long as the salaries of appointed administrators were guaranteed) and consultation with elected representatives in the appointment of the governor's executive councillors.

Great Britain finally abandoned its resistance to responsible government in settler colonies after the adoption of free trade in 1846 made it unnecessary to maintain a closed economic system. In 1847 Nova Scotia's lieutenant-governor, Sir

John Harvey, was instructed to choose advisers from the party that had a majority in the assembly. Reformers were victorious in an election held later that year, and on 2 February 1848 a Liberal government under the leadership of James Boyle Uniacke became the first 'responsible' administration in the British Empire. By 1855 all the remaining Atlantic colonies had followed Nova Scotia's lead. This milestone in the region's political history did not mean that the colonies were fully independent: the Colonial Office still kept a watchful eye over defence, external affairs, legal matters, and constitutional amendment.

Although the colonial franchise was quite wide, extending to men of modest means, political power was concentrated in the hands of the commercial and professional élites. Most of these men were conservative in their political outlook and wanted little to do with the liberal and radical ideas that by mid-century were being debated in Great Britain and the United States. Women, no matter what their property status, were disqualified from voting, along with Native people, landless labourers, wards of the state, and relief recipients. As for Labrador, it was entirely ignored in the debate over political rights, as were the inhabitants of the Newfoundland's French Treaty shore.

Despite—or perhaps because of—the closed circle in which it operated, responsible government in the early years was a messy and muddled affair. Administrations were often unstable, with 'loose fish' crossing the floor when they differed from their party on issues great or small. Bureaucratic processes were embryonic, patronage appointments commonplace, and alliances reflected religious affiliations—all to the detriment of good government. Governors continued to meddle even though (like the British monarch) they were supposed to stand apart from the daily routine of political life and follow the recommendations of their executive advisers.

Conclusion

These difficulties notwithstanding, the rituals of responsible government took root with surprising speed. By the 1860s political parties had emerged in all the colonies, borrowing the names (and often the programs) of their Liberal and Conservative counterparts in Great Britain, and colonial leaders had begun to move beyond religious and ethnic allegiances to define new community goals. With political visions increasingly defined by industrial progress, public works, and material well-being, politicians even found themselves discussing a plan for colonial union.

Chapter 9

Confronting Confederation, 1860–73

Between 1867 and 1873 the three Maritime colonies were swept into a new political arrangement with the colony of Canada, while Newfoundland and Labrador held aloof from Confederation until 1949. Nevertheless, all the Atlantic colonies faced the same economic and social challenges in the middle decades of the nineteenth century. The new world order characterized by faster communications, liberal political regimes, and galloping industrialization demanded new values and smart strategies. If they could not keep up with the pace of change, the Atlantic colonies faced marginalization in a world where literacy, railroads, and factories stood supreme as the symbols of progress.

The Context of Confederation

The 1860s was a critical decade for the North Atlantic world. In 1861 the United States erupted in a bloody civil war that pitted the industrial North against the slave-owning South. Nationalist movements in Europe took the German and Italian states along the road to nationhood, while the efforts of French emperor Napoleon III to establish an imperial regime in Mexico ended with the execution of the leader of his puppet government, Archduke Maximilian, by a Mexican firing squad in 1867. Imperial regimes everywhere were on the defensive. Even Great Britain, rapidly building an empire based on industrial supremacy and free trade, was determined to reduce its political and military commitments in those settler colonies where British traditions were taking root. No similar loosening of the imperial apron strings was planned for colonies where the majority of the people were non-British. Above all else, nationalist movements in Ireland, which had been annexed to Britain in 1801, would be vigorously resisted.

Influenced by developments in Europe, the United States, and Latin America, British North Americans began to imagine new destinies for themselves. The American Civil War had convinced many colonial politicians that republicanism had its flaws and that the colonies were better off under the British flag and parliamentary system—but how could they defend their small jurisdictions against a triumphant North determined to dominate the whole continent? The only way to do so, it seemed, would be to beat the Americans at their own game. Could the colonies not, with the help of Great Britain, build a transcontinental nation to rival their giant neighbour to the south?

Like their European counterparts, supporters of British North American unity

Timeline

1860	Prince Edward Island Land Commission appointed.
1861–5	American Civil War.
1861	Trent Affair.
1862	Collapse of negotiations with the Canadians on plans to build an Intercolonial Railroad.
1864	Charlottetown and Québec Conferences on Confederation; Tenant League founded.
1865	Pro-Confederation government defeated in New Brunswick.
1866	Fenian raid on New Brunswick; pro-Confederation government elected in New Brunswick; London Conference on Confederation.
1867	Confederation of New Brunswick, Nova Scotia, Ontario and Quebec; secession movement begins in Nova Scotia.
1869	Anti-Confederates in Nova Scotia accept better terms; Newfoundland decisively rejects Confederation.
1871	Treaty of Washington.
1873	Prince Edward Island joins Confederation.

were inspired by dreams of economic development. This was especially the case in the United Province of Canada (after 1867, Ontario and Québec), where industrial development and escape from a crippling railway debt were predicated on acquiring Rupert's Land—the vast territory controlled by the Hudson's Bay Company. The major impediment to Canada's dreams of a western empire was the political deadlock between its two parts that had been cobbled together in 1840: a largely French-speaking and Catholic population in Canada East (formerly Lower Canada) and an English-speaking and Protestant population in Canada West (formerly Upper Canada).

Following the collapse of yet another coalition government in the spring of 1864, a constitutional committee was established to seek a solution to the United Canada's political problems. Chaired by George Brown, editor of the *The Globe* and leader of the Reform party in Canada West, it recommended a federal union of all the British North American colonies. To see the project through to fruition, a 'Great Coalition' was established headed by Brown, the leaders of the Conservative-*Bleu* Party—John A. Macdonald from Canada West and George-Étienne Cartier from Canada East—and Alexander Galt, an early proponent of Confederation and spokesperson for the powerful business community of Montréal. It was a formidable alliance.

The Atlantic Colonies at the Crossroads

The Atlantic colonies initially had little interest in British North American union. Instead, they continued to focus their attention on the larger British Empire connected by the sea—that is, until railways began to dominate the agenda. Political and economic leaders in both Nova Scotia and New Brunswick saw their own colony taking advantage of its location to become the gateway to the continent. This goal seemed even more appealing when the fallout from the American Civil War made it clear that if war broke out between Great Britain and the United States, an ice-free port on the east coast would be essential to the security of the United Canadas, and that an all-British railway route linking the colonies together would have both military and economic benefits.

War seemed imminent in November 1861, when a Northern warship seized the *Trent*, a British steamer, on the high seas and arrested two Confederate agents. Although the two men were eventually released, tensions remained high, and Great Britain sent 15,000 troops to supplement the 3,000 soldiers already stationed in the colonies. Arriving in winter, they had to march overland to Québec City from New Brunswick—convincing proof of the need for a railway connecting the Maritimes to the Canadas.

Nova Scotia's Joseph Howe was an indefatigable promoter of railways. When he assumed the premiership of Nova Scotia in August 1860, he made railway building one of his top priorities. His favourite project was a line linking Halifax to the St Lawrence, generally referred to as the Intercolonial Railway. As early as 1849 Howe had proposed such a line at a Halifax conference on the implications for the Atlantic colonies of free trade. Howe's railway projects, which managed only to link Halifax with Windsor and Pictou, fell far short of his larger goal and were the main reason that the provincial debt reached a total of $4.5 million in 1863. By that time there seemed little hope that the Intercolonial would proceed. The collapse, in 1862, of railway talks with representatives from the United Canadas seemed to be the final nail in the coffin. British capitalists had little enthusiasm for a railway project that required negotiations with a rabble of dysfunctional colonies, most of them teetering on the brink of bankruptcy.

Howe's government was defeated by the Conservatives in 1863. Under Charles Tupper, who assumed the premiership in 1864, the Conservatives continued to support public works and other progressive programs such as publicly-funded schools. A medical doctor, Tupper had represented Cumberland County since 1855. With substantial investments in his constituency's coalmines and a keen sense of its strategic location with regard to any railway built between Nova Scotia and New Brunswick and points further west, Tupper was a great booster of enterprise both public and private. The Intercolonial held the promise for Nova Scotians of new markets in New Brunswick and Canada, but the colony lacked the financial resources to proceed. Under Tupper's watch, the provincial debt would reach $8 million by 1866.

New Brunswickers were also caught up in the mania for railways. In 1835, capitalists from New Brunswick and Great Britain formed the St Andrews and Québec Railway Company to attract traffic from the Canadas and the United States. The company ran out of money before achieving its objective, but the idea of an Intercolonial railway continued to inspire support among New Brunswick's political and business leaders. So too did the idea of a link to Maine. The era of

Reciprocity created a keen interest in north–south lines of communication, and a promoter from Maine, Joseph Alfred Poor, seemed poised to help make the idea a reality. When Poor declared bankruptcy in 1855, New Brunswick pressed ahead with a line linking Shediac to Saint John and continued making plans to extend its European and North American railway into the United States.

In 1861 Reform Premier Charles Fisher, an active supporter of railway construction, was brought down by a conflict-of-interest scandal relating to the purchase of Crown Lands. His successor, Samuel Leonard Tilley, wanted the Intercolonial, but with a $5-million railway debt and annual revenues of only $600,000, New Brunswick could not move forward on its own. Without the support of the Canadians and financial assistance from Great Britain, neither of which was forthcoming, the project would never succeed.

Prince Edward Island was slow to jump on the railway-building bandwagon. As a result its public debt in the 1860s remained under control. Islanders found export markets for the products of their farms and fisheries in the United States under Reciprocity and, like other Maritimers, boasted a healthy shipbuilding industry. Even the persistent land question seemed to be on the verge of resolution. Under the voluntary Land Purchase Act of 1853, Premier George Coles began using provincial funds to buy out some of the absentee landlords so that tenants could become landowners. Although the landlords and the Colonial Office resisted his efforts, by 1860 nearly 40 per cent of the island's residents were freeholders.

The increased accessibility of land under freehold tenure inevitably highlighted the hardships of those who continued to pay rents. In 1860 Conservative Premier Edward Palmer, himself a landlord, appointed a three-man commission to inquire into the land question. Nova Scotia's Joseph Howe, along with Halifax

Document: The Prince Edward Island Land Commission

In their report, submitted in 1861, the Prince Edward Island Land Commissioners included evidence from the hearings they had held throughout the colony. The document is thus an excellent source of information about the tensions between landlords and tenants on the Island. The following testimony by Nicolas Conroy, a Liberal member of the Island's Assembly, describes how new landlords such as Samuel Cunard became more efficient than their predecessors in enforcing rent payments. Together with his son Edward, Cunard owned more than 80,000 hectares, much of it acquired in the late 1830s.

> In 1835, when I first settled in Tignish, no proprietors were recognized in Lots One and Two. There had been some competitors for proprietorship, but previous to that period, though the people were asked, and even pressed to pay rent, still they always refused. I was present when the first

recognition of a proprietor took place on Lot Two. . . . Mr Peters, now Judge Peters, who was at the time agent for Mr Cunard, . . . desired me as I knew the people to accompany him . . . I did so. When we arrived, many of the inhabitants were assembled. Mr Peters told them, Mr Cunard was the proprietor of the Lot, and wished them to attorn to him as their landlord; but they refused, just as they had refused to attorn to Mr. Hill, some years previous. They were free, and desired to remain so if possible. Mr Peters then spoke to them of the wealth and power of Mr Cunard in Halifax. He said he was an influential gentleman in that City, and to hold out against him would be preposterous. The better way was, to pay rents; he would protect them; and they would have an honorable gentleman for their land-lord. After much coaxing, and half threatening they signed a paper which he wished them to subscribe. Some time after this Mr Peters and Mr Palmer came to some arrangement respecting Lot One. They accordingly sent word to the people, saying that they were coming to get them to take leases. The people met them, but unanimously refused to have anything to do with them. Messrs Peters and Palmer remained a week, and were on the eve of leaving, when, unfortunately, the people began to misunderstand each other—one thought the other was going to get his farm, and so forth, and the result was, all made a rush to the proprietor to attorn. I was present, I saw the rejoicing proprietors on that occasion. . . . The leases were for a term of 999 years, and at 1s sterling an acre. In addition to this, they signed notes of hand for £10, to be paid up the 25th March, then last past. Your Honors will remember that another year's rent was then nearly due, so that by the coming 25th of March, which was about one month hence, they were involved in £15 arrears. Now, some who signed those notes of hand, were very poor, and for them to make good their notes, was impossible. In the meantime, the proprietors pressed and threatened them, so that the greater number left their farms from sheer inability to pay these arrears. This I would call a real grievance.[1]

lawyer J.W. Ritchie and New Brunswick Liberal politician John Hamilton Gray, submitted a report that was sympathetic to tenant demands. It recommended that the tenants be given the right to purchase land from their landlords and to have arrears in payments prior to 1 May 1858 forgiven. In cases where tenants and land-lords could not agree on a fair price for the land, it would be established by arbi-tration. The landlords were livid, and although Palmer's government passed legis-lation to implement the commission's recommendations, royal assent was withheld on a 'technicality'.

The rejection of the commissioners' award fuelled the resolve of the aggrieved tenants and their supporters to put an end to the colony's feudal landholding sys-tem once and for all. In 1864 a Tenant League was formed to support a tenant

The Roman Catholic Cathedral in St John's, Newfoundland, engraving by A. Ruger, 1878. To the right of this imposing building are the Presentation and Mercy convents, to the left St Bonaventure's College. Consecrated in 1855, it overlooks the harbour and represents Bishop Michael Fleming's determination 'to have a temple superior to any other in the island'. Courtesy John FitzGerald.

takeover of rented land, with rates of compensation for landlords to be set by the townships. Members vowed to withhold rent payments, and when soldiers tried to serve writs on those in arrears, violence inevitably ensued. Finding the resources to solve the land question became the central focus of Island administrators.

In Newfoundland, where Liberals were mainly Roman Catholic and Conservatives overwhelmingly Protestant, denominational tensions continued to characterize political life in the years following the adoption of responsible government in 1855. There were also tensions within the Liberal camp. After the 1861

Table 9.1   Population of Eastern British North America, 1851–71

	1851	1861	1871
Ontario	952,004	1,396,091	1,620,851
Québec	890,261	1,111,566	1,191,516
Nova Scotia	276,854	330,857	387,800
New Brunswick	193,800	252,047	285,594
Prince Edward Island	62,678*	80,857	94,021
Newfoundland†	–	122,638	146,536

* Figure is from 1848

† Figures are from 1857 and 1869

Sources: 'Series A 2-14. Population of Canada by province, census dates, 1851 to 1976', in *Historical Statistics of Canada*, 2nd edn, ed. F.H. Leacy (Ottawa: Minister of Supply and Services, 1983) and James Hiller, 'Confederation Defeated: The Newfoundland Election of 1869', in James Hiller and Peter Neary, eds, *Newfoundland in the Nineteenth and Twentieth Centuries: Essays in Interpretation* (Toronto: University of Toronto Press, 1980).

election, a major riot in St. John's involving rival Liberal factions resulted in troops firing on the crowd, killing three people and wounding twenty. This event prompted compromise. Religious leaders voluntarily withdrew from overt political activity, and the political élites gradually shaped an unwritten agreement whereby public patronage, and seats in the legislature and on the executive council, would be awarded to each denomination in proportion to its size. Premier Hugh Hoyles signalled the new attitude by offering cabinet seats to a number of Roman Catholics. This denominational compromise was an important step, allowing the evolution of political parties based on factors other than religion.

The Road to Confederation

It was in this context of economic and political transformation that the Confederation issue burst on the scene. Nova Scotia's Conservative Premier Charles Tupper inadvertently started the Confederation ball rolling by promoting the idea of Maritime Union. Discouraged both by the collapse of the negotiations with the Canadians on the Intercolonial project and by the general parochialism of colonial politics, he reasoned that the Maritime colonies would have more clout with British investors if they pooled their resources. Early in 1864 Maritime Union was debated in the Nova Scotia assembly, whose members agreed to send delegates to a conference on the subject. New Brunswick supported this initiative; Prince Edward Island ignored it.

The idea of Maritime Union would almost certainly have remained dormant if politicians in the United Canadas had not been seeking solutions to the political deadlock in their own legislature. On hearing of the developments in the 'Lower provinces', the Canadians sought permission to attend the proposed Maritime Union conference, held in Charlottetown early in September 1864. The location insured the involvement of Islanders and was more convenient than other Maritime capitals for the Canadian delegates who arrived by boat. The meeting quickly expanded to include discussion of the Canadian proposal for a federation of all the British North America colonies. A month later, the delegates reassembled in Québec to hammer out a detailed agreement. Joined by two representatives from Newfoundland (invited as an afterthought), the delegates produced 69 resolutions, which became the basis of the British North America Act.

Since legislative union was unacceptable to most of the delegates, the Confederation agreement envisaged a federal system with two levels of jurisdiction: national and provincial. Members of the federal House of Commons were to be elected on the basis of population, giving the two sections of the United Canada, with their far greater numbers, overwhelming control. The appointed Senate was designed to provide a regional counter-balance, but was dominated by the Canadians because the Atlantic delegates failed to insist on equal provincial representation, settling instead for equal *regional* representation—the Maritimes, Québec, and Ontario—with four additional seats to be allocated to Newfoundland if it decided to participate. Coupled with the agreement that senators would be appointed for life by the federal government, this structure ensured that, as Phillip Buckner puts it, 'the Senate would have

The delegates to the Charlottetown Conference, September 1864. LAC, C-733.

no moral authority to challenge the governing party in the House of Commons' and at the same time 'limited its effectiveness as the guardian of regional interests'.[2]

The federal government was assigned the most significant powers, including control over interprovincial trade and transportation; foreign policy and defence; criminal law; currency and banking; and Indian Affairs (Aboriginal people, not surprisingly, had no say in this decision). The federal government also controlled all the major sources of taxation. The provinces had jurisdiction over commerce within their borders, natural resources, civil law, municipal administration, education, and social services. Agriculture, immigration, and fisheries would be joint responsibilities.

It is highly unlikely that internal pressures alone would have produced a Confederation agreement. External forces were also important, especially the threat posed by the United States. As the Civil War came to an end, Secretary of State William Seward began making noises to the effect that it was the 'manifest destiny' of the United States to control the whole continent. The purchase of Alaska from Russia in 1867 became the first step in the American thrust northward. The situation of the British North American colonies was further complicated by the Fenian Brotherhood, Irish nationalists whose leaders concocted a scheme to invade British North America from American soil—a clever way, they thought, of provoking a war between Britain and the United States that might give Ireland a better chance of achieving independence.

Neither the colonies nor Britain wanted a war with the United States.

Indeed, the Colonial Office strongly supported the idea of British North American union as a way of reducing imperial responsibilities, especially military commitments, in North America. (By 1871 British troops had been withdrawn entirely except from Halifax, where they would remain until the first decade of the twentieth century.) To compound what was developing into a full-scale military crisis, Washington served notice in 1864 that it would terminate the Reciprocity Treaty in 1866, causing consternation among those who relied on American markets. Confederation suddenly looked more interesting.

Selling Confederation

Since none of the leaders who attended the 1864 conferences had a mandate to negotiate political union, they were obliged either to call elections or to have the Confederation agreement endorsed by their legislatures. The Québec resolutions passed easily through the legislature of the United Canadas, but the Atlantic colonies were less enthusiastic.

In St John's Premier Hoyles found little support for Confederation either in his party or in Newfoundland at large. He therefore postponed a decision on the matter. Only 5 per cent of the island's trade was with British North America, and talk of railway building and military preparedness intensified well-founded fears that Newfoundland would be saddled with taxes from which it would receive little benefit. Among those of Irish descent, Confederation conjured up memories of the hated union of Great Britain and Ireland, and invoked fears that newly-won rights with respect to schools and political patronage would be jeopardized.

In Prince Edward Island, Conservative Premier John Hamilton Gray also shelved the issue. His own party was divided on the Québec resolutions, and few Islanders saw much advantage in a union that gave their colony only five seats in the Commons and did nothing to resolve the 'land question'. So contentious was the issue in Nova Scotia, where Joseph Howe became the spokesman for the anti-Confederate cause, that Tupper was forced to delay introducing the Québec resolutions into the legislature.

New Brunswick's Premier Tilley took a more direct route. In March 1865 he led his badly-divided party to a resounding electoral defeat at the hands of anti-Confederates led by Albert J. Smith. Strong forces intervened, some intentionally, others fortuitously, to put the Confederation movement back on track. Smith's anti-Confederate government broke into warring factions, and Lieutenant Governor Arthur Hamilton Gordon, in a high-handed manoeuvre, forced another election in May 1866. This time Tilley, promising major revisions to the Québec agreement, won a convincing victory. Support from Roman Catholic bishops and timber merchants, a timely invasion by the Fenians, and, finally, money from the Canadians and their Grand Trunk railway allies all helped to effect this reversal of fortunes. It would not be the last time that patronage rather than policy was used to legitimize Confederation in the Atlantic region.

In April 1866 Tupper made his move. With the assistance of Lieutenant-Governor William Fenwick Williams, a native of Nova Scotia and a decorated mil-

Biography: Samuel Leonard Tilley

With the exception of John A. Macdonald, no one played a more prominent role in the early years of Confederation than Samuel Leonard Tilley. He was born in Gagetown, New Brunswick, in 1818, a descendant of Loyalists on both sides of his family. At the age of 13, he began an apprenticeship with a pharmacist in Saint John, and in 1838 he and his cousin, Thomas Peters, opened their own 'Cheap Drug Store'. A year later Tilley was so deeply moved by a sermon that religious conviction thereafter governed his life. He taught Sunday school, served as a warden in the Church of England, and embraced the temperance movement. In 1854 he reached the highest office of the Sons of Temperance when he was named Most Worthy Patriarch.

Elected to the New Brunswick assembly in 1850, Tilley became a major player in the movement for responsible government, which was fully achieved in 1854. As provincial secretary he was a moving spirit behind the 1855 Prohibition Bill, but opposition to it was so great that he was defeated in the election of 1856 and the measure was rescinded. Regaining his seat in 1857 along with his position as provincial secretary, he became premier of the colony in 1861. With Joseph Howe, Tilley worked tirelessly to secure British and Canadian backing for an Intercolonial railway. When the Canadians withdrew from the deal in 1862, he refused to give up the dream and pushed an enabling bill through the assembly.

By the summer of 1864 Tilley was convinced of the need 'to bind together the Atlantic and Pacific by a continuous chain of settlements and a line of communications for that [was] the destiny of this country, and the race which inhabited it'.[3] He fought two bitter elections in New Brunswick over the Confederation issue and was appointed Minister of Customs in John A. Macdonald's first cabinet.

An early proponent of tariff protection for New Brunswick's infant industries, Tilley twice drew the wrath of commercial interests in the Maritimes with his initiatives. The tariff structure that he introduced in December 1867 helped to fuel the secession movement in Nova Scotia and it was Tilley who made the initial overture to Howe about accepting 'better terms' rather than abandoning Confederation. As Minister of Finance, Tilley introduced the 1879 tariff legislation that became the keystone to Macdonald's National Policy. High tariff walls to protect Canadian industry was a measure that would define the nation's economic strategy until the Canada–US Free Trade Agreement went into effect on 1 January 1989.

itary officer, Tupper twisted enough arms to ensure passage of a resolution in the Nova Scotia legislature authorizing continued discussion of British North American union. Significantly, Tupper's resolution made no reference to the Québec 'scheme', which had been thoroughly discredited by the anti-Confederate forces in the colony.

The final negotiations were conducted in London in the fall of 1866. Although no substantive changes were made to the constitutional arrangements forged in Québec in 1864, Tupper managed to secure a clause in the British North America Act providing for the 'immediate' construction of an Intercolonial railway 'by the Government of Canada'. The Maritime delegation also ceded to the federal government exclusive control over the fisheries—the original agreement had provided for joint jurisdiction as with agriculture and immigration—and export duties on coal. Despite a strong lobby from Halifax's Archbishop T.L. Connelly for a clause providing legal support for separate schools in the Maritimes, the delegates could not be moved, with the result that separate schools were constitutionally recognized only in Ontario and Québec.

Notwithstanding his failure to get major concessions from the Canadians, Tupper remained optimistic about the potential of Confederation to stimulate industrial development in Nova Scotia. In justifying the transfer to the federal government of the power to levy coal duties, he told the members of the Nova Scotia assembly in the spring of 1867 that 'the possession of coal mines, together with other natural resources must, in the course of time, make Nova Scotia the great emporium for manufactures in British America'. He went on to explain that 'in taking out of the power of any Legislature to double the amount of royalty, we were giving a guarantee to capitalists who might come and invest their money in these coal mines'.[4] In short, Nova Scotia would be open for business if Tupper had his way.

With little debate, the British North America Act passed in the British Parliament in March 1867, and on 1 July 1867 Ontario, Québec, New Brunswick, and Nova Scotia came together to form the Dominion of Canada. The *Morning Chronicle*, a Liberal newspaper in Halifax, appeared with a black border of mourning to mark the occasion, while the New Glasgow *Eastern Chronicle* carried a mock birth notice: 'On Monday last, at 12:05 a.m. (premature) the Dominion of Canada—illegitimate. This prodigy is known as the infant monster Confederation. . . .'

Nova Scotia's Secessionist Movement

Nova Scotians had good reason to feel they had been hoodwinked into joining the new union. Neither voters nor their elected representatives had given their approval to the proposals that ultimately became the basis for Confederation. Even worse, they felt that they had been literally 'railroaded' into a bad bargain. Commercial elements in the colony were particularly wary of a political structure initiated by 'Upper Canadians' who might pursue trade and tariff policies that would cripple their prospects.

In the elections held in September 1867, Nova Scotia voters finally had their say and they made their views clear. Thirty-six of 38 seats in the provincial assembly were won by candidates running on anti-Confederate tickets; only Tupper survived a contest that elected 18 anti-Confederates to the 19 seats available to the province in the House of Commons.

So determined were the Nova Scotia separatists that some of them even saw union with the United States as preferable to Confederation. In 1869 an Annexation League was formed to promote this alternative. Support for annexation was especially strong in southwestern Nova Scotia, which was virtually a suburb of Boston, and in Cape Breton, where coal interests were keen to restore access to American markets. At a meeting held in the summer of 1869, the annexationists drew up a manifesto, which they circulated around the province:

> Our only hope of commercial prosperity, material development and permanent peace lies in closer relations with the United States. Therefore be it resolved that every legitimate means should be used by members of this convention to sever our connection with Canada and to bring about a union on fair and equitable terms with the American Republic.[5]

Nova Scotia's opposition to Confederation represented more than wounded local pride. As constituted in 1867, the Dominion of Canada was little more than the United Canadas writ large, and was designed to serve the needs of the larger colony. The capital of the new nation was Ottawa, the former capital of the United Canadas, and the civil service was Canadian in structure and personnel. With their small populations compared to Québec and Ontario, the Maritime provinces could never dominate either the House of Commons or the cabinet table. The financial arrangements established by the British North America Act were particularly disadvantageous to small provinces. By absorbing the revenues from customs duties, Ottawa took away the chief source of funds for colonial administrations and offered the less populous colonies a per capita grant formula that would prove inadequate to fund their provincial responsibilities.

Nova Scotians were not opposed to becoming part of a larger political entity: imperial union, with colonial representation in London, was Howe's preferred option, while Maritime Union and annexation to the United States also had their supporters. What rankled was the obvious Canadian bias in the constitutional arrangements of 1867. This is not to say that the Maritime colonies would have fared better outside the Dominion of Canada—the fate of the Newfoundland government in the 1930s is often cited as proof that Confederation at least allowed the Maritimes a 'shabby dignity' in hard times.[6] Nevertheless, most of the predictions of the anti-Confederates proved correct in that the Maritimes did indeed have difficulty making their way in the new political structure.

In 1868 Howe led a delegation to London seeking repeal of the hated union, but the British had no interest in granting his request. Faced with growing support for annexation at home, Howe—ever loyal to Britain—agreed in 1869 to an accommodation with Ottawa that gave seats in the federal cabinet to two anti-Confederates and promised the province a ten-year bridging subsidy of about $800,000, with additional compensation for those public buildings that were transferred to federal control. Largely because of the lingering separatist sentiment in Nova Scotia, Prime Minister John A. Macdonald immediately authorized construction of the Intercolonial Railway.

Macdonald also tried to represent Nova Scotia's interests as a member of the British delegation that met with American representatives to settle a variety of issues left over from the Civil War. At the top of his agenda was a new reciprocity treaty. Although protectionists in the United States were too strong to permit such

A GAME OF SEE-SAW.
[SKETCHES FROM THE CAPITAL.]

J.W. Bengough, "A Game of See-Saw', *Canadian Illustrated News*, 4 May 1872. In the 1872 election, Maritime opposition to Confederation was sufficiently muted to give the federal Conservatives a large majority of seats. One reason, this cartoon suggests, was Macdonald's success in gaining entry to American markets for Canadian fish. Courtesy of Chinook Multimedia, Edmonton.

a concession, he managed to ensure that the Treaty of Washington, signed in 1871, provided free entry for Canadian fish into the American market, as well as compensation, to be determined by arbitration, for American access to Canadian inshore waters—terms that also applied to Newfoundland.

While Nova Scotians—and Canadians generally—had hoped for more from the Washington negotiations, they accepted what was on offer. Only two Nova Scotian MPs voted against the treaty, and in the federal election of 1872 two-thirds of the MPs from Nova Scotia supported Macdonald. Nevertheless, the province's continuing financial problems and the difficulties faced by both the primary and the commercial sectors guaranteed that anti-Confederation sentiment could easily be rekindled in the future.

Courting the Islands

Meanwhile, Macdonald made efforts to entice Newfoundland and Prince Edward Island into Confederation. Determined to unite Canada from sea-to-sea, he had already managed to incorporate Rupert's Land into the new nation in 1869, and British Columbia would follow two years later.

Despite widespread opposition to the idea, Confederation remained on the political agenda of Newfoundland's Conservative premier, Frederic Carter, who perhaps doubted the colony's ability to prosper on its own. In the months preceding the 1869 election, he persuaded the assembly to accept draft terms for union more generous than those proposed in the Québec resolutions. Canada was prepared to offer a special annual grant of $175,000 in exchange for the surrender of the island's Crown lands, an agreement that no export tax would be levied on its fish, and a promise that Newfoundlanders would not be drafted into the Canadian militia.

With no overwhelming debt and little tangible advantage to be gained from union, voters were not impressed. Anti-Confederate forces, led by the eloquent and persuasive merchant Charles Fox Bennett, won two-thirds of the seats in the assembly, and the margin of victory was enough that Confederation would not re-emerge as a viable political issue until the 1940s. Most Newfoundlanders apparently believed that their country had the resources to support an independent future.

Prince Edward Islanders, by contrast, eventually warmed to Macdonald's blandishments. The main issue in their 1867 election was not Confederation but the funding of denominational schools. Supported by a majority of the Roman Catholic voters, the Liberals defeated the Conservatives. Once in office, however, they proved equally unwilling to embrace denominational funding. Consequently, they lost much of their support and in turn suffered defeat in the 1870 election. The triumphant Conservatives under James Pope, a leading businessman and supporter of Confederation, formed the new government in alliance with the Roman Catholic independents who had broken away from the Liberals.

An apostle of progress, Pope built a railway line that wound a serpentine route through many of the Island's communities. Islanders soon found, as others had before them, that railway building was hard on the pocketbook. Meanwhile the land question remained unresolved. Although the Tenant League had collapsed in the autumn of 1865, when confronted by two companies of British troops called in from Halifax, the historian Ian Robertson argues that it succeeded in convincing many landlords that the system was impossible to sustain.[7] In May 1865 Samuel Cunard and Laurence Sullivan, who together owned 20 per cent of the land in the colony, announced that they would be selling, not leasing, their land, and others began to follow their lead. Only the lack of funding made a general policy to manage the transition from leasehold to freehold elusive.

Pope argued that the answer was to let Ottawa come to the rescue. Although he lost the 1872 election, his successor, Robert Haythorne, continued building railway lines and chalking up debts. To alleviate a financial burden that was rapidly becoming untenable, Haythorne's government negotiated a Confederation agreement and took it to the electorate in March 1873. Pope then returned to power—not because he opposed Confederation but because he promised to drive a harder bargain with Ottawa. In the end he succeeded in securing most of the concessions that Islanders had wanted in 1864 and more besides. Prime Minister

Canada in 1873.

Macdonald agreed not only to assume the railway debt and help to buy out the remaining absentee proprietors, but also to establish year-round communications with the mainland and give Islanders the six Commons seats that they demanded.

Conclusion

The debate over Confederation in the Atlantic region was defined to a striking degree by economic considerations. At the risk of oversimplification, it might be said that anti-Confederates tended to look east and south—to the North Atlantic, Britain, the oceanic trades, and the promising American market—whereas supporters of Confederation looked west, seeing the future in economic integration with the central provinces and expansion to the Pacific. Both groups recognized the need to adjust to a world in which Britain had abandoned imperial protectionism for free trade, reduced its defence commitments, and accepted colonial demands for responsible government, and in which the Americans had retreated behind a wall of protectionism. These changes were compounded by the spread of new technologies, based on coal, iron, and steel, that threatened traditional industries based on wood and wind. In a time of flux, it seemed to many people in the Maritimes that political consolidation made sense. Newfoundlanders took much longer to accept that their future was as a North American, not a North Atlantic, country.

Chapter 10

The Industrial Challenge, 1873–1901

The three Maritime provinces and Newfoundland had chosen separate political destinies, but in the last three decades of the nineteenth century they followed parallel paths. While the Maritimes worked out their position within a federal state dominated by Ontario and Québec, Newfoundland had to deal with an imperial government that hoped the colony would soon see the error of its ways. Relations with central governments, whether in London or Ottawa, were inevitably characterized by ambivalence and frustration. Most Maritimers became increasingly conscious of being Canadians; but at the same time, like Newfoundlanders, they remained proud members of the ever-expanding British Empire.

Maritimers faced a difficult transition from the traditional staple export trades to a more diversified economy characterized by industrialization and continental integration. Newfoundlanders tried to follow suit, but with limited success. The adjustment was all the more difficult because it took place in a context of extended economic recession, and aggressive competition from central Canada and the New England states.

Primary Industries in Transition

Industrializing processes forced changes on all sectors of the economy. Of the primary industries, agriculture—central to the Maritimes' economy—did better than most. Output increased, if modestly. Falling prices forced some farmers into subsistence agriculture, often in combination with other occupations such as lumbering and fishing. Others turned to livestock and dairy farming to supply a growing urban market, or focused on specialties for export. Orchards proliferated, especially in the Annapolis Valley, while potatoes became an important crop in Prince Edward Island and the Saint John River Valley. By the 1890s fox farming was increasing in popularity. Except for apple growers exporting to Great Britain, agricultural producers had difficulty finding foreign markets after the end of reciprocity in 1866. Newfoundland, where there were few commercial farms, relied heavily on imported livestock and foodstuffs, and St-Pierre provided a market for Cape Breton produce.

The forest industry, the traditional engine of the New Brunswick economy, was badly damaged by the decline in the British markets both for lumber and for wooden ships. During the 1870s Saint John lost 29 per cent of its population. A disastrous fire on 20 June 1877, causing losses estimated at $27 million, was a fur-

Timeline

1875	Caraquet riots.
1876	Intercolonial Railway completed.
1877	Saint John fire.
1879	Protective tariff imposed under National Policy; Provincial Workmen's Association established.
1881	First Acadian National Convention.
1882	Nova Scotia Steel and Coal Company founded at New Glasgow.
1885	Treaty of Washington concessions regarding fisheries expire.
1886	Secession motion in Nova Scotia.
1890	Newfoundland attempts to negotiate reciprocity.
1891	Intercolonial Railway reaches Sydney and Yarmouth.
1892	St John's fire; Dr Wilfred Grenfell arrives in Labrador.
1893	Nova Scotia legislature rejects women's suffrage; Dominion Coal Company established at Glace Bay.
1894	Newfoundland bank crash.
1897	Newfoundland Railway completed.
1900	Dominion Iron and Steel Company begins building steel mill at Sydney; Nova Scotia Steel and Coal Co. at Sydney Mines; Prince Edward Island becomes the first province in Canada to adopt prohibition.
1901	Bank of Nova Scotia moves headquarters to Toronto.

ther blow. Nevertheless, logging and sawmilling remained important industries, and in the 1890s Saint John was Canada's leading lumber producer. Maritime lumbermen extended their activity to Newfoundland, first assaulting the pine forests of the Humber River valley, later establishing sawmills in the watersheds of rivers along the island's east coast.

All three Maritime provinces suffered as shipbuilding gradually declined into insignificance. With iron (later steel) hulls and steam taking over the marine world, wooden sailing ships were confined to the coastal trades, fishing, and some long-distance freight routes. Increasingly, the Maritimes traded with central Canada and the United States rather than the Caribbean (where markets declined along with the sugar industry), and without government encouragement and protection there was little incentive to build iron or steel vessels or to maintain a sizeable merchant marine. Although locally built cargo schooners remained in use until the 1940s, small-vessel fleets gradually contracted everywhere except in Newfoundland, where expansion continued until 1919.

A famous photograph of a small boy with two prize codfish at Battle Harbour, Labrador, *c.* 1900. VA 21-18, The Rooms, Provincial Archives Division.

The swarm of small Newfoundland schooners reflected that colony's continued reliance on the cod and seal fisheries, as well as the absence of reasonable road and rail connections until the turn of the twentieth century. In the 1880s the fisheries represented 67 per cent of goods production, compared to 13 per cent in the Maritimes, and employed 85 per cent of the workforce. The Newfoundland economy was therefore especially vulnerable to falling international prices for salt cod and seal oil. There was little fisheries diversification, apart from the development of an offshore bank fishery in the 1880s. This was a response to government restrictions on the sale of bait to foreign offshore fleets, particularly the French banking fleet, whose product competed with Newfoundland exports. Lobster canning, an industry started by Maritimers, became increasingly important. Salt cod remained the staple, however, tied to increasingly congested markets in southern Europe and the Caribbean.

Nova Scotians, by contrast, had expanded the range of their fisheries by mid-century to include Labrador, the Gulf of St Lawrence, and the offshore banks. Federal bounties helped to stimulate this expansion, which stalled with the expiry, in 1886, of the concessions granting easy access to US markets for fish under the Treaty of Washington. In response, many Nova Scotian skippers and crew moved to Gloucester and other New England ports. The demand for saltfish also fell in this period. Among the businesses that went bankrupt as a result was Charles Robin and Company, the largest inshore cod firm in the Maritimes. Although salt-fish production declined, bank fishing continued to be an important industry, centred in Lunenburg and adjacent ports. Inshore fishers came to rely less on codfish and more on salmon, sardines, oysters, and lobsters. The 1880s and 1890s brought a lobster canning boom throughout the region. Maritimers were well-placed to meet the demand for fish, both fresh and frozen, from the United States and central Canada, primarily because of improvements in railway connections and refrigeration technology.

An Industrial Revolution in the Maritimes

Coal, abundant in Cape Breton, northeastern Nova Scotia, and to a lesser extent in southern New Brunswick, was the key component in the efforts of Maritime élites to join the industrial revolution. When the Reciprocity treaty expired in 1866, the United States slapped prohibitive duties on Nova Scotia coal. Maritime coal producers then turned their attention to markets in central Canada. The success of this strategy depended on the completion of a railway to the St Lawrence and the imposition of a protective tariff to keep out cheaper imports. When the Intercolonial Railway linked Halifax and Saint John to Lévis in 1876, Maritime producers finally had their long-desired access to central Canadian markets. Extensions to Sydney and Yarmouth were in place by 1891.

The National Policy budget of 1879 set off a binge of investment in secondary Maritime industries. There were two zones of development: in the south, the ports of Halifax, Saint John, and Yarmouth, where imported staples such as cotton, spices, and sugar were processed for sale elsewhere; and in the north, the corridor defined by the Intercolonial, where manufacturing was based on coal, iron, and steel. By 1885 Nova Scotia and New Brunswick supported eight cotton mills, three sugar refineries, two confectionaries, two rope works, and a glass factory.

The National Policy also imposed a duty on imported coal: initially 50 cents a ton, rising to 60 cents the following year. The Maritimes accounted for most of the coal produced in Canada, and shipments to the Québec market increased dramatically, but the region's producers were not able to supply much more than 10 per cent of the total demand. High-quality anthracite coal for domestic use came largely from the United States, as did the bituminous coal used by industries west of Montréal.

The development of a flourishing iron and steel industry seemed to confirm Nova Scotia's industrial pre-eminence. In the last decades of the nineteenth century two companies were established in the province that by the turn of the new century emerged as corporate giants. Founded in Pictou County in 1882, Nova Scotia Steel and Coal became, for a time, Canada's leading producer of iron and steel products. Using iron ore from Bell Island, Newfoundland, the company integrated its operations at Sydney Mines in 1900. A second corporate success story began with the creation of the Dominion Coal Company in 1893. Spearheaded by Boston financier Henry M. Whitney, Dominion Coal was granted, in 1899, a

Workers at the Intercolonial Railway shop in Moncton. Completed from Halifax to Lévis in 1876, the Intercolonial helped to make Moncton, the railway's eastern headquarters, a major distribution and manufacturing centre. Moncton Museum Collection.

99-year lease on all unassigned coal resources in Cape Breton in return for a royalty. Armed with this assurance, Whitney incorporated the Dominion Iron and Steel Company and began construction of a primary steel mill at Sydney in 1900. Small rolling mills were established in Halifax and Saint John, as well as Amherst, where in 1893 J. Rhodes, Curry, and Co. built the first railway cars to be manufactured in Canada.

The Intercolonial Railway and other lines that were built in this period were the key to economic development in many Maritime communities. Strategically located towns such as Moncton, Truro, Windsor, and Yarmouth produced textiles, foundry goods, furniture, and processed foods that found markets near and far. On the surface at least, the Maritimes appeared to be making a successful transition to an industrial economy.

Yet as Table 10.1 shows, the gross value of production in the manufacturing sector increased only by 32 per cent between 1880 and 1900—about the same as forestry—and as a percentage of the total actually declined by 3 per cent. In 1901 manufacturing employed only 28 per cent of the workforce (47 per cent were in primary production and 25 per cent in services). Maritime factories tended to be smaller and less efficient than those in central Canada, which meant lower pay for workers and lower profits for owners. Handicapped by a relatively small local market, managerial inexperience, and a long recession, they fought an uphill battle against central Canadian competitors.

Increasingly reluctant to invest in regional enterprises, Maritime banks looked for safer and more profitable places to do business. A clear sign of this shift was the Bank of Nova Scotia's decision to move its headquarters to Toronto in 1901. Meanwhile, to 'rationalize' production and protect their profits, central Canadian interests moved into the Maritimes. Dominion Cotton Mills and the related

Table 10.1 Gross Value of Production ($000), Maritimes

	Agriculture	Forestry	Mining	Fishery	Manufacturing	Total
1880	41.9	13.3	3.1	14.9	42.6	115.9
1900	58.7	17.2	14.4	20.3	56.4	167.1
Change (%)	40.1	29.3	364.5	36.2	32.4	44.1

Percentage of Gross Value of Production, Maritimes

	Agriculture	Forestry	Mining	Fishery	Manufacturing
1880	36	12	3	13	37
1900	51	10	9	12	34
Change	15	(–2)	6	(–1)	(–3)

Source: David G. Alexander, 'Economic Growth in the Atlantic Region, 1880–1940', in Alexander, *Atlantic Canada and Confederation. Essays in Canadian Political Economy*, Eric W. Sager, Lewis R. Fischer, Stuart O. Pierson, comps (Toronto: Memorial University and University of Toronto Press, 1983), 58–9.

Canadian Coloured Cotton Company, both of Montréal, took over the region's cotton mills, while Diamond Glass, also of Montréal, bought the three glassworks at Trenton and eventually closed them. It was the same story in coal, sugar, and cordage. By 1895 only spices, confectionary—most notably Ganongs in St Stephens and Moirs in Halifax—and manufacturing related to iron, steel, and local staples remained under regional control.[1] Small manufacturers as well as traditional trades were vulnerable to the marketing, through branch businesses, of goods produced elsewhere. With the completion of nation-wide railway systems, mail-order companies such as the one run by Timothy Eaton in Toronto extended their reach to the most remote corners of the country.

Newfoundland's National Policy

Newfoundlanders were also caught up in dreams of new industries and diversification. Realizing that political independence had to be underpinned by a stronger economy, the government led by Sir William Whiteway in the late 1870s and early 1880s adopted a local version of the National Policy, trumpeted as the 'Policy of Progress'. The centrepiece was a railway across the island—the first track was laid in 1882—which, like the Canadian Pacific Railway, was designed to link the east and west coasts and stimulate the development of land-based industries. Tariff policy was adjusted to protect small manufacturers in St John's. Convinced by Geological Survey reports that the island contained valuable natural resources in abundance, railway enthusiasts predicted rapid growth in agriculture, forest industries, and mining.

Another dimension of this policy was a determined attempt to gain unrestricted access to the resources of the French Treaty Shore. Having long claimed

Document: The Royal Commission on Labour and Capital, 1889

The industrial revolution was built on the backs of workers who initially had little say in the conditions of their employment. In 1886 the Canadian government responded to concerns about the exploitative nature of industrial capitalism by establishing a Royal Commission on Labour and Capital. The commissioners heard nearly 1800 witnesses, many of them from Nova Scotia and New Brunswick.

The following testimony by Joseph Larkins, a young factory worker in Halifax, was published in the commission's 1889 report. It reveals the tendency of entrepreneurs, pressured by stiff competition, to hire children under 16 who were paid less than adults for doing the same work. Reformers demanded that legislation be passed to regulate the employment of children, and to provide compensation for workers injured on the job.

Q. How old are you? A. I am 11 years.

Q. What is the matter with your hand? A. It got hurt in the machinery.

Q. How? A. It got caught in the rollers.

Q. What rollers? A. The rollers of a cracker machine—a biscuit machine.

Q. How long were you working in the biscuit factory? A. About seven weeks.

Q. Was it part of your work to look after the machinery? A. No; I was taken in as a packer and was then put to work on the machinery.

Q. How much wages did they give you? A. A dollar a week first, and then a dollar and a quarter.

Q. How much do they give you now? A. Nothing at all.

Q. How long is it since you were hurt? A. Nine weeks Thursday.

Q. And have they not given you anything? A. No; except for the week when I was hurt.

Q. Did you ask for employment? A. My mother asked for a job for me, and they said I could get a job biscuit packing; then they changed me to where the machinery was.

Q. How long were you working at the machinery before you were hurt? A. I could not say.

Q. What were you doing at the machinery? A. I was brushing the dough off according as it came through.

Q. Are other boys your age employed in the concern? A. I could not say. There was a boy about the same size.

Q. Did you lose any fingers? A. I lost one.

Q. Did you lose any of the joints in the others? A. I think I will lose a second finger.

Q. Who paid the doctor? A. I could not say.

Q. Who took you to the doctor? A. A man who was there. The doctor put seven or eight stitches in. . . .[2]

an exclusive right to fish between Cape St John and Cape Ray, France maintained that settlement, and by implication economic development, in that region was illegal because it would interfere with the fishery. As a result, the growing numbers of settlers on the Shore were not represented in the legislature, had no local government, and were denied Crown land grants as well as mining and timber licences. Although the French Shore fishery was declining as the bank fishery based at St-Pierre expanded, France was reluctant to give up its privileges. For its part, the British government was wary of precipitating a diplomatic crisis. Whiteway succeeded in extending the authority of the colonial government to the Shore, but with some important limitations.

In the short term at least, the Policy of Progress failed to alter the island's economy in any significant way. Nevertheless, employment in primary industries fell by 20 per cent between 1874 and 1901, while employment in secondary and service industries increased. The economic imperialism of central Canada reached the island when, in 1890, the railway project was taken over by the Montréal-based contractor Robert G. Reid, who had close links with the CPR and the Bank of Montréal. The latter became banker to the Newfoundland government after the crash of the colony's two private banks in 1894. Like the Maritime provinces, Newfoundland lost control of its financial institutions, and its currency became tied to the Canadian dollar. During the 1890s mainland steel companies took over the huge deposits of iron ore at Bell Island in Conception Bay, shipping it to their blast furnaces at Cape Breton.

Societies in Transition

In the last three decades of the nineteenth century, people throughout the Maritimes and Newfoundland were on the move from country to town, and from the Atlantic region to other areas of North America. The lure of urban jobs in factories, service industries, and emerging professions such as medicine, teaching, and engineering drew young people like a magnet and was typical of wider North American trends. Since the Atlantic region lacked a major metropolis such as Montréal, Toronto, Boston, or New York to absorb young talent, they became part of what was described by contemporaries as 'the exodus'. New England was the main attraction, but there were few parts of North America where migrants from the Atlantic region could not be found.

Out-migration was both an effect and a cause of the region's shaky economic performance. As early as the 1860s, the Maritimes began to suffer net migration loss, which reached a peak in the 1880s but continued at a significant rate until the 1930s. Between 1871 and 1881 the population grew by 13.5 per cent; thereafter growth dropped to 1.2 per cent between 1881 and 1891, and 1.5 per cent between 1891 and 1901. After 1891 the population of Prince Edward Island began to decline in absolute terms. In all, some 250,000 people left the Maritimes between 1871 and 1901. Women were more likely to leave than men, the young more likely than the middle-aged, anglophones more likely than francophones, and rural areas were particularly hard hit. In the view of the historian Judith

Fingard, the 'exodus of the last quarter of the nineteenth century may have result-ed in the decapitation of Maritime society.'[3]

The hemorrhage was not quite as severe in Newfoundland, but the trends were similar. In the 1880s the population grew by only 3 per cent, and for the first time more people left the colony than arrived from elsewhere. Most districts on the southeastern Avalon declined in absolute numbers.

The emphasis placed on out-migration has masked the attention paid by pol-icy makers to immigration. Immigration was a major priority in Ottawa, which assumed responsibility for funding the immigrant bureaucracy, including quaran-tine facilities in Halifax, Saint John, and Québec City. New Brunswick was par-ticularly aggressive in seeking immigrants after the completion of the Intercolonial Railway opened up new areas for settlement, implementing a generous land grants policy in 1872. Over 800 immigrants arrived that year, reaching a high of 3,714 in 1889, most (though not all) from Britain. The Maritimes also became a receiv-ing area for 'home children'—orphaned or destitute British children who were shipped to 'the colonies' to begin a new life, many of them as domestic servants or farm labourers.

The Mi'kmaq and Maliseet were subject to the same pressures as their non-Native neighbours, but for them the barriers to modernization were virtually insurmountable. As cheap factory goods increasingly flooded the market, income from sales of crafts began to decline and, for all practical purposes, Native people were barred from industrial ventures by lack of capital, local prejudice, and the rigid provisions of the Indian Act.

Following Confederation, those living on reserves became 'Status Indians' under the jurisdiction of the federal government. The 1876 Indian Act consoli-dated policies across Canada on the Ontario model, with little concern for region-al and cultural differences. Based on the premise that Aboriginal people were inca-pable of integrating into 'civilized' society, the Act insisted on their close supervi-sion, making it difficult for them to change their sub-standard living conditions. They could neither vote nor drink alcohol, and risked losing their status if they pursued higher education or took up a profession. Native women who married white men automatically lost their Indian status. Freezing the Mi'kmaq and Maliseet in patriarchal, pre-industrial social and economic arrangements, the Indian Act made integration into the larger Maritime society all but impossible.

Newfoundland had neither reserves nor any equivalent to the Indian Act. The approximately 200 Mi'kmaq living there—mainly in the Conne River area—made their living as guides, mail carriers, and trappers, and by fishing, hunting cari-bou, and selling basketry. For most of the nineteenth century they had the island's interior largely to themselves, but the situation changed for the worse in the 1890s with the building of the railway, the subsequent development of forest industries, and the arrival of sport hunters.

In Labrador the Innu relied heavily on trapping furs, which they traded at North West River, Davis Inlet, and elsewhere. By the 1890s, however, white and mixed-blood settlers living in Hamilton Inlet were encroaching on their hunting territory, causing angry confrontations. Meanwhile, the Inuit population of about

1,000 was assumed to be on the way either to extinction or to absorption into white society. With up to 1,200 Newfoundland fishing schooners arriving each summer, diet, clothing, and housing all began to change, and fishing for cod and char became the mainstay of the local Inuit economy. As contact with whites increased, Inuit proved susceptible to diseases brought from elsewhere, such as measles and influenza. In the 1890s, some Inuit brought back typhoid fever, having been put on display at the Chicago Exhibition.

Political Machinations

Inadequate federal subsidies meant that all the Maritime provinces experienced severe financial problems. Prince Edward Island—which, unlike Nova Scotia and New Brunswick, did not receive timber and mineral royalties—was particularly hard pressed since by 1900 it relied on federal subsidies for 64.5 per cent of its provincial budget. The Island government therefore had no choice but to retrench, going so far as to abolish the secret ballot (which was more expensive than open voting) and introduce statutory road labour. At the same time, Islanders were preoccupied with the federal government's failure to provide the 'efficient and continuous communication' with the mainland promised by the Confederation agreement. Only in the mid-1880s, after making a direct appeal to the imperial government, did they get a better ferry (although there was considerable support for a fixed link in the form of a tunnel).

In New Brunswick the economic recession of the mid-1880s exposed the weakness of the province's industrial base and underscored the steady decline of the once world-renowned shipbuilding industry. Discontent was manifested in a loose alliance of all political interests that coalesced under Andrew G. Blair in 1886 to become a powerful Liberal machine. Although Blair resorted to such popular cost-saving measures as abolishing the Legislative Council, he was at a loss to find a way to bring prosperity to his province. Ottawa, preoccupied with a second uprising in the Northwest and completing the Canadian Pacific Railway, seemed deaf to demands that attention be paid to the Maritimes, especially in provinces that persisted in electing Liberal governments.

Frustration with Ottawa led Nova Scotia's Liberal Premier W.S. Fielding to introduce a motion in the Nova Scotia legislature in 1886 calling for Maritime union as a preliminary to secession from Canada. The responses from New Brunswick and Prince Edward Island proved lukewarm, and even Nova Scotia voters effectively repudiated Fielding's proposal in the 1887 federal election, when Macdonald's Conservative government won a majority of seats in the province and nationally. As a fallback position, Fielding took up two new causes: provincial rights within Confederation and free trade with the United States. These policies were supported by a number of provinces with Liberal premiers, as well as the federal Liberal Party, now led by Wilfrid Laurier. Blair and Fielding attended the first interprovincial conference in 1887—a harbinger of what would prove to be long-standing tensions between federal and provincial jurisdictions in Canada.

The idea of reciprocity was also popular in Newfoundland, where fish

Ice boats waiting to cross the Northumberland Strait. Until the twentieth century, when ferries became powerful enough to negotiate the ice in Northumberland Strait, winter crossings were often perilous. Sometimes passengers and crew were left stranded for days. From 1827 to 1918, small iceboats such as these were used to carry mail to and from the mainland. PEIPARO, Acc. 2353/225

exporters, facing heavy French and Norwegian competition in Europe, were looking for new markets. Asserting its rights within the Empire, the Newfoundland government asked for and received permission to open talks with the American government. When its representative, Robert Bond, and the American Secretary of State, James Blaine, concluded a draft reciprocity treaty, there was surprise in London, consternation in Ottawa, and outrage in Halifax. If Newfoundland was allowed to gain advantages outside Confederation that Nova Scotia could not obtain within it, secession might well become more than a threat. The treaty was swiftly killed by London.

Humiliated and angry, Newfoundland retaliated by imposing extra duties on imports from Canada and refusing to issue bait licences to fishermen from Nova Scotia. Canada countered with similar measures. The crisis eventually blew over and the two sides met in Halifax in 1892 to discuss their differences, but nothing was resolved. The Newfoundlanders were unwilling to talk about Confederation, and the Canadians maintained their objections to a separate Newfoundland reciprocity treaty. Since London and the courts had already ruled that Newfoundland could not discriminate against other British subjects, Canadians were confident that their interests would prevail.

As in the past, political divisions prompted by economic concerns were complicated by issues of class, ethnicity, and religion. Labour unrest—a product of urbanization, industrialization, and new political ideas—became increasingly common. The centre of organized labour activity was the Nova Scotia coal fields, where increasingly repressive and unsafe corporate practices led to the formation of Canada's first industrial union, the Provincial Workmen's Association, in 1879. A relatively conservative organization, the PWA sought to advance the position of miners as skilled tradesmen, and lobbied the provincial government on safety, workmen's compensation, and other issues with considerable success, but it did not challenge the industry's structure, nor did it promote collective bargaining. As a result, coal strikes were restricted to individual fields: Pictou in 1886–7, Springhill in 1890 and 1897, Joggins in 1896. Nova Scotia's mines nevertheless saw some of the most protracted strikes in Canada in the late nineteenth century. Other sectors experienced strikes as well—for example, the Saint John and Halifax waterfronts—but the labour movement was too decentralized and scattered to have much overall impact.

If strikes reflected growing class divisions, prolonged debates over education revealed other cleavages: religious, ethnic, and linguistic. The basic question was how far public school systems should (or could) go to accommodate social diversity. The Newfoundland solution, finalized in 1873, was to cut the education budget in three and allow a denominational school system with separate Roman Catholic, Church of England, and Methodist schools. Over time, compromises emerged in Nova Scotia and Prince Edward Island whereby Roman Catholic schools were allowed to operate with provincial funding.

Such an accommodation was more difficult to achieve in New Brunswick. In the wake of the Common Schools Act of 1871, the provincial government insisted on a fully non-sectarian system in which all vestiges of religion were prohibited. Outraged, Catholics refused to pay school assessments and appealed to Ottawa for disallowance. The federal government declined to intervene on the grounds that education was a provincial responsibility, and the courts ruled the act to be constitutional. Thus fortified, the provincial government went to the polls in 1874 and, emerging victorious, began legal actions against those refusing to pay school assessments.

Resistance was especially fierce among the Acadian population. Since only one Acadian child in six received any schooling, and few attended for more than five or six years, there was little incentive to pay taxes to support schools of any kind, let alone schools that excluded Catholic teachings. Tensions culminated in the Caraquet riots of 1875, in which two people died. A compromise then emerged: where numbers warranted, Roman Catholics could be taught by members of religious orders and have religious instruction after school hours. For Acadians, though, the availability of French language instruction remained a serious problem, since New Brunswick, like the other provinces, insisted on the use of English in schools.

The schools dispute served as a rallying point for the scattered but increasingly self-conscious Acadian community, which by the 1870s numbered about 90,000, half of them in New Brunswick. Longfellow's poem *Evangeline* (1847), a love story set against the background of the Deportation, had begun to circulate in French transla-

The original Acadian flag, 1884, conceived by Father Marcel-François Richard. Photo Léo Blanchard, Musée acadien, Université de Moncton.

tion during the 1860s. Adopted for use in the Collège St-Joseph at Memramcook (founded in 1864), the poem seemed to the growing Acadian élite to be 'the poetic distillation of their history, the true legend of their past'.[4] It became, in effect, a unifying narrative at a time when Acadians were trying to establish a collective identity. At the first Acadian national convention, held in 1881 at Memramcook, the majority of delegates decided to adopt the Feast of the Assumption (15 August) as the national holiday, rather than that of St-Jean-Baptiste, thus choosing distinctiveness over closer ties with Québec. The 1884 convention, at Miscouche, adopted an Acadian flag—the French tricolour (which at that time was also used in Québec), with a yellow star signifying devotion both to the Virgin Mary and to the papacy— and 'Ave Maris Stella' became the national hymn. The Société Nationale l'Assomption, founded in 1881 (now the Société Nationale de l'Acadie), provided leadership and continuity by promoting Acadian interests. Several newspapers appeared—among them *L'Évangeline* in 1887—and in the 1890s new colleges were established at Pointe de l'Église in Nova Scotia and Caraquet in New Brunswick.

More reluctant than anglophones to leave the region, Acadians also had a high fertility rate; accordingly, their numbers increased both absolutely and as a percentage of the Maritime population. In New Brunswick, which lost 76,000 people to the United States during the last two decades of the century, Acadians made up 24 per cent of the population by 1901, and had replaced the Irish as the largest Roman Catholic group. Not surprisingly, it was in that province that the issue of cultural

Acadian National Identity

Between 1881 and 1890 Acadians met in three large congresses in each of the Maritime provinces: Memramcook, New Brunswick; Miscouche, Prince Edward Island; and Church Point, Nova Scotia. The inspiration came from a meeting in Québec City in 1880, when francophones from all over North America were invited to a convention held on Saint-Jean-Baptiste Day. There was a special committee for Acadians, which was well-attended. Joseph-Octave Arsenault, a prominent political leader in Prince Edward Island, encouraged Island Acadians to attend the Saint-Jean-Baptiste convention, in part because they were experiencing massive out-migration prompted by a lack of available agricultural land. As this newspaper summary of his comments at a parish assembly in Egmont Bay indicates, Arsenault was aware of efforts underway in Québec to open rural areas for group settlement and hoped that a similar approach might help to preserve the distinct Acadian 'national' identity from the homogenizing tendencies of industrial cities.

> It is here, under national banners, that we the Acadian people will find the strength and resources to gain respect for our rights which have been ignored for too long, and to preserve the integrity of our national character and the language we love and that our mothers taught us; in short, everything that is of concern to our nation: religion, education, science, industry, and colonization. He made us realize that we could benefit from joining our Canadian brothers to form one national family. Above all, the Honourable Arsenault emphasized the question of colonization. Since this issue is on the programme of the convention, it would be very much in our interest to be represented, if only to discuss a subject that concerns us so much; our properties are already too small and we shall soon be forced to seek settlements elsewhere for our children, and that will certainly be in Canada.[5]

uniformity—a sensitive issue throughout Canada—surfaced in the Maritimes. At a time when a revived cult of Loyalism, with its strongly imperial overtones, was spreading among Protestant New Brunswickers, Herman H. Pitts used a difficult schools dispute in Bathurst to launch a determined campaign in favour of 'equal rights'. The same euphemism was used in Ontario to identify a movement designed to end 'concessions' to Roman Catholics and francophones, and to promote an evangelical Protestant reform agenda that included non-sectarian schools, prohibition, sabbatarianism, political reform, and—eventually—limited female suffrage. A central (and divisive) figure during the 1890s, Pitts was ultimately rejected by an electorate that opted for accommodation over confrontation.

The Pitts crusade was an unattractive manifestation of the reform movement that began to take root in the region in the later nineteenth century: a mix of (usually Protestant) religion, imperialism, and faith in progress. Rooted in cities and churches—including the Salvation Army, which arrived in the mid-1880s—it addressed many of the problems associated with industrial development. The temperance movement was already well-established, and there had been widespread support in the Maritimes for the 1878 Scott Act, which permitted municipalities to bar the sale of alcohol. Newfoundland had similar legislation, and organizations such as the Sons of Temperance and the Women's Christian Temperance Union were active across the region.

Reformers were equally concerned with public health, urban renewal, the rights of women and children, social and economic justice, and moral uplift. Increasingly, they looked to the state to enact aspects of their program, a prospect not always welcomed by political leaders who understood the potentially divisive nature of some issues on the 'social gospel' agenda. In 1900 Prince Edward Island became the first province in Canada to legislate prohibition, but other provinces were slow to follow the Island's lead.

Although married women gained rights relating to child custody, marital property, and the municipal franchise in the Maritimes, women's right to vote at the provincial level was denied. In 1893 the Nova Scotia legislature passed, by a narrow margin, a motion for female suffrage but it was quashed in committee by Attorney General J.W. Longley, who was appalled by the prospect of Nova Scotia's leading the nation in such a controversial measure. The Women's Christian Temperance Union presented a suffrage petition to the Newfoundland legislature in 1891, but motions in support were defeated in each of following two sessions. Together, caution and lack of money dictated that such social intervention as did occur should be largely the work of the churches and voluntary organizations such as the YMCA and the YWCA, city missions, and children's aid societies.

A dramatic example of the social reform activism associated with the 'muscular Christianity' of the era was the work of the tireless Dr Wilfred Grenfell. Within Newfoundland and Labrador he was a controversial figure who offended church leaders by attacking denominational education, accusing the mercantile establishment for alleged exploitation, and thinking the government was corrupt and incompetent. Nevertheless, his ceaseless energy and activism helped to improve health care and stimulated the emergence of a public health movement that became primarily concerned with a tuberculosis epidemic then sweeping the colony. Similar anti-TB campaigns were also undertaken in the Maritimes, where death rates from tuberculosis were lower but still significant.

Close economic and ethnic ties in the region helped to ensure that many people were swept up the rising tide of imperial sentiment that characterized the closing decades of the nineteenth century. The New Brunswick-born George Parkin, in his own words 'the wandering evangelist of Empire', became in the 1880s a leader of the Imperial Federation Movement, designed to draw Great Britain and its colonies closer together. Portraits of Queen Victoria could be found in many homes, and her diamond jubilee was celebrated with enthusiasm in 1897. The same year marked the 400th anniversary of Cabot's voyage. With Maritimers claiming Cape Breton as the first land sighted, and Newfoundlanders Cape

Biography: Wilfred T. Grenfell

Grenfell's name is still associated with northern Newfoundland and Labrador, the area to which he devoted his working life after his first visit in 1892, at the age of 27. An English evangelical Christian who had recently qualified as a doctor, he was employed by the Royal National Mission to Deep Sea Fishermen to investigate the condition of fishers engaged in the Labrador fishery.

Each spring hundreds of schooners sailed from the island of Newfoundland to the Labrador coast. Some fished as 'floaters', following the fish, salting their catch on board and carrying it back to their home ports for drying. Others carried crews of 'stationers' who fished from fixed locations and dried their catches there. Grenfell found widespread poverty and a serious need for medical facilities, both for the fishermen and for the residents ('livyeres').

Over the following years he raised money to build hospitals and nursing stations that eventually extended from Newfoundland's Northern Peninsula to Lake Melville in Labrador, with a headquarters at St Anthony. More than this, Grenfell attempted to reshape the economy and society of the region, arguing that poverty, ignorance, and malnutrition were the causes of most disease. He encouraged the formation of cooperatives; promoted improvements in both hygiene and diet; started a sawmill and an industrial crafts program; tried to improve educational facilities; and, in the hope of providing a new source of food, clothing, and jobs, introduced reindeer (the experiment failed).

In many ways the Grenfell Mission was a colony within a colony. Its staff came from the United States, Britain, and Canada, as did the money that supported it. Grenfell himself had to spend much of the year on fund-raising tours; though known as 'Grenfell of Labrador', he never spent a winter there. He was the dynamo, but the actual work of the mission was done by remarkably dedicated staff members and, in summer, unpaid volunteers.

Grenfell died in 1940. Although there can be no doubt that he, and his mission, did much good, the region's structural economic and social features proved intractable, at least during his lifetime.[6]

Bonavista, ceremonies were held at both Halifax and St. John's. In both cities traditions were invented and embellished, speakers in each case celebrating Cabot as the founder not only of their respective countries, but of the British Empire of which they were proud members.

Conclusion

As the long depression lifted in the late 1890s, the region was in some ways much the same as it had been 30 years earlier; in others much changed. Farms, forests, and the sea still underpinned life in the region, but a quarter of Maritimers now lived

in towns; new industries had become established; mining had expanded significantly, along with the service sector; and the economy (in the Maritimes at least)
no longer relied so extensively on the old staple trades. Political divisions and local
rivalries remained deeply entrenched, but by the turn of century transportation
links were in place across the region: the Newfoundland railway was completed in
1897, and regular ferry service across the Cabot Strait began the next year. At the
same time many people throughout the region shared common enthusiasms,
whether for the Empire, for temperance, or for social reform. Despite bitter disputes
over education, levels of literacy had improved considerably, and a more sophisti-
cated society was emerging. There were signs that not all was well—the control
exercised by central Canadian banks and corporations was especially troubling—
but as the twentieth century dawned there was some reason for optimism.

Chapter Eleven

The Promise and Peril of a New Century, 1901–19

For almost two decades after 1900, most Maritimers and Newfoundlanders would have said that they lived in an age of social and economic achievement and promise. It was only as the Great War drew to a close that the mood shifted. Expectations of growth and security vanished in the face of the Spanish Flu epidemic, a wave of strikes, and the onset of economic and financial difficulties. The twentieth century, as it turned out, brought disillusionment and uncertainty.

The Busy East

Optimism was not unfounded at the turn of the century. The populations of Nova Scotia and New Brunswick were growing, if modestly—only Prince Edward Island experienced a net loss—and between 1900 and 1920 the gross value of production expanded in every sector except the fisheries. Agriculture was stimulated by strong demand for potatoes and apples in central Canada and the rapidly growing West, as well as expanding urban markets in the Atlantic region itself; Britain was still importing apples and sawn lumber in large volumes; and demand for fashionable silver fox pelts sparked a boom for breeders on Prince Edward Island. Meanwhile, the annual output of coal increased from approximately 2.9 million short tons in the 1890s to 6.5 million in 1916–20. In this instance, the regional market was all-important, much of the coal being consumed by the expanding iron and steel industry.

The history of the fisheries in this period arguably represents a missed opportunity. By the turn of the century, the trend was clearly towards the production of fresh and frozen fish, and steam trawlers were making their appearance. New Englanders moved most of their vessels from the Grand Banks to grounds closer to shore, and rapidly developed a large trawler fleet. By 1908 the French had between 10 and 15 trawlers on the banks (which put into Sydney for ice and coal) in addition to their fleet of over 200 sailing vessels. If fishermen in the Atlantic region hoped to compete for the common resource located on their very doorstep, they would have to modernize their practices.

Maritimers, especially Nova Scotians, proved cautious. While they were prepared to adopt the gasoline engine and the motor boat, invest in bait freezers (at Canso and Halifax, for example), and respond to the demand for fresh fish, there was strong opposition to trawlers from inshore fishermen and schooner owners

Timeline

1902	Sealers strike in St John's.
1904	The *entente cordiale* settles the Newfoundland French Shore dispute.
1906	Federal subsidies to provinces revised.
1907	Canada passes Lord's Day Act.
1908	William Coaker founds the Fishermen's Protective Union in Newfoundland; *Anne of Green Gables* published; automobiles prohibited on Prince Edward Island.
1909–11	Strikes in Nova Scotia's coal industry, including a 22-month strike by coal miners in Springhill.
1909	Formation through mergers of Dominion Steel Company; Glace Bay miners form local of United Mineworkers of America; the region's first pulp and paper mill opens at Grand Falls, Newfoundland; J.A.D. McCurdy becomes first person in the British Empire to fly an airplane.
1910	Prohibition legislated in Nova Scotia.
1911	International Court at The Hague rules on American fishing rights.
1912	Saint John adopts commission government.
1914	Outbreak of the Great War; Newfoundland sealing disasters.
1916	Newfoundland Regiment decimated at Beaumont Hamel on 1 July.
1917	Conscription imposed in Canada; explosion in Halifax Harbour.
1918	Prohibition across Canada; women's suffrage legislated in Canada and Nova Scotia; Great War ends on 11 November.
1918–19	Spanish influenza epidemic.
1919	Women's suffrage legislated in New Brunswick.

who feared—with reason—damage to fish stocks and the dominance of large corporations. Accordingly, in 1915, trawlers were forbidden to fish within 12 nautical miles (22 km) of the coast. As a result, the Canadian trawler fleet grew slowly in comparison to its competitors, and the Atlantic fishery stagnated. Saltfish production declined from an annual average of 693,000 cwt (35,206,025 kg) early in the century to 448,000 cwt (22,759,450 kg) by 1914, in spite of rising prices. The value of Nova Scotia's fresh fish exports increased by almost 50 per cent between 1901 and 1911, but the total could have been even higher.

In Newfoundland, as on the mainland, the fishery remained much as it had been. Merchants in St John's invested in steel-hulled steamers for sealing, passenger, and freight services, and showed considerable interest in product diversification. They also experimented with steam trawling. However, conservatism and lack of capital prevented significant change. Had the Canadian and Newfoundland governments been willing and able to emulate the American and French governments by actively encouraging the fishery, the story might have been very different.

The steel and coal industries, by contrast, seemed to be fulfilling the promise of the National Policy. Nova Scotia now produced 44 per cent of Canadian pig iron and over 80 per cent of the coal mined in Canada. Many communities along the Intercolonial route were booming. Between 1901 and 1911 the population of Cape Breton County increased by 49 per cent, and 60 per cent of the region's industrial workforce was to be found between Moncton and Glace Bay. Little wonder that a new regional business magazine, founded in 1910, was called the 'Busy East of Canada'.

In Newfoundland a short-lived sawmilling boom followed the completion of the trans-island railway, in which Maritime, American, and Scottish investors were prominent. But it soon became obvious that the colony's stands of good timber were limited, and that its forests were best suited for the manufacture of wood pulp. That opportunity attracted the English newspaper tycoons Harold and Alfred Harmsworth, who reached an extraordinarily generous deal with the Newfoundland government in 1905. Four years later the region's first pulp and paper mill opened at Grand Falls on the Exploits River. As the supporters of the Policy of Progress had hoped, the colony had a new staple industry, and the first settlement of any size in the island's interior.

There was also interest in the natural resources of Labrador. In the 1890s, a series of remarkable pioneering surveys conducted by A.P. Low for the Geological Survey of Canada confirmed the existence of huge iron ore deposits in the interior and the potential of the Grand (now the Churchill) Falls for hydroelectricity. These resources were too remote for development at that time. Instead, attention focused on exploiting the Labrador forests. A grant of timber concessions on the Hamilton (Churchill) River to a Nova Scotia company in 1902 raised once again the long-standing question of who owned the Labrador interior.

In 1898 the Canadian government, without consulting Newfoundland, had legislated a new northern boundary for the province of Québec. The line was drawn westwards from the Eastmain River on James Bay to Hamilton Inlet until it met the coastal strip, which in Canada's opinion, was all that Newfoundland rightfully controlled. The governments of Québec and Canada thereupon began protesting the timber licences, but the Newfoundland government refused to cancel them. By 1907 all parties had agreed to submit the question of where the boundary lay to the Judicial Committee of the Privy Council. The decision was slow in coming.

Newfoundland's gross value of production increased by 22 per cent between 1901 and 1911. Although it was a respectable showing against the Maritimes' 33 per cent, Newfoundland's economy continued to be disadvantaged by its tiny domestic market and its distance from larger markets elsewhere. In the Maritimes,

Railways in the Atlantic Region, 1914. Adapted from Shirley E. Woods, *Cinders and Saltwater: The Story of Atlantic Canada's Railways* (Halifax: Nimbus, 1992).

Railways in the Atlantic Region, 1914. Adapted from Shirley E. Woods, *Cinders and Saltwater: The Story of Atlantic Canada's Railways* (Halifax: Nimbus, 1992).

Nova Scotia & New Brunswick Railways, 1914

Railway Legend

1. Cape Breton Rly Extension
2. Cape Breton Main Line (ICR)
3. Sydney and Louisburg Rly
4. Inverness Rly
5. Musquodoboit Rly
6. Halifax & South Western Rly
7. Halifax & Yarmouth Rly
8. Coast Railway
9. Dominion Atlantic Railway
10. Central Rly of Nova Scotia
11. Nova Scotia Southern Rly
12. Middleton & Victoria Beach Rly
13. Great American & European Short Line
14. Springhill & Parrsboro
15. Chignecto Marine Rly (abandoned)
16. N.B. & Prince Edward Island Rly
17. Buctouche & Moncton Rly
18. Kent Northern Rly
19. Chatham Branch Rly
20. Caraquet & Gulf Short Rly
21. International Railway of New Brunswick
22. National Transcontinental Rly
23. Canada Eastern Rly
24. Fredericton Rly
25. Western Ext. E. & N.A. (CPR Short Line)
26. Saint John & Quebec Rly
27. New Brunswick & Canada Rly
28. St. Martins Railway
29. Elgin & Havelock Rly
30. Salisbury & Albert Rly

difficulties were intensified by the disappearance of the region's financial sector by 1913, severe competition from branch businesses, and further takeovers and mergers promoted by central Canadian interests.

In Amherst, for example, one of Canada's busiest manufacturing towns, the firm of Rhodes, Curry was amalgamated with two Montréal businesses in 1909—in a deal masterminded by the New Brunswick native Max Aitken—and eventually closed down. In 1901 Henry M. Whitney sold his share of Dominion Coal and Dominion Iron and Steel to Montréal interests and in 1909 the company was amalgamated with the Cumberland Coal and Rail Company at Springhill to form the Dominion Steel Corporation. With close links to the Bank of Commerce and the Bank of Montréal, Dominion Steel controlled most of the Nova Scotian coalfields. The company also had an eye on the Nova Scotia Steel and Coal Company but it eluded them—at least for the moment.

Holding at least 179 directorships among them, the directors of Dominion Steel were the high priests of the Gilded Age in Canada. They lived in opulence in Montréal and Toronto and built elegant summer homes in communities such as St Andrews. Sir William Van Horne's estate on Minister's Island, New Brunswick, included a model farm and a swimming pool filled by the ocean tides twice a day. As David Frank points out, these men integrated the Nova Scotia coal and steel industries into the national economy, but in so doing they contributed to the crises that those industries faced at the end of the First World War.[1] Together, political and economic fragmentation, and the competition between towns and governments to attract investment, meant that the region had no defence against either economic imperialism or dependency.

Labour Unrest and Social Reform

Industrial expansion was accompanied by labour unrest. Between 1901 and 1914 there were 411 strikes in the Maritimes—evidence of a workforce that was becoming more class-conscious, more heavily unionized, increasingly influenced by syndicalism, and aware of the way competition between industrial giants was being waged on the back of labour. It faced employers who had no particular attachment or loyalty to the region, and who were prepared to fight workers with any weapons at their disposal, safe in the knowledge that they could count on the support of all levels of government.

A particularly bitter dispute occurred in 1909, when Glace Bay miners, disillusioned with the PWA, formed a local of the United Mineworkers of America (UMW) led by Scottish-born James B. McLachlan. Dominion Steel refused to recognize the union, brought in strike breakers (Newfoundlanders among them) protected by troops obligingly provided by the federal government, and gradually wore the strikers down. The same happened at Springhill, where miners held out for 22 months in 1909–11.

Newfoundland also experienced labour militancy. Between 1901 and 1914 there were 120 strikes in St John's, mostly by unskilled workers. Bell Island miners, longshoremen, fish curers, and fishing crews struck as well, and in 1903 3,000 sealers refused to board the steamers in St John's harbour until the owners agreed to improvements in pay and conditions. Remarkably, 42 per cent of those strikes were successful, and 21 per cent ended in compromise.

With trade unions firmly established in St John's and Grand Falls, William Coaker decided to organize rural 'toilers', as he called them: fishermen, loggers, and sealers. The Fishermen's Protective Union was launched in 1908 at Herring Neck in Notre Dame Bay. A populist who took his cue from Canadian farmers' movements, Coaker wanted economic, social, and political reforms that would ensure fair treatment for his members—hence the FPU's motto, *suum cuique* ('to each his own'). The response was immediate and impressive except in predominantly Roman Catholic districts, which followed a conservative church hierarchy opposed to unions and class-based politics. The FPU established a trading company and a newspaper, and eventually built a town (Port Union) in Bonavista Bay. It also became a political party, winning eight seats in the 1913 election. Serving as the official opposition in all but name, the FPU promoted an ambitious reform program with goals that ranged from government control of fish grading and marketing to non-denominational night schools.

Labour organizers joined professionals, church leaders, and women's rights activists in an impressive coalition to demand a growing list of reforms. These 'progressive' thinkers believed that society could be improved by legislation and regulation in many areas of life, including the sale of alcohol, Sabbath observance, sexual practices, urban development, working conditions, public health, and the treatment of women, children, and animals. When provincial governments were slow to respond, social reformers established powerful voluntary organizations to lobby governments and find alternative ways of implementing their ideas.

The progressive forces scored some victories. The federal Lord's Day Act, passed in 1907, controlled what people could do on Sundays. In 1910, Nova Scotia (Halifax excepted) followed Prince Edward Island's lead a decade earlier by adopting prohibition. After much prodding, Nova Scotia Premier George Murray introduced legislation to improve working conditions, provide compensation to workers injured on the job, and establish the Nova Scotia Technical College, which opened in 1909. In the hope of promoting efficiency and honesty in public life, Saint John in 1912 became the first city in Canada to replace the old system of ward elections, which could be dominated by small cliques, with a commission-style council elected by all voters on a city-wide basis. A government-appointed commission was instituted in St John's in 1914. Although this reform in municipal government was designed to usher in an era in which appointed experts would determine best practices, commission governments, too, were often open to influence.

Politics in the Industrial Age

Reformers wanted a better society, but politicians were preoccupied by the challenge of finding money to pay for expanding government responsibilities. In 1906 Ottawa revised its subsidy policy, but the increases for the Maritimes were much

lower than those granted to Québec, Ontario, and British Columbia. Such discrimination reflected the region's diminished power and influence in
Confederation. In the redistributions of 1892 and 1903 the Maritimes lost eight
seats in the House of Commons, and the reductions might have continued over
the years had it not been for a 1915 agreement that no province could have fewer
MPs than senators. The meanness of that concession spoke volumes about the dis-
advantages faced by small provinces compared with giants like Ontario, Québec,
and Manitoba—each of which more than doubled its size in 1912 by absorbing
huge, resource-rich sections of the Northwest Territories. In 1908 New
Brunswick's Conservative Premier J.D. Hazen called for a 'United Acadia' to
counter the region's declining power in Ottawa, but there was little response.

Maritimers who did well in federal politics had little time to devote to the
region's problems. With the opening of the Prairies and continuing discontent in
Québec, the cabinet's attention was invariably focused elsewhere. Robert Borden,
an earnest Halifax lawyer who became prime minister in 1911, is a good example. While he responded to Prince Edward Island's demand for a decent winter
ferry service and supported African Canadians in their wish to participate more
fully in the First World War, he was preoccupied with national and international
issues for most of his term of office.

Meanwhile, as the Maritime provinces were becoming marginalized in
Ottawa, Newfoundland was a very junior player in London. Although recognized
as one of the dominions from 1907, it carried less weight than the others, and the
imperial government had no compunction about overriding its decisions. A
happy exception was the 1904 agreement, part of the Anglo–French entente cordiale, that ended the French Shore dispute and was a genuine compromise
between Britain, France, and the colony. Admittedly, Britain had smoothed the
way to compromise in 1902 by granting Newfoundland permission, over
Laurier's objections, to attempt once again to negotiate reciprocity with the
United States.

A draft treaty was arranged in 1902, but this time it was effectively killed in
the US Senate. In response, the government of Sir Robert Bond in 1905 launched
a campaign of harassment against American vessels engaged in the winter herring
fishery in the Bay of Islands. London swiftly intervened, unilaterally imposing a
modus vivendi pending arbitration on the interpretation of the 1818 fisheries convention (which applied to Canadian as well as Newfoundland waters), and forbidding by imperial order-in-council the seizure or arrest of any American vessel.
Colonial protests against this heavy-handed treatment were disregarded. The even-
tual arbitration at The Hague in 1911 largely upheld Britain's—that is, Canada's
and Newfoundland's—arguments relating to American rights under the 1818 convention, and made important recommendations concerning the delineation of the
three-mile marine limit and the definition of bays.

These arcane diplomatic manoeuvrings had nothing to do with everyday
concerns about economic development and social reform. Most Newfoundlanders
found Bond's crusade irrelevant, and they defeated his government in 1909 (after
a tied election in 1908 and a subsequent political hiatus).

Cultural Currents

Cape Breton made communication history twice in the early years of the twentieth century. In 1902 Guglielmo Marconi's Wireless Telegraph Company began to operate the first transatlantic link from Glace Bay, Nova Scotia. The previous year, Marconi had used kites flying from Signal Hill in St John's to pick up the first wireless signal sent across the Atlantic. In February 1909 J.A.D. McCurdy and F.W. Baldwin, under the auspices of Alexander Graham Bell's Aerial Experiment Association, made the first controlled manned flight in the British Empire. With McCurdy at the controls, their plane, the *Silver Dart*, soared over the ice of Lake Bras d'Or near Bell's home in Baddeck. By that time Bell's contribution to the invention of the telephone had made his name a household word

Improved communications helped to fuel the growth of sporting activities in the region. By 1900 baseball had emerged as the most popular sport in the Maritimes: there were many local amateur teams, and professional teams, many of them on tour from the United States, drew large numbers of spectators. Horse racing was particularly popular in Prince Edward Island, which by the 1880s had more than two dozen racetracks. Newfoundlanders were soccer enthusiasts. While competitive sports were all the rage, other sports activities, from boating and bicycling to hunting and fishing, engaged people from all classes and cultures and both genders.

Maritimers often made their sporting reputations south of the border. In 1905 Nat Butler, a Halifax native who began his bicycle racing career in Boston, broke all records at the Winter Velodrome in Paris in 1905. Four African Canadian boxers—Nova Scotia's George Dixon and Sam Langford, and Prince Edward Island's George Godfrey and George Byers—won acclaim both at home and in the United States for their success in the ring.

Members of the middle classes enthusiastically consumed not just novels and poetry but non-fiction, often historical, and many published their own work. Bliss Carman and Charles G.D. Roberts, two of the so-called Confederation poets, celebrated the sea and landscape of their Maritime boyhoods. The most successful writers were Nova Scotia's Margaret Marshall Saunders and Prince Edward Island's Lucy Maud Montgomery, who launched international careers with their first novels, *Beautiful Joe* (1894) and *Anne of Green Gables* (1908). In these and subsequent works, both women tapped into the growing demand for fiction that sentimentalized rural life and the values they believed it represented. In Newfoundland, Norman Duncan's stories sympathetically explored the lives of outport fishing families. Three literary periodicals began publication in St John's in the early years of the century, and it was a golden age for ballads and poetry—including the 'Ode to Newfoundland' (1902), which became the national anthem.

Journalists and boosters were also hard at work, often at the behest of the railroads and the emerging tourism industry. They scripted Evangeline's *Acadia*, conjuring an image of Nova Scotia as 'a gently rolling and fertile land filled with Old World Charm'.[3] So widespread was Evangeline's appeal in this period that she became the subject of Canada's first feature film in 1913. On Prince Edward Island,

Skating behind the college at Caraquet, New Brunswick. Hockey became an increasingly popular sport in the Maritimes in the second half of the nineteenth century. PANB, Père Joseph Courtois fonds, P38-109.

the prohibition of automobiles in 1908 helped to preserve the pastoral image so important to the development of tourism, while elsewhere, fishing and hunting were heavily promoted. Overall, the literature helped change the image of rural people from that of backward bumpkins to that of picturesque, stalwart 'folk', living enviably simple lives. With an apparently straight face, the Reid Newfoundland Company assured potential tourists that 'no people in the world maintains a more comfortable and contented existence than the Newfoundland fisherman'.[4]

The reality was somewhat different. The loss of life in the Newfoundland seal fishery in the spring of 1914 was the highest in the history of that dangerous industry. Loaded with pelts taken in the Gulf, the SS *Southern Cross* sank with its crew of 174 men in a storm somewhere off Trepassey Bay. Meanwhile, out on the floes off the northeast coast, the crew of the SS *Newfoundland* was left on the ice for 53 hours during a blizzard. Seventy-eight men died of exposure or drowning, their bodies brought back to St. John's 'stacked like cordwood'. In retrospect, these twin tragedies appear as local harbingers of the world crisis that was to erupt the following August.

The Great War

When Great Britain declared war against Germany in August 1914, Canada and Newfoundland, as members of the British Empire, were automatically involved.

Biography: Lucy Maud Montgomery

Lucy Maud Montgomery is arguably better known around the world than any other Atlantic Canadian. Born in 1874 in Prince Edward Island, she lost her mother at an early age and was raised by her grandparents in Cavendish. She was educated at Prince of Wales College and spent a year at Dalhousie University. Although she began making money from the publication of poems and short stories in the expanding magazine market in the 1890s, her fame derived from the publication in 1908 of *Anne of Green Gables*. The red-haired orphan girl sent to work on an Island farm quickly won the hearts of readers all over the world.

Lucy Maud Montgomery (1874–1942) became one of North America's most popular authors following the publication of *Anne of Green Gables* in 1908. PEIPARO Acc. 3110/1.

In 1911, following the death of her grandmother, for whom she was the primary caregiver, Montgomery married the Reverend Ewan Macdonald. The couple moved to Ontario, where Ewan ministered in a number of Presbyterian churches. Between raising two sons, coping with her husband's debilitating depressions, and attending to the endless round of public duties demanded of a minister's wife, Montgomery continued to write. She produced 22 novels, including seven sequels to *Anne*, as well as 450 poems and 500 short stories. One of her most enduring legacies is 'The Island Hymn', the unofficial anthem of Prince Edward Island. In addition, from 1889 to 1942 she kept a diary chronicling the more serious and darker aspects of her life. Selected diary entries have been published in five volumes that Montgomery fans have read no less avidly than her novels.[2]

Not that people in the region objected. They remained imperial enthusiasts, and at first responded willingly. Militia regiments were called out in the Maritimes, and Halifax headquarters staff began a recruitment campaign, first to bring the regiments up to strength, and then to provide additional overseas drafts. Involving clergy, teachers, and the press, the war effort soon became all-consuming.

Newfoundland had no militia and hence no militia department. The Newfoundland Regiment was raised by the Newfoundland Patriotic Association (NPA), founded in August 1914 by Governor Sir Walter Davidson in consultation with the prime minister, Sir Edward Morris. Composed mostly of prominent St John's men from a variety of political and religious backgrounds, the NPA functioned as the unofficial war ministry for three years, with a wide range of responsibilities. Its creation reflected a desire to place the war effort above political and denominational rivalries.

Voluntary enlistment rates in the Maritimes were higher than in Québec and Saskatchewan, but lower than in other provinces. In Newfoundland the proportion of the population that volunteered was similar to that in the Maritimes, although an appallingly high number of medical rejections reduced the numbers of those who actually served. In Canada in 1917 and in Newfoundland, the native-born and those living in rural areas were least likely to volunteer, and the rate was reduced further in the Maritimes by the importance of war-related industries such as coal mining, steel production, and agriculture. Including those compelled to enlist under conscription, implemented in both Canada in 1917 and Newfoundland in 1918, some 72,500 men from the Atlantic region joined the allied army. Others served at sea, in the air, or in the forestry corps. About 300 women from the Maritimes and 43 from Newfoundland went overseas as nurses. Among those travelling with the First Canadian Division in October 1914 was Pictou County's Margaret MacDonald, the matron in charge of 101 volunteer nurses who were the first women to become full-fledged members of the Canadian Expeditionary Force.

By 1916 the difficulty in filling the escalating demand for soldiers gave ethnic minorities, who were initially not welcome as recruits, a chance to enlist for overseas service. Mi'kmaq were for the most part integrated into existing units, but most Blacks were hived off into the No 2 Construction Battalion under the command of white officers. Attached to the Canadian Forestry Corps, the battalion produced lumber for the trenches and coal mines. The efficiency of white soldiers, it was argued, would be reduced if they were forced to fight on the battlefields alongside Black recruits.

Of those who went overseas, about 14 per cent of Canadians and 25 per cent of Newfoundlanders were killed. In town centres throughout the region, war memorials testify to the appalling death toll. A great blow was inflicted on the newly-formed Newfoundland Regiment at Beaumont Hamel on 1 July 1916, the first day of the Battle of the Somme. The anniversary is still observed each year, and the battlefield is preserved as a memorial park.

Women throughout the region, schooled for generations to embrace volunteer work, 'did their bit' to support the war effort. In Newfoundland a Women's Patriotic Association (WPA) was formed at the outset of the war under the presidency of Lady Davidson. With branches throughout Newfoundland and Labrador, it attracted 15,000 members within a few months. By 1916 women and children of both sexes had produced, among other 'comforts', 62,685 pairs of socks—an astonishing number which achieved legendary status abroad. The WPA became involved with the Red Cross and health care, as well as general welfare issues, and raised money for a range of causes. Women in the Maritimes were also heavily engaged in war-related activities, often working through the Red Cross and the St. John Ambulance. In Halifax, a busy port throughout the war, women's volunteer services were stretched to the limit.

The Newfoundland Regiment, D Company, on the march near St John's, 1915. E-22-45, The Rooms; Provincial Archives Division.

The demands on everyone in the Halifax area were dramatically increased on 6 December 1917 when the French munitions ship *Mont Blanc*, loaded with TNT, collided with the Belgian relief ship *Imo* in the city's harbour. The resulting explosion, the largest man-made blast before Hiroshima, levelled the city's North End, killing nearly 2,000 people and injuring 9,000. As word of the tragedy spread, help poured in from around the world. Massachusetts and Newfoundland were among the most generous contributors to the devastated city, testimony to the close family ties connecting these Atlantic coast communities.

The horror of the explosion brought the war closer to home and contributed significantly to a growing mood of disillusionment. The mounting death rate overseas, rampant inflation, food restrictions, and a series of tawdry scandals further dampened the enthusiasm that had characterized the war effort in the early days. When Prime Minister Robert Borden's Conservatives formed a Union government with the badly split Liberals in 1917, and imposed compulsory military service on men between the ages of 20 and 35, class and cultural divisions deepened. Even the granting of suffrage to female relatives of men serving overseas prior to the December 1917 election—a move crudely calculated to win votes—initially spoiled what turned out to be a major step in women's political emancipation. Conscription was widely opposed in the Maritimes, and the majority of electors

Beaumont Hamel

The Allied war plan for 1916 called for a major offensive by French and British troops in the region of the Somme. British troops—which included Canadians and Newfoundlanders—were in the majority, and preparations were complete by late June.

The offensive began at 7.30 a.m. on 1 July. In the Beaumont Hamel area, the plan called for a 5,000-metre advance led by the 86th and 87th Brigades, while the 88th (1st Essex and Newfoundland regiments) attacked other German positions. The plan proved to be irrelevant. Withering enemy fire caused the advance to falter, but the commanding general, mistaking German flares for a signal from the 87th Brigade that it had succeeded, ordered the 88th to advance.

The Newfoundlanders went over the top at 9.15 a.m. It was all over in 30 minutes. Unprotected by artillery, they advanced into heavy fire concentrated on the gaps in the British wire from which they emerged. 'The only visible sign that the men knew they were under this terrific fire,' wrote one observer, 'was that they all instinctively tucked their chins into an advanced shoulder as they had so often done when fighting their way home against a blizzard in some little outpost in far off Newfoundland'.[5] Most were cut down before they reached the British front line.

The Regiment at the front on 30 June had consisted of 25 officers and 776 non-commissioned officers and other ranks. After the battle, 233 were listed as killed, 477 as wounded or missing. For a small country this was a devastating loss.

Beginning in 1917, 1 July was observed as Memorial Day, Newfoundland's own national day of remembrance. Although the Regiment fought other battles, Beaumont Hamel became iconic. As an expression of the sterling qualities and imperial loyalty of Newfoundlanders, the failed offensive was transmuted into an occasion for solemn patriotic pride. Memorial Day is still observed today, although now it coincides, perhaps uneasily, with the upbeat Canada Day celebrations.

in both Prince Edward Island and Nova Scotia voted against the Union government. So, too, did most Acadians in all three Maritime provinces.

As the evidence of profiteering mounted and the gap between rich and poor grew, labour unrest increased and the incidence of strikes increased dramatically. The Maritimes experienced more than 30 strikes in 1918 alone, and the Newfoundland Industrial Workers Association, with 3,500 members, successfully struck against the Reid Newfoundland Company in the spring of that year. Calls for the conscription of wealth as well as manpower grew louder. Farmers became disenchanted when the government refused to honour its promise to exempt their sons from the draft, and fishing crews could not afford the loss of young men. Although Acadians were not as uniformly opposed to the war as their counterparts in Québec, they resented not only the anti-francophone tone of the con-

After the Halifax Explosion, December 1917. This photograph of women travelling downtown from Africville reveals the extent of the devastation along the waterfront. City of Toronto Archives, Fonds 1244, Item 2451.

scription debate but also the heavy-handed tactics used against 'deserters.' In New Brunswick, one Acadian resister was seriously wounded and 26 others were taken to Saint John under military escort for resisting compulsory service.

The same factors led to a full-blown crisis in Newfoundland, where Morris manoeuvred the three political parties into a National Government and then promptly departed for London and a peerage, leaving his successors to bring in conscription. As unpopular in Newfoundland as in the Maritimes, conscription created tensions between urban and outport districts. A militia department replaced the NPA in 1917 and, as on the mainland, income and profits taxes made their first appearance—as did prohibition, which was already more or less in place everywhere else in the region except Halifax. Ottawa imposed nation-wide prohibition in 1918.

Social unrest and cultural tensions during the war emerged against a background of general economic prosperity. Although the fur-farming bubble burst, and the overseas markets for apples temporarily collapsed, the steel industry expanded as many factories converted to munitions manufacturing; fisheries and agriculture generally did well; and lumbermen supplied pit props to British coal mines. The gains were undermined to some extent by inflation, rising freight rates, and a shortage of shipping, but the region's economic performance during the war still provided grounds for optimism, which government propaganda did its best to encourage. These were, as Ian McKay notes, the 'last years of abundant hope'.[6]

Post-war Challenges

The end of the war was greeted with relief, if not jubilation. In any event, people were preoccupied with the Spanish influenza epidemic that was raging throughout the Atlantic region along with the rest of Canada. The impact was particularly devastating in Labrador, where the infection was carried by the Moravian mission ship *Harmony*. As many as a third of the Inuit in the area of the mission died between November 1918 and January 1919. The worst affected settlement was Okak: of a population of 263, only 56 women and children survived. An observer described the appalling scene:

> When the Harmony left Okak, people were beginning to fall sick. . . . Crews went off to their sealing places only to fall sick and die. . . . the dogs played havoc with the corpses. At Sillutalik 36 persons died, but only 18 remained to be buried. The only visible remains of the others were a few bare skulls and a few shankbones lying around in the houses.[7]

The epidemic had a lasting impact on northern Labrador. Recoiling from the tragedy and facing persistent economic difficulties, the Moravians gradually reduced their activities and handed over their trading stores to the Hudson's Bay Company in 1926.

Veterans returned home to perfunctory welcoming ceremonies, and inadequate government help with the challenges of reintegration into a society that had been subjected to severe strain. Their discontent merged with a militant class consciousness sparked by wartime injustices, and fanned by the success of the 1917 Bolshevik Revolution in Russia. There were riots in Sydney and Halifax, in which veterans played prominent roles, and in 1919–20 a wave of labour unrest swept the Maritimes resulting in 93 strikes, including general strikes at Amherst and on the Miramichi. The recession that arrived in 1920 blunted the effectiveness and much of the militancy of the labour movement. With companies experiencing severe difficulties amid the cut-throat competition of the post-war period, workers faced a drab future.

There was no strike wave in Newfoundland, where problems in the Italian market brought the wartime fishery boom to a sudden end in the fall of 1918. Overextended fish merchants, pressed by their bankers, faced heavy losses and the possibility of a general market collapse. The crisis was so acute, and the political situation so unstable in 1919, that attention was diverted from Newfoundland's humiliation at the Paris peace conference.

During the war the dominion (as it officially called itself from 1918) had been represented in the Imperial War Cabinet and at the Imperial War Conference, but at Paris its fragile status was clearly exposed. Manoeuvring between the United States' objections to separate dominion representation and the justifiable expectations of the dominions themselves, the British government decided to sacrifice the claims of the least influential dominion in order to obtain representation for the others. Newfoundland found itself sidelined, excluded not only from the list of signatories of the Versailles Treaty but also from the list of original members of the League of Nations. There could not have been a clearer demonstration of Newfoundland's subordinate place in the imperial hierarchy.

While Newfoundland politics after 1918 became personal and factionalized, Maritime voters increasingly threw their support to new political parties. The comfortable give-and-take of political power between Liberals and Conservatives came to an end in the wake of the war with the emergence of Farmer and Labour parties in New Brunswick and Nova Scotia and the Progressive Party at the federal level. Meanwhile, no one was certain what impact female suffrage would have on electoral politics. Women were granted the federal vote on the same basis as men in May 1918. Nova Scotia had already passed similar legislation the previous month and Prince Edward Island followed suit in 1922. New Brunswick granted women the right to vote in 1919 but withheld the right to hold elected office until 1934. Newfoundland finally adopted the British model in 1925, extending the franchise to women over the age of 25.[8]

Conclusion

The First World War destroyed the confidence and optimism that had prevailed in the early twentieth century. Pride in wartime achievements abroad was tempered by post-war frustrations and disappointments at home. Only time would tell if the political turmoil of 1919 was part of the new world order to which the Great War had played midwife or just a brief, if troubling, interlude in the region's long history. Two things were certain: the stakes in the industrial age were high and the competition was keen. Unless the Atlantic region could sustain economic growth and staunch the tide of out-migration, the prospects for the future would be bleak.

Chapter Twelve

Between the Wars, 1919–39

Between the end of the First World War and the beginning of the Second the Atlantic region faced adverse economic conditions. Poverty, unemployment, and labour unrest were endemic throughout the period and out-migration continued at alarming levels until the onset of the Great Depression. Facing severe financial problems, all governments in the region were forced to turn to Ottawa or London for assistance. The fundamental reasons for the economic crisis were beyond the region's control. The boom and bust cycles of the global economy created a roller-coaster ride that culminated in the stock market crash of October 1929. Although the worst was over by 1933, except possibly in Newfoundland, recovery would be difficult and prolonged.

Economic Uncertainty

Some sectors of the economy coped with the roller-coaster ride better than others. Between 1920 and 1939, the gross value of production in the Maritimes actually increased by 17.3 per cent and more than doubled in Newfoundland, but the overall figures disguise uneven experiences. Agriculture in the Maritimes and the fishery in Newfoundland declined after 1929, while manufacturing took a hit from which it never recovered. In many other areas of North America, economic development was focused on the production of mass consumer goods such as cars, radios, and home appliances, but with industry increasingly concentrated and owned in central Canada, the Atlantic region failed to make the transition.

The fisheries that sustained many families, in whole or part, continued to languish. In the Maritimes the production of saltfish, whether dried or green, virtually collapsed. The extent of the decline was reflected in the size of the Lunenburg fleet of saltbankers, which dropped from about 140 to 20 vessels between 1919 and 1939. Given the uncertainty of international markets for saltfish in this period, it is little wonder that Maritime fishermen sought other ways of making a living. European markets for saltfish were slow to recover after the war, demand for Canadian fish in the Caribbean and South America weakened, and the competition from Norway and Iceland became aggressive. Newfoundland also emerged as a serious competitor, increasing its low-priced exports to the West Indies and Brazil when European markets became unstable.

Timeline

1919–23	Intercolonial Railway integrated into Canadian National Railways.
1921	Scotia and Dominion Steel merge to form British Empire Steel Corp. (BESCO); launch of the *Bluenose*; W.F. Coaker's attempt to regulate the Newfoundland fishery fails.
1922	Cape Breton miners' strike; women in Prince Edward Island gain the right to vote.
1923	Cape Breton steelworkers' strike.
1925	Cape Breton miners' strike; Royal Commission on the Coal Mining Industry in Nova Scotia chaired by Sir Andrew Rae Duncan; newsprint mill opens at Corner Brook; women's suffrage legislated in Newfoundland.
1925–9	Prohibition ends in Newfoundland, Nova Scotia, and New Brunswick.
1926	Duncan Royal Commission on Maritime Claims; Moravians lease their trading stores to Hudson's Bay Company.
1927	Maclean Royal Commission on the Fisheries of the Maritime Provinces; Labrador boundary defined by the Privy Council.
1929	Great Depression begins.
1933	Report of the Newfoundland (Amulree) Royal Commission.
1934	Responsible government suspended in Newfoundland.
1939	Second World War begins.

To make matters worse, the United States raised its tariffs and revoked the permission it had given Canadians to land fish in American ports. As a result, 1921 was the worst year for the Atlantic fishery in four decades. There was some recovery thereafter, largely in the fresh fish sector, which was stimulated by the expanding demand of fish processing firms. By the mid-1920s Nova Scotia boasted 11 trawlers and Halifax was beginning to emerge as the centre of a modern industrial fishery. Resistance to modernization of the fishery remained strong, however, and was reinforced when a 1927 royal commission on the fisheries (the Maclean commission) recommended restrictions on steam trawling. By 1939 the trawler fleet was reduced to three. Together, uncertain markets and resistance to change stunted the overall development of the Maritime fisheries. Instead of pursuing technological innovation, they continued to rely on cheap labour, to the detriment of both the well-being of the workers and the value of the catch, which sank to approximately what it had been in 1880.

The Newfoundland government met the fisheries crisis with a dose of state intervention as prescribed by William Coaker, founder of the Fishermen's

Protective Union and, after 1919, Minister of Fisheries. Coaker's support for conscription had damaged his prestige and divided his union, but he was still regarded with suspicion by the 'long-coated chaps' of St John's. Nevertheless, he pressed ahead with government inspection of fish and control over exports. The new regulations had a short life, and were effectively scuttled by the exporters they were designed to assist. It was only in 1933, in the depths of the Depression, that a merchant-supported government finally created a Salt Codfish Board to control exports. Coaker then turned his attention to finding alternative employment for poverty-stricken fishing families, and enthusiastically supported plans developed by the Reid Newfoundland Company to establish a second newsprint mill at Corner Brook, which began production in 1925—just as the post-war boom in paper prices ended.

Built by British interests, the Corner Brook mill was sold to International Power and Paper in 1927, an American firm that was also expanding in the Maritimes. IPP developed hydro power at Grand Falls in New Brunswick, and built mills at Dalhousie and Bathurst. Other firms constructed pulp mills at Edmundston and Atholville in New Brunswick, and at Liverpool, Nova Scotia. The pulp and paper mills made up in part for the decline in sawmilling, which faced a twofold challenge: the costs of lumber production were increasing as the more accessible stands of trees disappeared, and there was stiff competition from Pacific coast producers, who could now ship efficiently through the recently completed Panama Canal to the east coast and Britain.

The apple industry recovered its coveted British market following the Great War and expanded production. In 1933 growers sold 82 per cent of their bumper crop of more than 8 million bushels (nearly half of the entire Canadian output) overseas. The competitive position of Maritime apples depended on price, not quality, with the result that growers concentrated on medium-quality cooking apples for their profits. By the 1930s American, British Columbian, and Australian apples were making serious inroads, and consumers everywhere were turning to the larger dessert varieties. Maritime producers would have to plant new orchards, develop new packing techniques, and improve their marketing skills or be left behind.

The potato industry, which relied on markets in the United States and the Caribbean (mainly Cuba), expanded during the 1920s. Prince Edward Island seed potatoes found a ready market, and potato acreage expanded at the expense of other types of farming. Although some Maritime farmers focused on dairy, chicken, and beef production for local consumption, most did not specialize, and their operations gradually became unsustainable. As a percentage of total gross value of production in the Maritimes, agriculture fell from 34.3 per cent in 1920 to 27.8 per cent in 1939. Farm families needed other sources of income, and many farmers had to take seasonal jobs to make ends meet. During the 1930s, family farms became a refuge for those who lost their jobs in the urban centres, but the general trend was clear. Young people who could do so abandoned the rural life for jobs in cities, often outside the region. In the 1920s the Maritimes' population increased by less than 1 per cent, and both Nova Scotia and Prince Edward Island experienced absolute declines.

There was also trouble in the industrial belt that had grown up along the Intercolonial route. Between 1919 and 1923, the regional railway was integrated into Canadian National Railways, a Crown corporation with scant sympathy for Atlantic problems and aspirations. Freight rates, now determined outside the region, quickly increased by 140 to 216 per cent, making it virtually impossible for Maritime producers to compete in the central Canadian market. With the end of railway expansion, the market for rails and railway equipment contracted sharply. The region's iron and steel industry had difficulty adapting because it was hampered by lack of capital and the difficulty of competing with central Canadian producers.

The result was a sudden downsizing: between 1919 and 1921, the labour force employed in iron and steel declined by 85 per cent, and in manufacturing generally by 40 per cent. This contraction in turn hurt the region's coal industry, since iron and steel had absorbed 25 per cent of its output. Nor was this the only problem that coal producers faced. The Québec market had been lost during the war and would take time to regain. High freight rates and cheaper American imports effectively blocked sales west of Québec, where hydro power and oil were gaining ground. For Maritime producers to compete, they would have to reduce their prices—but the costs of production in Cape Breton, where the shafts extended under the seabed, were inevitably higher than elsewhere because of the long distance to and from the coal face, and the need for expensive ventilation and drainage systems.

Overall, the manufacturing sector was badly crippled in the early 1920s as plants closed or were consolidated into central Canadian companies. The net value of production declined from $325 million in 1920 to a low point of $192.5 million in 1924, and employment fell significantly below the levels of the 1890s. As S.A. Saunders pointed out as early as 1939, the Maritimes failed to make the transition from heavy industry geared to railway and nation-building, to light industry producing consumer goods.[1] The consequences would be felt for the remainder of the twentieth century.

Maritimers Take A Stand

Maritimers were not passive in the face of these blows to their economic aspirations. In Nova Scotia, members of the newly-formed Labour Party entered a loose alliance with alienated farmers to win 11 seats in the 1920 provincial election, making the Farmer–Labour coalition the official opposition to the reigning Liberals, who had held office since 1882. Later the same year the United Farmers did equally well in New Brunswick, where they already had 141 locals and ran a wide range of cooperatives. On Prince Edward Island fishermen's organizations emerged and, like the farmers, began to form cooperatives to compete with corporate interests.

Union membership had grown dramatically during the war. Although the post-war recession blunted labour militancy, Cape Breton remained a battlefield. In 1921 Nova Scotia Steel and Coal merged with Dominion Iron and Steel to form the British Empire Steel Corporation (BESCO), with headquarters in

Lawren S. Harris, 'Glace Bay'. A member of the Group of Seven, Harris visited Cape Breton in 1921. This stark image of a miner's family appeared on the cover of the July 1925 issue of the *Canadian Forum*, which included an article on the strike-bound island. LAC, C-110249

Montréal. The following year BESCO announced a 37.5 per cent wage cut for miners. Already hit by plant closures and reductions in hours, the UMW local in Cape Breton called for 'the complete overthrow of the capitalist system' and went on strike. Alarmed by this local eruption of bolshevism, authorities called in soldiers and special police to crush labour activism. A year later the troops returned to put down a steelworkers' strike. An unprovoked mounted charge through the Whitney Pier district of Sydney led coal miners to walk out in sympathy, and union leaders 'Red' Dan Livingstone and J.B. McLachlan were arrested. Two years later, a protracted and bitter strike by coal miners ended in the death of William Davis, a thirty-seven year old miner, who was shot by the police. At a subsequent district convention, the day of his death, 11 June, was declared Davis Day—a date that is still commemorated in Cape Breton.

By this time, all workers in the coal and steel industries had suffered severe wage cuts and BESCO was on the edge of bankruptcy. It was cold comfort for the miners that a 1925 provincial royal commission on the coal industry found the size of the original wage cut unjustified. Chaired by British lawyer-industrialist Sir Andrew Rae Duncan, the commission criticized the company for bad faith and intransigence, but since neither the commission nor the provincial government was prepared to consider genuinely radical solutions, the tensions continued.

The rise of western Canada and the dominance of Ontario and Québec underlined the minority status and increasing political marginalization of the Maritime provinces. Federal leaders were inevitably more sympathetic to the demands of the more powerful regions, tending to view the Maritimes as backward and their leaders as chronic grumblers with no good reason for complaint. Unable—sometimes unwilling—to counter hostile and unsympathetic federal policies and attitudes, Maritime members of parliament exerted little influence on national policy. In the 1921 federal election, voters in Nova Scotia and Prince Edward Island registered their hostility to the Conservatives under Borden's successor, Arthur Meighen, by awarding all their seats to the Liberals. Only New Brunswick showed some resistance to the trend, returning five Liberals, five Conservatives, and one Progressive to Ottawa. Although the Conservatives were defeated, it soon became clear that the Maritime vote counted for little. At the head of a minority Liberal government, the new prime minister, William Lyon Mackenzie King, was held hostage by the spectacular success of 65 Progressive Party candidates, most of them from constituencies in the badly alienated Prairie provinces and rural Ontario.

By now Maritimers already had a long roster of grievances against Ottawa. Federal subsidies to all three provinces were parsimonious in the light of the generous financial terms granted Alberta and Saskatchewan when they achieved provincial status in 1905. And where was the compensation to the Maritimes for the huge chunks of former Hudson's Bay Company territory awarded to Manitoba, Ontario, and Québec in 1912? Ottawa showed no signs of moving on these issues. Nor was it prepared to act on freight rates—indeed, in 1922 it prepared to restore the advantageous Crow's Nest Pass rate, while allowing Intercolonial rates to increase dramatically.

An all-pervasive sense of grievance finally found political expression in the Maritime Rights movement. A genuinely regional phenomenon, Maritime Rights was dominated by professionals and businessmen—the Conservative Party and the Maritime Provinces Board of Trade both played conspicuous roles in the movement—but it received widespread support from people of all classes and cultures. Farmers were especially supportive. Although the western-controlled farmers' movement had its own regional agenda, the two groups shared a sense of indignation at the declining power of the country's rural areas. In Nova Scotia the Conservatives, led by the industrialist E.N. Rhodes, fought the 1925 election under the banner of Maritime Rights, winning 40 out of 43 seats. The Conservative premiers of New Brunswick and Prince Edward Island, J.B.M. Baxter and J.D. Stewart, were quick to climb on the bandwagon, although the frugal Islanders, who believed in minimal government and usually ran a budget surplus, never adopted Maritime Rights with the same enthusiasm as other provinces.

Maritime Rights campaigners made sufficient noise for even the unsympathetic Mackenzie King to take notice. Needing support from the Maritime members in the House of Commons to sustain his minority government, he reluctantly appointed a royal commission on Maritime Claims, chaired by the same Sir Andrew Duncan who had investigated the problems in the coal industry. In a carefully worded report released in 1926, the commission recommended increased subsidies, lower freight rates, development of the harbours at Saint John and Halifax, a subsidy for the steel industry, and improved ferry service to Prince Edward Island (Duncan had been convinced of the need for the latter by his trip to Charlottetown). It avoided any discussion of tariffs or special grants to ensure that services in the Maritime provinces would not fall behind those in the rest of the country.

Well-received in the Maritimes, the report met heavy opposition in Ottawa. The result was a compromise that, according to historian E.R. Forbes, 'changed Duncan's program for Maritime rehabilitation into a plan for Maritime pacification . . . to be achieved with the fewest possible concessions'.[2] And it worked. Though the federal government refused to budge on the subsidy issue, Maritime Rights leaders gratefully accepted the Maritime Freight Rates Act (1927), the Dominion Fuel Act (1927), port development for Saint John and Halifax, and a new ferry for Prince Edward Island. With that, the movement petered out.

Biography: Mona Wilson and Public Health

In the inter-war years, governments in the Atlantic region were hard pressed to provide the level of health services that wealthier jurisdictions could afford. Thus the task of improving public health tended to fall on nurses and voluntary associations such as the Red Cross. In Newfoundland, for instance, the staff of the Newfoundland Outport Nursing and Industrial Association (NONIA), formed in 1924, brought modern ideas about health and nutrition to outport communities, and encouraged the production of handicrafts to help pay for nursing services.

On Prince Edward Island, the dynamic Mona Wilson played a remarkable role in advancing public health. Born in Toronto in 1894, she was educated at Johns Hopkins University and served overseas with the American Army Nursing Corps in the First World War. She joined the American Red Cross in 1919 and served in Vladivostock and the Balkans. After studying for her Public Health diploma at the University of Toronto, she became Chief Red Cross Public Health Nurse in Prince Edward Island in 1923.

Wilson and her small staff were responsible for the all Island's health needs. They introduced school medical inspections; established dental clinics, tuberculosis clinics, and camps for crippled children; organized province-wide smallpox and diphtheria vaccinations; and promoted eating fruits and vegetables, drinking milk, and maintaining scrupulous hygiene. Through the Junior Red Cross Clubs, children were taught that they should have a warm bath at least once a week, brush their teeth twice a day, cough or sneeze into a handkerchief, and sleep ten hours a night with an open window.

Mona Wilson is shown here conducting a school health inspection at the Charlottetown Model School in 1926.

When the province finally established a Department of Health in 1931, Wilson was appointed Provincial Director of Public Nursing. She held this position until her retirement in 1961, except during the Second World War, when she served as Red Cross Commissioner for Newfoundland. Wilson's contributions to Island life include the establishment of the Girl Guides, Zonta Club, and Business and Professional Women's Club. Found among her personal effects when she died in 1981 was a poem that she had kept since 1925. It summed up her approach to life:

BE STRONG!
WE ARE NOT HERE TO DREAM, TO PLAY, TO DRIFT;
WE HAVE HARD WORK TO DO AND LOADS TO LIFT.
SHUN NOT THE STRUGGLE; FACE IT
'TIS GOD'S GIFT.[3]

Trouble in Newfoundland

The Dominion of Newfoundland had no federal government to blame for its problems, which mirrored those experienced by the Maritimes. The postwar recession meant major losses for fish exporters, and many businesses declared bankruptcy between 1921 and 1923. In addition, the war had changed the nature of Newfoundland politics. With the collapse of the National Government in 1919, the three parties dissolved into factions and party labels came to mean little. There was, however, a broad distinction between conservative, St John's-based politicians, and those who were more populist and outport-oriented. The 1919 election saw a victory for the second grouping, a coalition between William Coaker's Fishermen's Protective Union and Richard Squires' Liberal following. Like all inter-war administrations, it found its freedom to address the economic crisis curtailed by a public debt that had grown substantially as a result of the war effort. As unemployment mounted and emigration increased to 1,000–1,500 people annually, there were demonstrations in St John's and, in 1921, mob scenes in the House of Assembly.

The building of the Corner Brook paper mill was a major achievement. However, the government had to take over the operation of the dilapidated railway—yet another financial burden. In 1923 the government collapsed amid charges that Squires had taken kickbacks from the mining companies on Bell Island and had turned the Board of Liquor Control into a covert bootlegging operation, the profits from 'private' sales going into his political account. The charges were largely substantiated by an independent inquiry. With Squires temporarily out of public life, the St John's-based conservatives took over, promising clean, stable, businesslike government. They also belatedly extended the franchise to women in 1925.

A piece of good fortune for Newfoundland came in 1927, when the Judicial Committee of the Privy Council ruled that the western boundary between Newfoundland and Canada in the Labrador peninsula should, for the most part,

Rum-Running

A significant regional industry in the inter-war years was the illicit liquor trade that emerged as a by-product of prohibition, which remained in place in most Canadian provinces following the war and became the federal law in the United States in 1920. With the fisheries languishing, many Maritimers were only too happy to make a living as rum-runners. Typically, liquor from Europe, the Caribbean, and Canada was delivered to St-Pierre-et-Miquelon. There Maritime vessels would pick it up and then legally carry it to 'rum row', just outside the American 12-mile limit, where they would wait for a fast motor launch sent by one of the American crime syndicates that made fortunes smuggling it into the country.

The tidy income made by bootleggers was not lost on provincial administrations looking to finance mother's allowances, old age pensions, and essential public works. One by one, provincial governments in the Maritimes abandoned prohibition and took control of liquor sales (and profits) themselves: Newfoundland in 1925, New Brunswick in 1927, and Nova Scotia in 1929. The US trade continued unabated until the American Congress finally gave up the fight and repealed prohibition in 1933. Only Prince Edward Island held out until after the Second World War, though the Island supported plenty of bootleggers.

follow the height of land. This bonanza meant little in the short term. When Newfoundland offered to sell the territory, neither Canada nor Québec was interested in buying. For the moment Labrador remained a potential rather than an actual asset, its resources too remote for effective development. The Newfoundland government provided only minimal services, preferring to leave Labrador in the hands of the missions and the Hudson's Bay Company. But this was scarcely a lasting solution.

Literature and Tradition

Amid the difficulties of the 1920s, there was an upsurge of romantic interest in the region's heritage and folklore. The image of the mid-nineteenth century as a mythical Golden Age for the Maritimes became firmly embedded with the publication in 1924 of F. W. Wallace's *Wooden Ships and Iron Men*, which idealized the hardy mariners and fishing folk of the sea-bound coast. Billed as 'Canada's Ocean Playground' as early as 1929, Nova Scotia led the region in the invention of tradition. The *Bluenose*, designed as a banking schooner and a racer, was launched at Lunenburg in March 1921. Only once defeated in races for the International Fishermen's Trophy sponsored by the *Halifax Herald*, the schooner entered local mythology as an enormously potent symbol, and its image has been on the reverse of the Canadian dime since 1937. Around the same time Nova Scotia's cultural élite discovered Peggy's Cove, conveniently near Halifax, which rapidly became 'the region's primary symbolic landscape', epitomizing the hardiness, simplicity, and virtues of the seafaring life, as well as the physical beauty of Nova Scotia's south shore.[4]

As a result of the new interest in the pre-industrial past, folklore became a subject of systematic study. Helen Creighton embarked on a lifelong career collecting Maritime folk songs and stories. Gerald S. Doyle, Elisabeth Greenleaf, and Maud Karpeles similarly collected songs in Newfoundland.

However well the 'cult of the folk' sold to tourists, the folk themselves were not eager to become cultural artifacts. In 1927 Frank Parker Day, one of the Maritime literary group known as the 'song fishermen', published *Rockbound*, a novel based on the thinly disguised people of Ironbound Island, off the south shore of Nova Scotia. The Ironbounders felt that Day had misrepresented and betrayed them, and in a letter to the *Lunenburg Progress-Enterprise* protested that they were not the 'ignorant, immoral and superstitious' people portrayed in the novel.[5]

Invented traditions were a standard feature of the developing tourist industry, which received government assistance throughout the region, mainly in the form of new roads. Major hotels were built at Halifax, Saint John, Charlottetown, Digby, Pictou, and St John's. The Newfoundland government created a Tourist and Publicity Commission, which, apart from the usual emphasis on fin, fur, feather, and scenery, began to trumpet what is now known as heritage tourism. It was following the example of Nova Scotia, where in the 1930s motoring tourists were encouraged to visit the newly constructed Cabot Trail or participate in

Champlain's 'Order of Good Cheer' at the reconstructed Port Royal. Under the Liberal premiership of Angus L. Macdonald (1933–40), Nova Scotians were urged to remember their Scottish heritage, and in 1939 Cape Breton acquired its own Gaelic College at St Ann's. It was not long before 'tartanism', complete with bagpipes, kilts, and crests, trumped all other local identities in the province.

The Depression

Conditions seemed to be improving in the late 1920s, but all hopes were dashed by the onset of the Great Depression. Prices fell, markets collapsed, and unemployment climbed even higher. The resulting social problems were accentuated by the fact that emigration was no longer readily available to serve as a safety valve: the US border was closed to all newcomers looking for work, and Canada for the first time restricted the entry of immigrants from Newfoundland. In 1930 the Smoot–Hawley tariff closed the US market to most products, and by 1931 almost one in five Maritime wage earners (19 per cent) was unemployed. Although this figure was only slightly above the national average, the Maritime provinces had fewer resources than most other provinces of Canada with which to participate in Ottawa's cost-shared relief programs.

The strain on all levels of government was extreme. By 1931 Guysborough County in Nova Scotia was virtually bankrupt, and several counties in northern New Brunswick soon found themselves in the same position. Provincial governments were also in difficulty. Personal income per capita had fallen to 71 per cent of the Canadian average by 1933, revenues stagnated, and borrowing drove debt charges to impossible heights: more than 30 per cent of revenue in Nova Scotia and more than 50 per cent in New Brunswick, where the government was on the verge of bankruptcy by the end of the decade. In 1933, 12 per cent of Maritimers were on direct relief, which in most cases paid only a pittance and sometimes was cut off in the summer. The Prince Edward Island rate of $1.93 per person per month (the same as in Newfoundland) was the second lowest in Canada.

Many people looked to charities, the churches, and the Red Cross for assistance. The worst hit were fishermen and urban labourers. As for the elderly, strictly means-tested pensions, introduced in the Maritime provinces between 1933 and 1936 at rates 20 to 40 per cent lower than the national average, were a convenient way to reduce relief rolls. There was near-starvation in some areas, and widespread malnutrition. But amid it all, Maritimers found the time, energy, and resources to send aid to the Prairies, where the wheat economy had collapsed as a result of falling world prices and a devastating drought.

The depression precipitated the final scenes in the drama of Newfoundland under responsible government. In 1928 Squires had returned to power. His government was soon engulfed by the Depression. Four years later, revenue had fallen by 21 per cent, spending had risen by 7 per cent; the debt had increased by 23 per cent; and servicing it now absorbed more than 60 per cent of government revenue. These bald figures represent an escalating crisis: low prices, poor catches, ris-

Crowds outside the Colonial Building, St John's, 5 April 1932. Accusations of corruption levelled against the Prime Minister, Sir Richard Squires, precipitated this demonstration, which turned into a riot. A-19-23, The Rooms, Provincial Archives Division.

ing urban unemployment, a quarter of the population on the dole (which was centrally administered), and the necessity of borrowing to maintain the basic operations of the state, even after swingeing cuts in public expenditure. When bank loans became ever more difficult to arrange, another futile attempt was made to sell Labrador, this time for $110 million, but there were no takers.

The atmosphere was especially tense in St John's, where the prime minister's opponents sensed blood and organized a march on the legislature on 5 April 1932. It turned into a violent riot, and Squires was lucky to escape unharmed. His party was virtually wiped out in the ensuing general election and the conservatives took over once again. Having assessed the financial situation, they suggested what Squires had consistently refused: a partial default on debt payments. There seemed to be no other alternative.

Alarm bells rang in London and Ottawa, where the possibility that a dominion might default on its debt was viewed with dismay. Newfoundland was given a proposition that it was not allowed to refuse: Canada and Britain would assist with the debt payments on condition that an imperial royal commission investigate the situation and advise on what to do in the longer term. Chaired by Lord Amulree, the commission reported in October 1933. It placed the primary blame for the debt crisis not on the depression, structural economic problems, or the cost of the war and the railway, but rather on 'persistent extravagance and neglect of proper financial principles', 'greed, graft and corruption', and general incompetence, along with various other shortcomings. Its central recommendation, fabricated by the Whitehall bureaucracy, was that the country's debt should be rescheduled and guaranteed by the British government. In return, Newfoundland would surrender responsible government and be administered by a British-appointed commission until such time as it was again 'self-supporting'.

Weary of persistent economic problems, disillusioned with the political élite, fearful of further violence and unrest, Newfoundlanders threw in the towel. There were very few dissenting voices. The legislature voted itself out of existence, and the Commission of Government took office in February 1934. Though welcomed at the time, the surrender of responsible government soon came to be seen (and is still seen) as a humiliation, and the analysis in the Amulree report as unfair. Joining Canada might have proved less of an indignity, but there was little support for Confederation on the island and none at all in Ottawa.

Responses to Hard Times

To help those most devastated by the economic crisis, two strategies were adopted across the region. The first was to provide unemployed people with land and encourage them to become self-sufficient farmers. This program was most popular in New Brunswick, where the government opened new areas for pioneer settlement and provided some minimal assistance. Acadians were particularly involved in the scheme, establishing a number of new settlements in the northern part of the province. In Nova Scotia some 600 vacant farms were made available, but most of the beneficiaries were unemployed miners and their families. Lacking the necessary agricultural skills, many of them soon drifted away. The results were similarly disappointing in Newfoundland, where the Commission government created eight land settlements and relocated approximately 365 families.

The second, more famous and influential strategy was developed by the Extension Department of St Francis Xavier University under the direction of Father Moses Coady. The Antigonish Movement, as it came to be known, focused on self-help through adult education and the establishment of cooperatives to do everything from marketing fish to building houses. Although co-ops were not new to the Maritimes, the Antigonish Movement provided a new impetus for them, especially in rural areas where the Roman Catholic church was strong. By the end of 1939, Antigonish claimed involvement in 2,390 study clubs and 140 credit unions throughout all three Maritime provinces.

The Newfoundland government established its own division of co-operatives in the mid-1930s, with Antigonish alumni as the director and field workers. There was considerable early success both in St John's and on the island's west coast. Less well-received was the Commission's insistence that, to prevent beriberi, dole recipients should use brown rather than white flour: unemployed marchers in St John's in 1935 responded with a banner reading 'We work for our cash; we want money not cattle feed'.[6]

The Antigonish Movement was inherently conservative, and its leaders had no interest in socialism or radical politics. Indeed, it has been accused of being more romantic than realist, and of failing to involve industrial and urban workers. Some people in the region were less willing to accept the status quo. Until it was banned by the federal government, there was support in the Maritimes for the Communist party, as well as the social-democratic Cooperative Commonwealth Federation (CCF), which won both provincial and federal seats in industrial Cape Breton within a decade of its founding in 1932. The upstart Reconstruction Party, which split from the Conservatives, attracted followers in eastern Nova Scotia in the 1935 federal election. Even the Ku Klux Klan reared its ugly head to scapegoat Roman Catholics, Blacks and other minorities in these difficult times.

The existence of these parties did not substantially transform Maritime politics, and there was no meaningful change in federal–provincial relations. In Nova Scotia a royal commission appointed by Macdonald's Liberal government recommended in 1934 that the federal government either base its subsidies to the provinces on their individual fiscal needs, or take over the entire responsibility for certain services. Real change had to await the report of the Royal Commission on Dominion–Provincial Relations (the Rowell–Sirois Commission), which appeared in 1940. Also important was the increasing acceptance during the Second World War of Keynesian economic principles, such as the use of government spending to offset capitalist boom and bust cycles. In the meantime, provincial governments had no option but to borrow money to pay for relief works and essential services.

In Newfoundland, the Commission government was a conservative caretaker regime subject to the supervision of the Dominions Office and the British Treasury. London wanted to see progress, but at the same time insisted on economy and avoidance of controversy: there were to be no awkward questions raised in Parliament about Newfoundland. The Commission's achievements were real: it reorganized the civil service, reformed taxation, introduced improvements in health and education, and encouraged modernization in the fishing industry. It also created the Newfoundland Ranger Force, whose members were to be at once policemen, administrators, and the government's eyes and ears in rural districts, including Labrador. Valuable as such initiatives were, most Newfoundlanders could see little change in their economic circumstances, and the inflated expectations that had been associated with the Commission's inauguration were soon replaced by disillusion. The Commission was no more capable than its predecessors of balancing the budget, reducing the debt, or finding work for the unemployed. By the late 1930s it was widely unpopular.

In the Maritimes there was a slow recovery after 1933, fuelled in part by ambitious road-building programs. Exports of lumber and apples were protected by the 1932 Ottawa agreements on imperial trade, an achievement of New Brunswick-born Conservative Prime Minister R.B. Bennett. Thanks to government subventions and increased tariff protection, steel and coal production revived. The lobster and fresh fish industries expanded, as did dairy and poultry farming. In Newfoundland mining was the only sector to show any significant

King George VI and Queen Elizabeth, Doaktown, New Brunswick, summer 1939. Visiting Canada and Newfoundland to generate support for the imminent war with Germany, the royal couple were greeted by enthusiastic crowds at every stop on their tour. PANB, P54-74.

improvement, though newsprint, as in the Maritimes, maintained its position. Yet prices remained low, markets uncertain, and employers drove down wages as far as possible. In terms of national income per capita, the region lagged behind. In the late 1930s, average income in Newfoundland was approximately $150; in the Maritimes $248; and in Canada as a whole $360.

To counter the general misery and mean-spiritedness of the 1930s, many people found solace in the mass consumer culture that was transforming North American society. Radio, movies, mail-order catalogues, glossy magazines, cars, and modern conveniences exploded on the market in the 1920s with dramatic effect. Under their magic spell, older values such as self-discipline, self-denial, duty, and religious observance began to give way to self-fulfilment and secular pleasures. Although Atlantic Canadians were on the periphery of this revolution, they were no less attracted to the new values than people elsewhere; all they lacked was the economic wherewithal to insist that they too have 'a chicken in every pot and a car in every garage', or at least indoor plumbing to replace the outdoor privy.

Conclusion

The inter-war years left an indelible mark on the Atlantic region. In the era when other areas of North America were making the transition, however uneven, to mass consumer society, the Maritimes and Newfoundland were left behind, while

Labrador remained another world altogether, one whose people had never yet voted in a democratic election. Much would change with the outbreak of the Second World War, but the image of the Atlantic region as the 'sick man' of North America would continue to have an impact long after it was no longer true.

Chapter 13

The Emergence of an Atlantic Region, 1939–49

The Second World War brought prosperity to the Atlantic region, but it was both artificial and uneven. Postwar readjustment was difficult and, as it had been 25 years before, in some ways disillusioning. The reforms undertaken during and after the war did little to change the fundamental structure of federal–provincial relationships, and no solutions were offered to the growing problems of regional disparity and dependency. In Newfoundland and Labrador, though, the war precipitated fundamental political and constitutional change. The suspended dominion became a Canadian province in 1949, and the term 'Atlantic Canada' came into use. Many citizens of the new province hoped and expected that joining Canada would solve major economic problems; in the long run they were to be disappointed.

The Military Occupation

For the duration of the war, the Atlantic region was essentially a military base extending from Labrador to the American border. As the part of North America nearest to the European theatre of war, the region provided an indispensable base for air and sea links to the United Kingdom. There was investment in military infrastructure, but the main permanent benefits of Canada's war effort went to Québec and Ontario, where the industrial component was centralized. Ottawa had little interest in using the opportunities presented by the war to promote regional development. The role of the Maritimes and Newfoundland was simply to shield the industrial heartland and provide the necessary conduit to Europe.

In the Maritimes approximately 47.5 per cent of the eligible male population joined the armed forces. Over 11,000 Newfoundlanders joined the British or Canadian forces, and several thousand more crewed merchant vessels. Unemployment disappeared as men and women from across the region either migrated to industrial jobs in central Canada or found work closer to home. Many of the local jobs involved building and strengthening military bases, not only in the Maritimes but in Newfoundland and Labrador, where the Canadian government assumed the responsibility for defence.

The most important military centre on the east coast was Halifax, followed by Sydney. Each had a large and potentially vital harbour, as well as a base for each of the three armed forces: army, navy, and air. All three services also had detach-

Timeline

1940–1	Unemployment insurance legislation passed in Canada.
1941	Anglo-American Leased Bases Agreement signed; Canadian High Commission established in St John's.
1942–4	U-boats sink vessels in Gulf and approaches, including the ferry *Caribou*.
1942	Newfoundland government takes over the north Labrador trade.
1944	Maritime provinces conduct inquiries on reconstruction; Canada adopts family allowance legislation.
1945	End of the Second World War; riots in Halifax, Sydney, and New Waterford; formation of National Sea Products Ltd.
1946–8	National Convention debates Newfoundland's future.
1947	Maritime coal miners' strike.
1948	Newfoundland voters choose Confederation with Canada.
1949	Newfoundland becomes a province; Hal Banks' union-breaking in Halifax.

ments at Saint John and Gaspé, while the Royal Canadian Navy had additional bases at Shelburne and Cornwallis; the Royal Canadian Air Force at Greenwood, North Sydney, Chatham, Moncton, Yarmouth, Shelburne, Debert, East Passage, Summerside, and Charlottetown; and the army at Debert, Edmundston, Sussex, Aldershot, and Little River.

The Canadian government had understood from the start that Newfoundland would have to be included in its defence planning, and RCAF planes began to patrol the waters around the island, using the seaplane base at Botwood. By June 1940 Canadian troops and aircraft were stationed at Gander, and before long both Botwood and Gander were placed under Canadian control, along with the Newfoundland militia. The Canadians built another air base at Torbay, a short distance north of St John's, starting in 1941, and the next year began to construct naval facilities there on behalf of the Royal Navy. HMCS *Avalon,* with 3,600 personnel by 1943, became the Canadian navy's second largest base. The Canadian government also rapidly constructed a huge new airfield at Goose Bay, Labrador, which was operational by the end of 1941. In total, the infrastructure established in Newfoundland and Labrador cost roughly $65 million.

Early in the war people in the Atlantic region had a real sense of being on the front line, vulnerable to German attack. Those fears eventually faded, even though German submarines continued to bring danger into home waters. In time, the forces stationed in the region came to concentrate not so much on defending North America as on providing protection for the convoys of merchant vessels crossing the Atlantic; the coastal vessels sailing to and from Québec, Corner Brook, and Bell Island; and the ferry service between North Sydney and Port aux Basques. In addition, Goose Bay and Gander were used as take-off points for the almost 12,000 aircraft ferried from North America to Britain during the course of the war. Other functions included the training of personnel, and the repair and maintenance of ships and aircraft.

In September 1940, the British and American governments agreed in principle that in return for 50 aging destroyers and other military equipment, Britain would allow the United States to lease base sites in Newfoundland, Bermuda, and the Caribbean for 99 years, 'freely and without consideration'. The Leased Bases Agreement, finalized in June 1941, was unpopular in Newfoundland since it gave the United States virtual sovereignty over its bases. Great Britain's wartime leader Winston Churchill felt it necessary to appeal to Newfoundlanders to accept the deal 'for the sake of the Empire, of liberty and of the welfare of all mankind'. The Commission government had no choice but to accept. The Americans built an army base at St John's, a naval and army base at Argentia, and an air base at Stephenville; leased part of St John's harbour; and stationed personnel at Gander and Goose Bay. At the height of the military occupation, in 1943, there were 10,000 Americans and more than 6,000 Canadians stationed in Newfoundland and Labrador—tangible proof of the country's strategic importance.

Protecting convoys from German U-boat attacks placed an immense strain on the Canadian navy and air force. Inevitably, rapid expansion meant that officers and crews often lacked training and experience; equipment was sometimes inadequate, and base facilities could be substandard. In particular, repair and refit capacity in the region was limited, in part because skilled tradesmen were in short supply, and more directly because the federal government decided to locate the major repair centre at Montréal—despite the danger posed by U-boats in the St Lawrence and the fact that the river was impassable to ocean-going vessels for half the year. British and American authorities questioned the decision to no avail.

Between May 1942 and November 1944, submarines sank 23 ships in the Gulf. In September and November 1942, four vessels were sunk at Bell Island with the loss of 69 lives; and in October the Newfoundland ferry *Caribou,* though escorted by a minesweeper, was torpedoed 40 miles off Port aux Basques with the loss of 137 passengers and crew. After a shaky start, Canadian aircraft and naval vessels managed to contain the U-boat threat, won the Battle of the St Lawrence, and played a significant role in the Battle of the Atlantic. Stories circulated of Germans landing in remote places along the region's long coastline—and an automatic weather station was in fact placed by the Germans on the north Labrador coast—but by 1944 the region was safe from direct enemy threats.

In July 1945 Halifax once again suffered a major explosion as a result of its role as a site for munitions storage. Fire and explosions racked the city for 24 hours after the *Halifax Magazine,* on the Dartmouth side of the Bedford Basin, caught fire. When Halifax residents north of Quinpool Road were ordered to evacuate their homes, many refused and instead lined the slopes of the harbour to watch the fireworks.

Bedford Basin, on the inner reaches of Halifax harbour, offered shelter to merchant ships and their naval escorts assembling for the dangerous voyage across the north Atlantic during the Second World War. Department of National Defence, LAC, PA-112993.

The Economic Impact of War

Notwithstanding the bias toward central Canada, the war boosted the Atlantic region's economy. Steel production and processing at Sydney and Trenton revived and expanded, and shipyards were busy at Saint John, Halifax, Dartmouth, and Pictou. Newsprint production increased, and overall employment in manufacturing expanded by 25,000 (74 per cent). Even the cotton industry bounced back, and for a time wool producers enjoyed a steady demand for their product, used in military uniforms.

The Halifax docks generally functioned well, thanks to the reorganization of labour, and the imposition of a minimum wage, which more than met the increase in the cost of living. There was a three-month strike in 1944, when the Dominion Steel and Coal Corporation (DOSCO)-owned Halifax Shipyards Limited challenged, unsuccessfully, the legality of the union dues check-off. War did nothing to resolve tensions in the coal industry, with its history of intense antagonism between workers and management. Vital as coal was to the war effort, production actually declined between 1941 and 1945, and there was serious labour unrest until 1943, when the federal government agreed to top up miners' wages. This

Biography: Clarie Gillis

Clarence Gillis was born in 1895 in Londonderry, Nova Scotia. In 1904 his family moved to Glace Bay, where his father worked in the mines and became a close associate of the union activist J.B. McLachlan. Because of this union activity, the entire family was expelled from company housing and forced to spend a winter living in a tent. Blacklisted, the elder Gillis worked from 1910 to 1923 in the United States.

At the age of 14, with a grade 5 education, Clarie began his career as a miner in No. 2 colliery in Glace Bay. When war was declared, he volunteered for service overseas and was wounded three times. Back in Cape Breton, Gillis played an active role in the coal miners' struggle against BESCO, supported the cooperative movement, and helped establish a local branch of the Canadian Legion.

In 1927 Gillis was elected president of the Phalen Local—known as the 'Red Local'—of District 26 of the United Mine Workers of America (UMW). After a group broke away from District 26 in 1932 to form the Amalgamated Mine Workers of Nova Scotia, he served as its vice-president, but by 1938 he was back in the UMW and deeply involved with the recently founded Cooperative Commonwealth Federation (CCF). After decades of bitter internal struggle, Cape Breton miners were ready to bury their differences and put their weight behind a political party dedicated to serving the interests of working people.

District 26 was the first union to affiliate with the CCF at the national level, and in a provincial by-election in December 1939 a miner named Douglas Macdonald won the riding of Cape Breton Centre for the party—its first seat east of Ontario. In the federal election of the following year Clarie Gillis won Cape Breton South and became the first miner to sit in the Canadian House of Commons. He was to hold the seat until the Diefenbaker landslide of 1958.

decision reflected both poor government control of skilled labour, and the inability (or unwillingness) of corporations and governments to find a permanent solution to the industry's problems. Allowing more than 1,000 miners to join the armed forces, and the number of coalface workers to decline by 29 per cent, proved to be an unwise move, as was the appointment of W.F. Carroll, a known anti-union Liberal, to chair a royal commission to investigate the industry in 1944.

As urban-based industries expanded to meet wartime needs, they drew labour away from the rural economy at the very time when demand for fish and farm products was increasing sharply. Between 1939 and 1945 the total farm income for the Maritimes rose by 98 per cent (from $25 million to $49 million). Apple growers faced disaster when the British market was abruptly closed at the beginning of the war so that capital and shipping could be diverted to the military effort. At the request of growers and shippers, the federal government stepped in to help, establishing marketing boards to dispose of some of the vast surplus and process the rest as juice, sauce, and pie filling. As a result, processing accounted for nearly 80 per cent of the crop in 1942, up from 11.4 per cent in 1938, and growers continued to get good returns as they waited for overseas sales to resume once the war had ended.

The war helped to stimulate astonishing gains in the fisheries: the value of Maritime fish landings increased 230 per cent (from $8 million to $27 million), while the value of Newfoundland's saltfish exports quadrupled, from $4.1 million to $16.7 million, over the same period. In the Maritimes and Newfoundland alike, governments encouraged modernization, offering financial incentives for the construction both of larger vessels (including trawlers and draggers) and of freezing plants. The establishment of the giant National Sea Products Limited in 1945 marked the arrival of mechanized, industrial fishing. This trend was endorsed in an influential report written for Nova Scotia's royal commission on reconstruction in 1944 by Stewart Bates. Soon to become federal Deputy Minister of Fisheries, Bates argued that the future lay with fresh fish, trawlers, centralization, consolidation, and the North American market. The Newfoundland government made almost identical recommendations the same year.

The militarization of the region also created economic spinoffs. Although rationing, shortages, and restrictive liquor laws limited what they could buy, people had money to spend. Servicemen and women received regular salaries, and the construction of military bases created a large number of jobs—about 20,000 in Newfoundland and Labrador alone in 1942. In the Maritimes, base development in communities such as Summerside, Greenwood, and Chatham generated economic growth and work for people in the surrounding area. Some bases became nuclei for new or vastly expanded towns, and displaced families and communities. French-speaking farmers in St George's Bay were expropriated to make way for the Stephenville base, while at Argentia two villages had to be closed down and their residents, and even cemeteries, moved a short distance away.

The construction of the Goose Bay airfield is considered, with reason, to be the watershed dividing the old Labrador from the new. Labradorians from all over the region, including some Inuit and Innu, came to build the base and establish the town of Happy Valley—originally called 'Refuge Cove' because there was no place to stay; workers had to live in tents and shacks. Another significant change came about in 1942, when the Hudson's Bay Company decided to abandon the trading posts it had leased from the Moravians in 1926. Now the Newfoundland government had no choice but to take over. Labrador could no longer be governed by proxy.

War and Society

The military presence was not an unmixed blessing for cities and towns still recovering from the depression. The 65,000 residents of Halifax, Canada's main Atlantic port, were particularly hard pressed to make room for some 100,000 additional people: military personnel, their families, and sundry camp followers, as well as industrial workers. With many unpaved streets and a dilapidated water system, Halifax was a dismal place for many of the new arrivals: rents were high, living

War brides arriving in Canada at Pier 21. Many of the nearly 48,000 war brides and their 22,000 children arrived in Canada through Pier 21. While they were destined for communities all across Canada, many of them found homes in the Maritimes. LAC, PA-47114.

conditions often disgraceful, hospitals and schools overstretched. The city had never been particularly open at the best of times, and the Depression had taken its toll on amenities such as restaurants and theatres. Thus it was left to volunteers to set up hostels and canteens, and arrange concerts. Conditions were similar in Sydney and Saint John, which also were required to host expanding military and civilian populations. In St John's, relations between townspeople and the military were generally good, the Americans being especially popular. The Americans sent military dependents home, and the number of Canadian dependents was capped, which helped to alleviate the strain on housing and food supplies.

When the end of the war in Europe was announced, on 8 May 1945, the city of Halifax erupted in two days of rioting and looting. The immediate cause may have been the authorities' decision to close down all shops, cafes, and liquor stores, which led frustrated revellers to break in and help themselves, but the violence spread, and the total damages amounted to more than $5 million. In the federal inquiry that followed, Rear-Admiral L.W. Murray was relieved of his commission for failing to control the men under his command, and 211 people, civilians as well as servicemen, were indicted for offences. There were also riots in Sydney and New Waterford, where, as in Halifax, the authorities had thoughtfully marked the day by closing down all shops, cafes, and liquor stores.

There were those who feared that the war had weakened traditional morality and encouraged 'licence'. Although attitudes towards alcohol, sex, and religion had been changing for some time, the war accelerated the process. Bootleggers and prostitutes plied their trades more openly than before and casual liaisons between servicemen and local women were not unusual. In an era when 'safe sex' was rarely discussed, the numbers of illegitimate children increased and venereal disease became a growing cause for concern.

The war also strained marriages and family life. With husbands absent for long periods, wives might find other partners; and absent husbands could similarly form new relationships. Wartime circumstances encouraged hasty marriages—in Newfoundland alone, more than 900 women married servicemen from either the US or Canada, while many young men from the region found brides in Europe. As the war came to an end, there were demands in the Maritimes for easier and cheaper divorce, and in Newfoundland, where divorce was a taboo subject, the courts for the first time agreed to handle formal separations.

Post-war Reconstruction

As the war began to wind down, Ottawa asked each of the provinces to take stock of its future. Nova Scotia appointed a Royal Commission on Provincial Development chaired by Robert McGregor Dawson, a political scientist at the University of Toronto. New Brunswick enlisted Norman A.M. Mackenzie, president of the University of New Brunswick, to chair a commission, while Prince Edward Island chose Dr J.E. Lattimer, chair of the Department of Agricultural Economics at Macdonald College, McGill University, to head its inquiry. All three commissions recognized that the prosperity brought by the war was transient, that the unequal distribution of wartime benefits had aggravated regional disparities, and that the economy remained dangerously vulnerable. Nevertheless, there was hope that a post-war slump could be avoided and there was a growing consensus that state intervention would help to prevent a return to the desperate conditions that prevailed in the 1930s.

The Rowell–Sirois Commission on Dominion–Provincial Relations had recommended equalization payments and national standards in basic services, reflecting a new approach both to federalism and to the poverty that existed side-by-side with the wealth created by the industrial system. Since the beginning of the war Ottawa had been seriously considering a national policy that incorporated some welfare state measures. Unemployment insurance was introduced in 1940 to cover industrial workers; in 1944, family allowances became the first in a series of universal programs; and in 1945 Mackenzie King proposed an ambitious federal reconstruction plan designed to address deficiencies in public works and social services.

Condemned by Ontario and Québec as 'state socialism', this approach was also opposed by Angus L. Macdonald, who regained the premiership of Nova Scotia in 1945, after a wartime stint as minister of national defence for naval services. Macdonald had witnessed at close range the extent to which federal politics was dominated by central Canadian interests and he had no wish to strengthen Ottawa's hand. As a result of provincial opposition the program was modified. In any event,

Family Allowances and Public Schooling

After the establishment of public schooling in the mid-nineteenth century, education reformers in the Maritimes began demanding that attendance be compulsory. Poor families, who depended on the labour of their children to make ends meet, often found themselves in trouble with truant officers once compulsory schooling up to a certain age was made mandatory. Attitudes changed when the federal government tied payment of Family Allowances to school attendance for children up to the age of 16. In Prince Edward Island François-E. Doiron, who monitored school attendance, noted in his 1946 report:

> The appointment of an Attendance Officer and the granting of Family Allowance, I believe, has been a forward step in education in this province. It is pleasing to note a very marked improvement in attendance in this inspectorate under the new system. In fact some of the schools are now overcrowded and hardly able to accommodate the increased number of pupils in attendance. It is true there are still some children of school age not going to school and trying to circumvent the work of the Attendance Officer, but as time goes on I believe the children will gradually become accustomed to attend regularly as they begin to realize that they cannot absent themselves from school with impunity as they have done in the past.[1]

it had never aimed to remedy uneven economic development, or to give any special consideration to the Maritimes. The federal government had no desire to play the interventionist role and focused on cutting its losses. It closed down DOSCO's steel plate mill, for example, and paid farmers to uproot their apple trees when the British market remained closed to Canadian producers after the war.

The failure of governments to address regional needs in post-war reconstruction had disastrous results. By the late 1940s Pictou and Cape Breton counties had the highest unemployment rates in Canada, and employment in secondary manufacturing was fast declining. Out-migration again became the solution to economic problems. Unions, meanwhile, faced anti-communist hysteria and intimidation. Nowhere was this more obvious than on the Halifax waterfront, where in 1949 goon squads orchestrated by the American labour leader Harold ('Hal') Banks used violence to break up the Communist-controlled Canadian Seamen's Union.

For the three Liberal premiers in the Maritime provinces—Macdonald in Nova Scotia, J.B. McNair in New Brunswick, and 'Farmer' Walter Jones in Prince Edward Island—the post-war picture looked bleak. Their provinces lagged behind most of the rest of the country in health and educational services, and their roads could no longer accommodate the growing traffic. Other parts of North America were beginning to take electricity and running water for granted, but many people in the Maritime provinces still lived without either. New Brunswick had the dubious distinction of having the highest illiteracy rate in Canada and a social welfare policy that invited ridicule. On Prince Edward Island, 405 of the 473 schools had only one room and 69 of those were beyond repair. Elsewhere in Canada, the trend was toward large consolidated schools, but where would the Maritimes find the money to build them? As the North American economy began to improve, out-migration accelerated. There seemed to be no end to the dreary tale of economic decline.

Newfoundland and Labrador join Confederation

The British government understood that Newfoundland's remarkable wartime prosperity was ephemeral, and that its economy remained narrowly based and fundamentally unchanged. It also accepted that Commission government could not continue indefinitely, but feared—with reason—that if Newfoundland returned to responsible government there would be another financial crisis sooner or later, and another application for British help. To ensure against that possibility, a $100 million reconstruction scheme was developed by the Newfoundland government and approved by the Dominions Office. When the British Treasury denied funding, an approach was made to Ottawa, where the reaction was equally negative. Canadian officials did indicate, however, that they would favour bringing Newfoundland into Canada, preferably without a prior return to responsible government. Thus the reconstruction scheme was buried and the two governments quietly agreed, late in 1945, that their objective would be Confederation

Ottawa was not enthusiastic about taking on what it saw as another Maritime province, but it now recognized that Canada had vital long-term interests in Newfoundland and Labrador. The war had demonstrated how important that country was for defence and aviation; the economic potential of Labrador was well understood; and Ottawa feared that the large American presence on the island might draw Newfoundland into the orbit of the United States. Moreover, reports from the Canadian High Commission in St. John's, established in 1941, suggested that Confederation might attract majority support.

In December 1945 the British government announced that citizens of Newfoundland and Labrador (the latter having the franchise for the first time) would elect a national convention to recommend the constitutional options to be placed on a referendum ballot. It was a calculated gamble, in that the British and Canadian governments could only hope that opinion in Newfoundland would come to favour Confederation: there were no guarantees.

The Convention sat from September 1946 to January 1948. From the beginning it contained a vocal confederate minority, led by Joseph Smallwood, journalist, farmer, and broadcaster; and the lawyer-turned-outport-businessman Gordon Bradley, who had been a member of the last Squires administration. Neither was a member of the colonial élite, which was largely anti-confederate. The Convention's debates concerning the country's condition and prospects, broadcast by the government radio station, were closely followed. Delegations were sent both to London and to Ottawa, where Bradley and Smallwood persuaded the federal government to formulate draft terms of union. Finally, after days of passionate discussion, Smallwood's motion to make Confederation an option was defeated, and the Convention recommended that the referendum choice be between continuing with Commission government and returning to responsible government. However, the British government overruled the Convention and placed all three options on the ballot. Anti-confederates responded with outrage: where were British justice and fair play now?

As a result of this decision the anti-confederates would have to mount an effective campaign to counter the confederate crusade, but they were divided and lacked effective leadership. Smallwood and his allies stressed how Confederation would improve social security payments and services while reducing the cost of living: in his words, the referendum gave voters 'the best chance that they EVER HAD to make Newfoundland a better place for themselves and their families'. Who opposed these goals? 'Water Street [merchants] . . . the rich and wealthy . . . the few fortunate, well-fed, well-clothed, well-housed people amongst us'. Confederation was the cause of 'the toiling masses' who wanted 'a NEW Newfoundland'.[2]

The referendum held on 3 June 1948, did not settle the issue: responsible government received 44.6 per cent of the vote, Confederation 41.1, and Commission government 14.3. Thus a second, run-off vote was scheduled for 22 July. Although the Avalon Peninsula, including St John's, was strongly anti-confederate, the Confederates were confident that victory was within reach. Stressing the economic benefits of Confederation, they also deliberately played the sectarian card. Members of every Orange lodge were reminded that many Roman Catholics—including members of religious orders, voting for the first time in history—opposed Confederation. Anti-confederates were viciously accused of disloyalty to Britain, while Confederation was presented as 'British Union'.

In the end, Confederation emerged with a majority of 4.6 per cent over responsible government. The geographical voting pattern was largely unchanged. What gave the confederates the edge was their success in attracting most of those who had supported Commission government in the first referendum—voters described by one member of the St John's élite as 'ignorant and avaricious outporters' who had 'handed over [Newfoundland] to Canada as a free gift'.[3] Although the victory was narrow in numerical terms, the fact that the confederates took every district off the Avalon Peninsula and in Labrador meant that they had won the equivalent of an electoral landslide. Three factors in particular contributed to the final result: the significant social and economic changes that had taken place in Newfoundland and Labrador since the early 1930s, genuine uncertainty about the wisdom of returning to independence, and the desire to benefit from the social programs offered by post-war federalism. Newfoundlanders and Labradorians had great hopes and expectations for their future as a province.

During the negotiation of the final terms of union, there were difficulties over fisheries administration. That Newfoundland had to place its main industry under federal control caused some justifiable shaking of heads. Financial arrangements also caused some concern. The final deal included a special 12-year transitional

'Shall We Say Grace?' This cartoon from *The Confederate*, 20 May 1948, draws on memories of the Great Depression to emphasize the message that the wealthy élites supported a return to responsible government, which (allegedly) had only brought misery to the common people in the past.

grant, as well as a federal undertaking, in Term 29, to establish a royal commission within eight years to determine what additional assistance might be needed to maintain adequate public services while keeping taxes comparable to those paid in the Maritimes.

The terms of union made no reference to the Aboriginal people of the new province. The island's Mi'kmaq were overlooked entirely until 1973, and although it was initially agreed that the federal government would accept responsibility for the Inuit and Innu, that provision changed during the final negotiations. Since the province had no reserves, and its Native people already exercised the right to vote, to introduce the Indian Act there would have been a large step backwards. Thus the two sides decided that the new provincial government would administer Native affairs, with the help of special federal grants. As a consequence the Aboriginal peoples of Newfoundland and Labrador until recently were treated differently from their counterparts in the rest of Canada, and over the years have received considerably less federal money.

By the end of 1948 the terms of union were settled, and Newfoundland became Canada's tenth province on 31 March 1949. Smallwood served as Newfoundland's first premier, and Bradley became its first representative in the federal cabinet. The ceremonies were subdued.

Conclusion

In 1949, then, a new region was born. 'Atlantic Canada' was a convenient term, but misleading in that the four provinces had no effective regional identity and often followed separate, at times conflicting, agendas. Although cushioned now by a kinder, gentler federalism, optimistic about the future, and part of a prosperous country, the region had to accept that the centralization of political and economic power was irreversible.

Chapter Fourteen

The Real Golden Age? 1949–75

According to the historian Eric Hobsbawm, the three decades following the Second World War were a 'golden age' of 'extraordinary economic growth and social transformation, which probably changed human society more profoundly than any other period of comparable brevity'.[1] Scarred by two world wars and the depression of the 1930s, almost everyone wanted to ensure that those experiences would never be repeated. At the same time, the Cold War underlined the opposition between two distinct routes to that end—capitalism and communism—and policy-makers on each side were eager to prove the merits of their own system. Governments at all levels played an important role in shaping a new world order that was designed to appeal to a broad spectrum of society.

In Canada, the federal government's commitment to economic planning, social welfare, and human rights created a receptive environment for Atlantic Canadians' efforts to pursue regional development. The result was economic and social transformation. This new golden age faded to bronze with the oil crisis of the 1970s, but it left a legacy of interregional co-operation, institutional development, and claims to entitlement that still inform pubic policy.

The Atlantic Revolution

During the immediate post-war years, the trends long associated with the Atlantic region—low incomes, high unemployment rates, mass out-migration—continued unabated. Indeed, conditions became relatively worse. In 1945 per capita income in the Maritimes was 24 per cent below the national average; by 1955 the difference had increased to 33 per cent. In that year Newfoundland, the nation's poorest province, recorded a per capita income 55 per cent below the national average.

Having promised Newfoundlanders that Confederation would usher in a new era, Premier 'Joey' Smallwood proved to be Atlantic Canada's most articulate and persistent spokesman for regional development. He recruited entrepreneurs from elsewhere and badgered what he called 'Uncle Ottawa' for financial aid. To improve his province's chances in that regard, he persuaded J.W. Pickersgill to run for the seat of Bonavista–Twillingate in 1953. As a former assistant both to Mackenzie King and to King's successor as prime minister, Louis St Laurent, Pickersgill was well-placed to manipulate the levers of federal power, and he gave Newfoundland a powerful voice in Ottawa.

Timeline

1954	Atlantic Provinces Economic Council founded; resettlement program begins in Newfoundland and Labrador.
1955	Canso Causeway opened; preliminary report of the Royal Commission on Canada's Economic Prospects.
1956	Ottawa passes equalization legislation.
1957	Industrial Estates Limited established in Nova Scotia.
1958	Ottawa approves Atlantic Provinces Adjustment Grants.
1959	Loggers strike in Newfoundland.
1960	Aboriginal people in Canada granted the right to vote on the same terms as other Canadians.
1962	Atlantic Development Board established; Halifax City Council decides to relocate residents of Africville.
1964	Bryne Report advocates municipal reform in New Brunswick.
1967	Cape Breton Development Corporation created.
1968	BRINCO signs deal to sell transport Churchill Falls power to Hydro-Québec through Québec.
1969	New Brunswick declared a bilingual province; Prince Edward Island development plan signed; Black United Front founded; White Paper on Indian Policy; Department of Regional Economic Expansion created.
1970	Deutsch Report recommends Maritime Union; Report of the Royal Commission on the Status of Women.
1971	Council of Maritime Premiers founded.
1972	Parti Acadien founded.
1974–5	Strike by trawler crews in Newfoundland.

The Maritime premiers were also eager to obtain federal support for regional development. Following his election victory in New Brunswick in September 1952, Progressive Conservative Premier Hugh John Flemming undertook an aggressive campaign to develop 'power for industry', and was outraged when the St Laurent government refused assistance for the Beechwood power project on the Saint John River. Prince Edward Island's Liberal Premier Alexander Matheson was similarly offended when Ottawa insisted that his province return $1.4 million mistakenly paid out in per capita grants. In Nova Scotia, Premier Angus L. Macdonald, who had had his fill of federal politics during his wartime stint in Ottawa, was suspicious of federal schemes of any kind. His death in April 1954 opened the way for a more interventionist approach under Robert L. Stanfield, who led a Progressive Conservative government from 1956 to 1967.

Premier J.R. Smallwood chats with Winston Churchill, Jr, at Labrador's Churchill Falls in 1966. Smallwood had promoted the hydro development as a project in the tradition of the British merchant adventurers, and the elder Churchill (who died in 1965) had provided practical support. But the hope that the Falls would turn Newfoundland and Labrador into a 'have' province has proved illusory. CNS, MUN

Business interests played a critical role in defining the post-war version of regional protest. In 1951 the Maritime Provinces Board of Trade established an office in Moncton to encourage regional co-operation. The Board sponsored a meeting with Atlantic premiers in 1953 and a year later helped create the Atlantic Provinces Economic Council, designed to spearhead development efforts.

Ottawa's decision in 1955 to appoint the Royal Commission on Canada's Economic Prospects, chaired by Walter Gordon, played into the regional agenda. In July 1956, when the Atlantic premiers met at the first of what would become regular conferences, Flemming presented a list of proposals that he hoped his fellow premiers would support: federal subsidies based on need, assistance for resource development, and fiscal, tariff, and transportation policies that would help to stimulate regional economic growth.

Blessed with treasury surpluses in the 1950s, the federal government looked for ways to accommodate what the historian W.S. MacNutt described as an 'Atlantic Revolution'.[2] Equalization payments to the poorer provinces were instituted in 1956. The following year, Ottawa offered concessions on freight rates and power development. At Pickersgill's insistence, seasonal fishery workers became eligible for Unemployment Insurance. Meanwhile, the preliminary report of the Gordon Commission, released in January 1957, singled out the Atlantic provinces as deserving 'positive and comprehensive' attention.

The Progressive Conservatives under John Diefenbaker also began to show greater sensitivity to regional concerns. During the 1957 election campaign, Conservative candidates developed a series of 'Atlantic Resolutions' based on Flemming's proposals and the recommendations of the Gordon Commission. Diefenbaker squeaked through to victory, and for the first time in Canadian history cabinet ministers from the Atlantic and Western provinces outnumbered those from Québec and Ontario. Several policies dear to the hearts of Atlantic ministers were implemented before the next election in March 1958. With a $25-million Atlantic Provinces Adjustment Grant, a $29.5-million loan to the Beechwood power development, subventions for coal, and aid to thermal power development, 25 Progressive Conservatives from the region were smiling when the Diefenbaker government won by a landslide.

Only Newfoundland failed to give the Conservatives a majority of seats. Smallwood had thrown his lot in with the federal Liberal party, and his influence remained dominant. He had generally stood at one remove from the 'Atlantic front' in the hope that his province's special status as the youngest member of Confederation would serve him better than the politics of regionalism. The strategy backfired. Smallwood had expected an annual grant of $15 million under Term 29, but in July 1958 the royal commission on the matter chaired by John McNair recommended only $8 million annually until 1962. A bitter confrontation erupted and the province eventually settled with the Liberal government of Lester Pearson for $8 million in perpetuity. In the short term, the row was a useful diversion from Smallwood's belligerent suppression of a loggers' strike in central Newfoundland in 1959, which so disgusted Diefenbaker that he intervened to prevent the dispatch of RCMP reinforcements.

The Atlantic provinces benefited from a succession of minority governments in Ottawa between 1962 and 1968. In the dying days of the Diefenbaker administration, the Atlantic Development Board (ADB) was established to orchestrate investment in the region. Then the Liberal Pearson government enlarged its functions and endowed it with federal money. Other federal programs were tailored to meet the region's needs. After Pierre Elliott Trudeau became prime minister in 1968, his government replaced the ADB with the Department of Regional Economic Expansion (DREE), which applied regional development principles to the entire country.

Planning in the Provinces

Spurred by infusions of federal money, politicians and planners in the Atlantic provinces and Ottawa embarked on ambitious programs. Development agencies were created to attract industrial investment and blueprints for social change multiplied impressively.

Newfoundland had the farthest to go and it went the fastest. Tapping into the cash surplus of $40.2 million bequeathed by the Commission, the government

Robert Chambers, 'The Order of Good Cheer—circa 1960', *Atlantic Advocate*, September 1960. This cartoon reflects the optimism that circulated in the region as the 'Atlantic Revolution', led by the region's premiers, got under way. With permission from the Chambers family.

induced European firms to invest in 16 new industries between 1950 and 1956. All but one of the investors were German. Few of these industries survived for any length of time, and the program exhausted much of the surplus and more besides. One of Smallwood's most unfortunate decisions was to hire a Latvian economist, Alfred Valdmanis, who as Director of Economic Development spent money extravagantly and was eventually convicted of taking kickbacks.

The best prospects for resource development appeared to be in Labrador, with which Smallwood was increasingly obsessed. Western Labrador was opened to development in 1954 with the completion of the Québec, North Shore, and Labrador Railway to Sept-Îles. The first mines were on the Québec side of the border, but in the 1960s new mines and new towns—Labrador City in 1962 and Wabush in 1964—appeared on the Labrador side.

Smallwood was intent on tapping the hydro potential of Labrador's Grand Falls (renamed Churchill Falls in 1965). In the early 1950s the province had leased the falls to the British Newfoundland Corporation (BRINCO), a consortium put together by the Rothschilds. Since Québec refused to allow transmission lines to run across its territory to customers in Ontario and the United States, and the federal government was reluctant to intervene, BRINCO was obliged to sign a long-term sales contract with Hydro-Québec. The terms of the 1968 agreement did not seem unreasonable at the time, but by the mid-1970s, when Churchill Falls went on-stream, energy prices were starting to climb. Québec reaped mammoth profits simply for reselling the electricity produced in Labrador—profits that it continues to collect. This debacle still haunts Newfoundland and Labrador

In 1954, as part of its diversification and modernization program, the Smallwood government began to encourage people living in small and remote outports to move to larger communities. A joint federal–provincial resettlement program followed in 1965. Approximately 30,000 people were relocated, and 250 communities disappeared between 1954 and 1970. Those who moved enjoyed better public services, including electricity and roads, but 'growth centres' often failed to provide the expected jobs, and abandoning a deeply-rooted way of life left many people with a profound sense of loss.

In New Brunswick a young Louis J. Robichaud led his Liberal party to victory in June 1960 and appointed a cabinet in which the majority of members were francophones. Determined to improve conditions in the poor, rural municipalities where most Acadians lived, Robichaud established the Royal Commission on Municipal Finance and Taxation, chaired by Edward G. Byrne. Its 1964 report documented the inequalities that characterized New Brunswick municipalities and recommended sweeping changes.

For his 'Programme of Equal Opportunity' to succeed, Robichaud needed a civil service with the capacity to implement it. He therefore imported administrators from Saskatchewan, where the defeat of the CCF government in 1964 had freed up a significant pool of talent. The most important member of the so-called 'Saskatchewan mafia' was Donald Tansley, who became Deputy Minister of Finance. Tansley's motto was 'Process Is the Policy', and he played a critical role in persuading Robichaud's cabinet members to think beyond their parochial interests.[3]

Many anglophones complained that Robichaud's administration represented a 'French takeover', but they could not stop the transformation of New Brunswick's political landscape. The centralization of health and educational services, the establishment of a francophone university in Moncton in 1963, and the decision in 1969 to declare New Brunswick a bilingual province—the only one in Canada—underscored the growing power of the francophone minority. Robichaud lost the 1970 election to the Progressive Conservatives under Richard Hatfield, but he resisted pressure to turn back the clock. The new political and cultural realities were in New Brunswick to stay.

Prince Edward Island also embraced the Atlantic Revolution. In 1969 Liberal Premier Alexander Campbell agreed to a 15-year Comprehensive Development

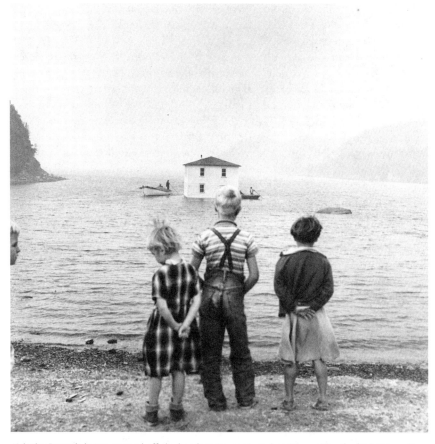

Malcolm Rogers's house, moored off the beach at Dover, Bonavista Bay, waiting for high tide so it can be hauled ashore. It had been floated from Fox Island as part of Newfoundland's outport resettlement program in the 1960s. B. Brooks, LAC, PA-154123.

Plan that promised an investment of $725 million ($255 million from Ottawa) to help restructure farming and fishing activities, improve infrastructure, and diversify the economy, most notably in the area of tourism. The agreement recognized that Prince Edward Islanders needed help if they were to maintain adequate services without sinking farther into debt. By 1971 the Island had slipped below Newfoundland as the poorest province in Canada and its per capita debt was higher than that of any other Atlantic province. Even so, many Islanders were offended by the apparent arrogance of the planners. Del Gallagher, who spearheaded the development program, was particularly unpopular, and jokes about 'Gallagher's Island', in reference to a popular American television series, became commonplace.[4]

The Stanfield government in Nova Scotia signalled its interest in economic planning with the creation in 1957 of Industrial Estates Limited to promote investment. By the early 1960s two Swedish firms, Volvo and Stora Forest, had been persuaded to locate in Nova Scotia. Michelin Tire arrived in the 1970s and became one of the province's largest employers with plants in Bridgewater, Granton, and Waterville.

The crisis in the coal and steel industries spurred further government intervention. With oil and gas rapidly replacing coal as the fuels of choice, and the demand for steel rails shrinking dramatically, Nova Scotia's industrial base collapsed. Following the recommendations of the 1960 Royal Commission on Coal, chaired by Chief Justice Ivan Rand, the federal government embarked on a program to develop alternative industries on Cape Breton Island, where the hardship was most acute. Money was pumped into Cape Breton Highlands National Park and the rebuilding of the fortress of Louisbourg, but these initiatives absorbed only a fraction of the workers facing unemployment. Cape Bretoners left in droves for jobs on the mainland, their departure made easier by the completion of the Canso causeway in 1955. To mitigate both human distress and unpleasant political repercussions, Ottawa created the Cape Breton Development Corporation in 1967, which purchased and operated the mines. The provincial government established the Sydney Steel Corporation, which bought the steel mill.

The push for economic development had positive and negative aspects. With government assistance, Halifax, Port Hawkesbury, and Saint John emerged as superports. A few home-grown entrepreneurs emerged—K.C. Irving, the McCain brothers, Frank Sobey, Harry Steele, and R.A. Jodrey in particular. At the same time, there was a price to pay for governments that jumped on the corporate bandwagon. To keep their investors happy, both Newfoundland and Nova Scotia passed restrictive labour legislation (Nova Scotia's became known as 'the Michelin bill'). K.C. Irving moved to Bermuda to avoid Canadian taxation even though his oil, transportation, and media empire benefited greatly from government assistance.

Eager to support economic development, political leaders notoriously backed a series of 'white elephants'. Clairtone Sound and the Point Tupper Heavy Water plant were serious embarrassments for the Stanfield government. Hatfield's image was tarnished when the Bricklin gull-wing sports car on which he had pinned his industrial hopes proved unviable. Throughout the region, government-assisted food- and fish-processing operations appeared and disappeared with unnerving regularity. Smallwood, ever a gambler on the next big project, fell victim to several dubious American entrepreneurs in the 1960s, among them John Shaheen. The premier's decision to back Shaheen's plan scheme for an oil refinery and petrochemical plant at Come By Chance prompted two of his most ambitious ministers, John Crosbie and Clyde Wells, to leave the cabinet in 1968. Three years later, a revived Progressive Conservative Party under Frank Moores defeated Smallwood's government.

Although politicians liked to conjure up visions of an 'Atlantic Community', they often disagreed on how to achieve regional development. Prince Edward Island felt cheated when the Atlantic Provinces Adjustment Grant was divided on a 30:30:30:10 ratio, and each province had its own ideas about which capital projects should have priority if and when Ottawa could be induced to provide funding. By the early 1970s Labradorians were starting to resent what they perceived as their exploitation by a provincial government that otherwise ignored them. A Labrador flag was created in 1974, and the New Labrador Party was formed in time for the 1971 provincial election, where it proved to be the spoiler.

In 1964 Robichaud added yet another controversial project to the mix: union of the Atlantic provinces. His francophone supporters might well have opposed such a move, but it was popular in Ottawa, which was growing impatient with Atlantic Canada's proliferating demands. At Robichaud's urging, the three Maritime premiers—Smallwood remained aloof—established a commission in 1968 to study the issue. It was chaired by Queen's University professor John Deutsch, who recommended unification in his 1970 report. Not surprisingly, this advice was largely ignored. The Commission's most important outcome was the creation of the Council of Maritime Premiers, established in 1971.

Social Adjustments

While political and business élites manoeuvred and negotiated, ordinary Atlantic Canadians were living the post-war revolution in their daily lives. The impact of economic restructuring is reflected in the statistics. During the 1950s alone, the numbers of people working in agriculture dropped by 49 per cent, in fishing and trapping by 37 per cent, in forestry by 24 per cent, and in mining by 22 per cent. The exit from primary pursuits continued through the 1960s. Each sector had its own cycle, but all were reshaped to meet the demands of an increasingly bureaucratized, centralized, mechanized, and, ultimately, computerized world.

Long an endangered species, the family farm survived only by adopting corporate practices. Quotas, marketing boards, and national standards spelled the end of part-time farming for any purpose apart from personal pleasure. Whereas one in five people had lived on farms in 1951, only one in 50 did so by 1981. Apple growers in the Annapolis Valley, faced with the permanent closure of the British market, were encouraged by generous government subsidies to uproot their trees and convert their acreage to mixed crops for a regional market. Most of them got out of farming altogether.

On Prince Edward Island, the National Farmers Union and the Brothers and Sisters of Cornelius Howatt—named after the island's most famous nineteenth-century anti-confederate—staged a protest in 1971 against development policies that they believed had contributed to the decline of family farming. They jammed the highway between Charlottetown and Borden with their tractors at the height of the tourist season, but general trends in agriculture were unaffected. Between 1951 and 1981, the proportion of Islanders employed in farming dropped from nearly 50 per cent to less than 10, and the number of farms to 3,154 from 10,137.

The story was the same in forestry, where mechanization had made it possible to fell and process more trees with fewer workers. In New Brunswick milling for the construction industry continued to thrive, but even there, as elsewhere in the region, the major product was pulpwood. By the 1980s the 19 pulp-and-paper operations in Atlantic Canada depended on foreign markets and faced intense competition. In the absence of tough environmental laws, companies were tempted to cut and run rather than follow the more costly forestry practices required to ensure a sustainable industry. A side effect of the over-exploitation of forest resources was a monoculture of softwood trees that invited periodic spruce bud-worm infestations.

In mining, restructuring produced mixed results. A growing demand for base metals such as lead, zinc, copper, and iron produced a mining boom in northern New Brunswick and western Labrador. The most dramatic new frontier was off-shore oil and natural gas, to which multinational investors were attracted by gen-erous tax incentives. On the down side, the steady decline of the coal industry meant hard times for many communities. Mine disasters in Springhill in 1956 and 1958 tragically underlined the inadequacy of safety measures in superannuated mines. The fluorspar industry on the Burin Peninsula appeared to be a success story, but the discovery that radon gas was causing cancer in workers, together with the availability of cheaper ore from Mexico, led to its closing in 1977.

Meanwhile, modernization and expansion in the fisheries set the stage for a dra-matic collapse before the end of the century. In the early 1950s Europeans began sending freezer trawlers to the banks fishery, signalling a major transition in the region's oldest primary industry. With the emphasis on the offshore banks and fresh or frozen fish, on the plant rather than the fish stage, and overwhelmingly on the American market, saltfish production declined. Meanwhile, a record 810,000 tonnes of groundfish was taken in 1968. Eager to tap a resource on its own doorstep, the Canadian government declared a nine-mile limit in 1964, a 12-mile limit in 1970, then a 200-mile limit in 1977, and encouraged massive investment. The number of people engaged in the fisheries began to rise for the first time in over a century.

The expansion of employment in the fisheries notwithstanding, most of the jobs created in the new 'golden age' were in the burgeoning trade and service sec-tors, and often tied to state spending. By the early 1960s government employment accounted for over 100,000 jobs in the Atlantic region—more than forestry and mining combined. The Department of Defence, its budgets fattened by spending associated with the Korean and Cold wars, employed 41,000 Atlantic Canadians in 1961. Many military bases received a new lease on life, and several new ones, such as CFB Gagetown in New Brunswick, were established. While Nova Scotia led the region in dependence on defence jobs—over 11 per cent of its labour force was employed in defence in 1961—all four Atlantic provinces benefited econom-ically from the federal government's decision to locate more than one-quarter of the nation's armed forces on the east coast.

The transition from primary to tertiary industries was difficult for many Atlantic Canadians. Those displaced from primary industries often lacked the skills required by the available jobs, and had to find work outside the region. Increasingly, skilled employment went to qualified immigrants. Employment in areas tradition-ally dominated by women—clerical, teaching, nursing, social work—expanded rap-idly, and as more women entered the paid workforce, their subordinate positions and unfair wage scales caused concern, as did changing gender relations within the family. At the same time the region's Aboriginal, Acadian, and African minorities questioned their unequal access to new economic opportunities.

The human costs of economic transformation were alleviated in part by government intervention in the form of Ottawa's welfare-state policies: universal family allowances (introduced in 1944), old age pensions (1951), hospital insurance (1957) and Medicare (1968), as well as the Canada pension (1965) and social assistance (1966) plans. Unemployment insurance expanded in the post-war period to cover a growing number of Canadian workers, including the seasonally unemployed. For those who never had much disposable income, these programs often meant the difference between dignified subsistence and outright destitution.

Political leaders saw formal education as the key to success in the new economy, and focused energy and funds on educational infrastructure. In the 1950s school enrolments in Atlantic Canada grew from 338,364 to 485,051, with most of the so-called baby boomers attending large new consolidated institutions. Vocational schools proliferated, and universities were transformed. In the 1940s most Atlantic Canadian universities were small, private operations, often with religious affiliations. By 1970 Atlantic Canada boasted an impressive network of state-funded universities and a total enrolment of 15,820 students, up from just 5,811 a decade before. The Maritime Provinces Higher Education Commission was established to control escalating costs and duplication of programs but university enrolments and budgets continued to rise, making higher education one of the most important industries in the region.

People's Politics

Businessmen, politicians, and bureaucrats were not the only ones responsible for the changes taking place in Atlantic Canada. Ordinary people also had an impact. Established organizations such as churches and unions adjusted to rapidly changing conditions, and new organizations to protest developments and encourage reform sprouted like mushrooms across the Atlantic Canadian landscape.

Structural changes in the workforce were reflected in the fortunes of the labour movement. From a high of 32 per cent in 1953, union membership dropped to a low of 21 per cent in the early 1960s. As white-collar workers—teachers, nurses, and government employees—began signing union cards, the percentage rose again. By the 1980s Newfoundland had the highest proportion of organized labour in the region—37 per cent—primarily because of a 1971 decision to grant collective bargaining rights in the fishery. The Newfoundland Fishermen, Food, and Allied Workers, under its feisty leader Richard Cashin, fought two successful actions: a strike at Burgeo in 1971 and a massive work stoppage by trawler crews in 1974–5. In Canso a protracted strike led by the United Fishermen and Allied Workers' Union in 1970 won concessions in prices and berthing facilities, only to be challenged by the Canadian Food and Allied Workers Union, which wanted to represent workers in all facets of the fisheries.

The fact that the region's business and government leaders tended to treat ordinary people as just another natural resource helped to build support for the New Democratic Party. Created in 1961 through a marriage of the old CCF and organized labour, the NDP gradually gained strength in the region. Support came initially from Cape Breton but soon spread elsewhere as white-collar workers began reconsidering their traditional political allegiances.

By the early 1970s the voice of labour had strengthened considerably. When Nigadoo Mines near Bathurst, New Brunswick, announced in January 1972 that it was suspending operations and throwing 300 employees out of work, it provoked an angry outburst from local people, who organized a 'Day of Concern'. Attended by Jean Marchand, the minister responsible for DREE; Premier Hatfield; and the leaders of both federal and provincial opposition parties, it sparked the creation of a $10-million temporary make-work program. Together, the protest and the response it received were testimony to the political climate of the day, when it was widely accepted that all levels of government had a responsibility to address poverty and unemployment.

The Day of Concern also reflected complex developments in New Brunswick's francophone community. Although not all francophones in the Maritimes were descended from Acadians, most identified with the deeply rooted Acadian heritage. Many working-class and younger francophones were becoming increasingly critical of the gradualist approach taken by their leaders. In 1968 the refusal of Moncton's mayor, Leonard Jones, to consider making the municipality bilingual precipitated a confrontation between the city council and students from the Université de Moncton. Student unrest flared again early in January 1972 after a showing of the National Film Board's *L'Acadie, l'Acadie*, and together with the mine closures, inspired the creation of the Parti Acadien. Although the new party's goal was to politicize francophones rather than to win seats, it fielded candidates in provincial elections between 1974 and 1984, and made headlines with its call for a francophone province—'Acadie'—in northeastern New Brunswick. Premier Hatfield's implementation of sections of the Official Languages Act helped to defuse some of the anger while confirming, once and for all, the bilingual character of the province.

Considerably fewer in numbers than their New Brunswick counterparts, francophones in Nova Scotia and Prince Edward Island had more reason to be concerned about their cultural survival. While 90 per cent of those of French heritage in New Brunswick claimed French as their mother tongue in 1960, only 45 per cent did so in Nova Scotia and Prince Edward Island. Francophones in Nova Scotia formed the Fédération Acadienne de la Nouvelle-Écosse in 1967, while the Société Saint-Thomas-d'Aquin, established in Prince Edward Island in 1919, took on a more active political role. In 1968 the Island's legislature became officially bilingual, and all four provinces gradually made concessions in the area of French-language schooling. Francophone groups began to organize in Newfoundland and Labrador during the early 1970s, forming the Fédération francophone de Terre-Neuve et du Labrador in 1973. With Moncton serving as the capital of the larger regional Acadie, French-language radio, television, arts, and cultural expression flourished.

As issues of human rights and social justice became part of the political agenda, members of the Black minority began to protest their second-class status. The Nova Scotia Association for the Advancement of Coloured People was organized in 1945, and the following year it raised money to help Viola Desmond fight segregation in the province's movie theatres. Although the case was thrown out of

Student unrest hit the Atlantic region in February 1968, when students at the Université de Moncton boycotted classes for ten days to protest fee increases and then (with the silent blessing of university presidents) led a province-wide 'sit-in' at government offices in Fredericton. Centre d'études acadiennes, Université de Moncton.

court on a technicality, the incident generated so much negative publicity that laws endorsing racial discrimination were soon abandoned. In 1954 the Nova Scotia government, spurred by the civil rights movement in the United States, quietly dropped a clause in the province's education act sanctioning separate Black schools, and the last segregated school was closed in the early 1960s. New Brunswick's smaller Black community formed its own Association for the Advancement of Coloured People in 1959. In the 1960s all provinces in the region passed human rights legislation and established monitoring agencies.

Encouraged by the Black Power movement in the United States and galvanized by the decision of Halifax city council to demolish the Black community of Africville, African Nova Scotians stepped up their efforts to fight discrimination

Africville

The plight of Blacks in Nova Scotia received international attention when the city of Halifax decided to demolish Africville. Located on the shores of Bedford Basin, Africville had been home to Halifax's Black population since the mid-nineteenth century. The community had been shamefully neglected. The city provided no water and sewage services or garbage collection, and had located the municipal dump nearby. Even after a serious fire in December 1947 drew attention to the lack of a water supply, the city authorities refused to act.

In 1962, without consulting them, the city council decided to relocate the people living in Africville and to use the site for industrial development. The residents' protests caught the attention of human rights activists. In 1965 both the CBC and *Maclean's* offered critical commentary, and in 1969 representatives of the US-based Black Panther movement arrived to lend support. Aaron Carvery, the last resident to reach a settlement with the city, was invited to City Hall in December 1969 and shown a 'suitcase full of money tied up in neat bundles'—$14,000—as an inducement to move.[5] He eventually received an apology for this outrageous attempt at a bribe, but the city pressed on with its plans for relocation. Most whites and a few Blacks argued that urban renewal was a necessary prelude to a better future for all Haligonians.

Residents were compensated for their property and offered alternative housing, but they resented being treated as if they were incompetent to decide what was best for them. The use of garbage trucks instead of moving vans to relocate some members of the community seemed to symbolize the city's attitude. The residents also feared the loss of community, but, if anything, the destruction of Africville galvanized community spirit. Because of the prolonged struggle, Africville has not been forgotten and has been immortalized in books, films, songs. Every year a picnic is held on the site of the former community, part of which is now a park.

and crippling poverty. The Black United Front was founded in Halifax in 1969, after a visit to the city by Stokeley Carmichael and other leaders of the Black Panthers. Working with grants from both the federal and provincial governments, BUF leaders sponsored workshops and projects designed to help African Nova Scotians to increase both their self-esteem and their material well-being. The Black Cultural Society, established in 1977, accomplished one of its major goals in 1983 with the opening of the Black Cultural Centre in Dartmouth.

Aboriginal people also adopted a more activist approach. After three centuries of decline, their numbers in the region had finally begun to increase, reaching 18,000 by 1981. Some of the more abhorrent features of the Indian Act had been dropped after the Second World War, and in 1960 status Indians were enfranchised. Ottawa's desire to abolish both the Indian Act and Indian status, articulated in an infamous 1969 White Paper, provoked a national effort to redress long-standing grievances and resist assimilation. By this time, the Union of New Brunswick Indians (1967) and Union of Nova Scotia Indians (1969) had been established.

In Newfoundland and Labrador, more funds were invested in Aboriginal health, education, and housing. In the late 1950s, however, the provincial government decided, in concert with the Grenfell and Moravian missions, to close the northern Inuit settlements of Nutak and Hebron and move their residents to communities farther south. Neither the people who were to be relocated nor the people who were to receive them were consulted. As the Labrador Inuit Association has put it: 'The government told [us] that our social and economic welfare would be improved. Instead, a social, cultural and economic disintegration occurred, the effects of which can be felt to this day.'[6] In 2005 Premier Danny Williams issued a formal apology on behalf of the government for the way the decision was made and the difficulties that the people and their descendents experienced as a result of the move.

The consequences of relocation were perhaps even more devastating for the semi-nomadic Innu who in the 1960s were settled at Sheshatshiu and Davis Inlet. Arguably no Aboriginal group in the region suffered more in this period than the Innu. The distress that accompanied the collapse of the fur trade was compounded by high rates of tuberculosis and the loss of traditional lands—without any compensation—to mining operations in western Labrador, military installations at Goose Bay, and the Churchill Falls project, including the enormous Smallwood

Biography: Sandra Lovelace

Sandra Lovelace was born in 1947 on the Tobique Reserve in New Brunswick. In 1970 she married an American, Bernard Lovelace, and moved to California. When her marriage ended a few years later, she and her children returned to Tobique, only to be denied access to housing and other rights provided under the Indian Act. Like all Native women subject to the Indian Act, Sandra Lovelace had lost her Indian status when she married a non-Native man.

In cooperation with Native women's organizations, as well as non-Native women's groups, Lovelace fought the case in the courts, and in 1979 she appealed to the United Nations. Two years later Canada was found in breach of the International Covenant on Civil and Political Rights. The Canadian government was slow to respond, in part because First Nations men opposed giving women equal rights to scarce reserve resources.

Under the Charter of Rights and Freedoms, adopted in 1982, double standards such as those sanctioned by the Indian Act could no longer be condoned. The Indian Act was finally revised in 1985 to ensure that Native women who marry non-Native men and their children no longer lose their status. In 2005 Sandra Lovelace was appointed to the Canadian Senate, the first Aboriginal person from Atlantic Canada to be awarded this privilege.

Reservoir. In 1973 both the Labrador Inuit Association and the Federation of Newfoundland and Labrador Indians were formed. The latter soon split into island and Labrador components, and in 1990 the Labrador Innu adopted the name Innu Nation.

Despite its poor economic prospects, the Atlantic region continued to attract immigrants in the post-war period. War brides and their children, most of them of British background, were followed by refugees and displaced persons from Europe and domestic workers from the Caribbean. After Canada's immigration laws were liberalized in the 1960s, people from all over the world began arriving in Atlantic Canada. Their presence had little impact on the overall cultural mix, in part because many of them moved on. With the exception of the Dutch, who tended to take up farming, most of those who stayed settled in urban centres. During the Vietnam War (1965–75) 'draft dodgers' from the United States slipped across the border, and many of them stayed.

In the Atlantic provinces as across North America, some of the most dramatic developments in the post-war period involved the changing status of women. Women flocked to jobs in the paid labour force, and began entering the universities in unprecedented numbers. Meanwhile, the plummeting birth rate, escalating divorce rate, and increasing incidence of single motherhood prompted traditionalists to make dire predictions about the future of the family. Most women now had no more than two children, if they had any at all, and increasingly both parents worked outside the home. The 'traditional' family was further challenged by gay and lesbian relationships that came out of the closet following federal legislative reforms in 1969.

In this period, Atlantic Canadian women joined their counterparts throughout North America in breaking down the barriers that stood in the way of achieving equality. Provincial branches of national women's organizations pushed for a variety of reforms. By the late 1960s, married women were eligible for civil service jobs that had previously been denied them, and quotas restricting women's entry into law, medical, and engineering schools had disappeared. Aboriginal women throughout Canada gained the right to serve on band councils in 1951. The achievement of Helena Squires, who had sat in the Newfoundland House of Assembly between 1930 and 1932, was finally matched in Nova Scotia when the former Kentville mayor Gladys Porter was elected to the legislature in 1960. In 1953 Muriel Fergusson, Fredericton's first female alderman, was named to the Senate, and in 1972 she became the first woman to be appointed Speaker. The Royal Commission on the Status of Women, which reported in 1970, eventually prompted provincial governments to establish commissions and advisory councils to address women's issues, to legislate equal pay and a fairer division of marital property upon divorce, and to fund women's centres and shelters.

Threats to peace, common during the Cold War, inspired regional responses. In 1960 Halifax became one of the first cities in Canada to form a branch of the Voice of Women, an organization devoted to peace and disarmament. Three years earlier, Pugwash, Nova Scotia, had been the site of a unique effort to put an end the nuclear madness that defined the Cold War. Twenty-two scientists from around the world, including the United States and the Soviet Union, converged on the summer home of the Nova Scotia-born industrialist Cyrus Eaton to discuss nuclear disarmament. In 1995 the Pugwash Conference on Science and World Affairs was awarded the Nobel Peace Prize for its efforts on behalf of world peace.

Environmental issues also inspired political activism. As early as 1962, in her groundbreaking book *Silent Spring*, Rachel Carson had singled out the 'rivers of death' created in New Brunswick by aerial pesticide spraying. In the 1970s Betty Keddy mobilized opposition to budworm spraying in New Brunswick, while Elizabeth May led a similar campaign in Cape Breton. At the same time, animal rights groups, especially the International Fund for Animal Welfare led by New Brunswick's Brian Davies, mounted a high-profile attack on the seal hunt, arguing that the practice of clubbing white-coated pups was brutal and threatened an endangered species merely to satisfy the fashion industry. Greenpeace joined in, bringing the French movie star Brigitte Bardot to the ice floes in 1977 and calling for boycotts of seal products in Europe and the United States. Newfoundlanders, for their part, were outraged both by the threat the anti-sealing campaign posed for the rural economy and by what they saw as an assault on their culture. Among the responses was a theatre production by The Mummers' Troupe in St John's entitled 'They Club Seals, Don't They?'

Cultural Awakenings

Theatre was not the only cultural industry that showed a new vitality in the 1970s. High and low, élite and popular, the arts flourished as never before, and the themes that artists addressed often reflected a growing interest in local history and heritage. Improvements in education, nation-wide radio and television networks, and federal support for Canadian culture all fed into a cultural awakening that continues to generate excitement in the Atlantic region and beyond.

In music the region has produced a roster of stars that stretches back to the 1930s, when Nova Scotia's Wilf Carter became a popular radio performer, better known in the US as Montana Slim. Hank Snow was a regular at the Grand Ole Opry in the 1950s, and Anne Murray rose to international fame with her rendition of 'Snowbird', composed by Prince Edward Island's Gene MacLellan. Carroll Baker won numerous Juno Awards, Stompin' Tom Connors became a Canadian icon, and although Stan Rogers grew up in Ontario, many of his songs were inspired by his Maritime roots. Edith Butler introduced Acadian folk songs to international audiences, while the Celtic traditions of Newfoundland and Cape Breton have inspired a remarkable number of popular performers, from The Wonderful Grand Band, Figgy Duff, and Rawlins Cross to Rita MacNeil, John Allan Cameron, the Rankins, and Natalie MacMaster. Following in the wake of Portia White, a gifted contralto who performed at New York's Carnegie Hall in 1944, African Nova Scotian musicians such as the a capella group Four the Moment found enthusiastic audiences.

Halifax's Neptune Theatre opened in 1963, and in 1964 the centennial of the Charlottetown Conference launched the successful Charlottetown Festival

In 1944 the Nova Scotia-born contralto Portia White (1910–68), who had already won national acclaim, made her New York debut. She later toured the United States, Europe, and the Caribbean. LAC, PA-192783

Theatre. Theatre New Brunswick followed in 1968. In St John's, the success of CODCO and the Mummers' Troupe, based in a former downtown union hall, laid the groundwork for the team that made *This Hour Has 22 Minutes*, a television phenomenon in the 1990s.

In the post-war period a new cultural maturity was being reflected in the regionally grounded work of poets and novelists such as Milton Acorn, Ernest Buckler, Harold Horwood, Percy Janes, Antonine Maillet, Alden Nowlan, and Ted Russell. They laid the foundation for the next generation of literary greats, which included George Elliott Clarke, Wayne Johnston, Rita Joe, Anne Marie Mac-Donald, Alistair MacLeod, David Adams Richards, Herménégilde Chiasson, and Maxine Tynes. Regional themes also inspired filmmakers. Don Shebib's award-winning film *Goin' Down the Road* (1969) exposed the plight of working-class Maritimers in Ontario, and Gordon Pinsent's *John and the Missus* (1974) was a gripping portrayal of outport resettlement in Newfoundland.

Artists such as Alex Colville and his students at Mount Allison University, including Christopher Pratt, Mary Pratt, and Tom Forrestall, developed representational art in a direction that has come to be called 'Atlantic realism'. New Brunswick artists such as Miller Brittain often portrayed the harsher side of Maritime life. The same was true of David Blackwood, who gained widespread acclaim for his images of the seal hunt and other aspects of traditional life on Newfoundland's northeast coast. In Prince Edward Island, artists such as Erica Rutherford revealed new ways of looking at the island landscape. By the end of the twentieth century, Native artists who had long been excluded from formal channels of art education and marketing in the region began to exhibit their work, among them Ned Bear, Shirley Bear, Teresa Marshall, Leonard Paul, Jonathan Sark, Alan Syliboy, and Gilbert Hay. The region's self-taught folk artists, including Maud Lewis, Joseph Norris, Arch Williams, and Joseph Cullen, added yet another dimension of locally rooted artistic expression.

In Newfoundland in particular, a large part of the cultural awakening involved questioning the assumption that Confederation was an unqualified good. By the mid-1970s, a new awareness of the province's history and culture was fuelling a sense of Newfoundland-Labrador nationalism and identity that would have serious implications for federal–provincial relations.

Conclusion

If the period from 1949 to 1975 represents Atlantic Canada's golden age, it was gold plated rather than pure metal. Modernization had brought impressive changes, many of the old economic and social patterns remained in place. Outmigration was slowing but not halted, economic stagnation was confronted but not vanquished, and 'have-not' status was still an ever-present reality. What *was* striking about the period, in retrospect, was the conviction that progress was possible. The closing years of the twentieth century would test the convictions of even the most enduring optimist.

Chapter 15

The Atlantic Region in a Global Context, 1975–2005

In 1973 a global oil crisis precipitated by the Organization of Petroleum Exporting Countries, brought an end to the post-war 'golden age'. Two years later, rising government deficits and 'stagflation' prompted Ottawa to impose wage and price controls and cut back on its spending. Meanwhile, neo-liberal economic arguments against government intervention, including assistance to poor people and outlying regions, gradually became the conventional wisdom. Policy-makers across the political spectrum focused on 'restructuring', and Atlantic Canadians faced new challenges no less daunting than those that had accompanied industrialization in the nineteenth century.

Contexts: National and International

The election of Margaret Thatcher in Great Britain (1979), Ronald Reagan in the United States (1980), and Brian Mulroney in Canada (1984) signalled the emergence of a neo-liberal order in the major Western nations, which in 1989 was reinforced by the collapse of communism in Eastern Europe. A comprehensive Free Trade Agreement between Canada and the United States took effect the same year and was extended to Mexico in 1992. Atlantic Canadians had no option but to adjust to 'globalization'—the code word for the movement to impose free-market capitalist principles not merely on international trade relations but on the internal affairs of nations around the world.

To make matters worse for 'have-not' provinces, Canadian federalism was facing serious challenges. They began with the election in 1976 of the Parti Québécois and continued through the sovereignty referendum of 1980 and the years of constitutional turmoil that followed. By the mid-1980s, western Canada—already outraged by Trudeau's national energy strategy—had become so alienated by Ottawa's apparent preoccupation with central Canada that it was ready to embrace its own regionally-oriented party. Founded in 1987, the Reform Party attracted so much support, especially in the two westernmost provinces, that in 1993 it effectively supplanted the Progressive Conservatives in Ottawa. Staunch proponents of the neo-liberal agenda, Reformers were outspoken in their criticism of government 'handouts' and those who received them—notably Atlantic Canadians.

In this hostile climate Atlantic political leaders found it increasingly difficult to get their issues on the national agenda, especially once Ottawa started slashing

Timeline

1973	Global oil crisis ends post-war boom.
1976	Parti Québécois wins power in Québec.
1977	200-mile limit declared.
1980	Québec referendum on sovereignty-association.
1982	Constitution Act; 84 crew members lost on the *Ocean Ranger*.
1985	Atlantic Accord; Report of the Royal Commission on Canada's Economic Union and Development Prospects.
1987	Atlantic Canada Opportunities Agency established; Reform Party founded; Meech Lake Accord.
1988	Canada–US Free Trade Agreement signed.
1992	Cod moratorium; Charlottetown Accord; North American Free Trade Agreement signed.
1993	Westray Mine disaster kills 26 men.
1995	Second Québec referendum.
1997	Confederation Bridge opens.
1999	Supreme Court decision in the Marshall case.
2001	Terrorists attack the World Trade Centre and Pentagon.
2003	Royal Commission Report on Newfoundland and Labrador's Place in Canada; Supreme Court rules on undersea boundary between Nova Scotia and Newfoundland.
2005	Federal agreement with Nova Scotia and Newfoundland on sharing royalties from offshore development; Nunatsiavut agreement.

transfer payments in an effort to bring the federal deficit under control. Beginning in the mid-1990s—just after the collapse of the cod fishery—these cutbacks had devastating consequences for a region with few financial resources to fall back on.

Globalization took a dramatic turn on 11 September 2001 when Muslim extremists attacked the Pentagon in Washington and the World Trade Centre in New York. In the days immediately following this tragedy, Atlantic Canadians opened their homes to thousands of passengers who were stranded when their planes were forced to land at the nearest available airport. The humiliated Republican President, George W. Bush, authorized the invasion of Afghanistan and Iraq, and drew a line between those who were for and those who were against him in his 'war on terror'. Since Canadians had refused to participate directly in the war against Iraq, relations with the United States became strained, and Atlantic

Canadians worried that their major trading partner might retaliate in ways that would damage their fragile economies.

Variations on the Theme of Neo-liberalism

Most Western nations tolerated the growing power of the state in the decades following the Second World War, but there had always been critics of this trend. Neo-liberals argued that Keynesian policies—deficit spending, tax incentives, transfer payments—created rigidities and inefficiencies that would cripple economic growth in a capitalist system. If governments simply reduced taxes, controlled inflation, and let the marketplace adjust to changing conditions, the economy would find an appropriate balance.

When inflation and economic stagnation arrived simultaneously in the 1970s, confidence in Keynes, planners, and interventionism declined. North American businesses, facing severe competition from Pacific Rim 'tigers', threatened to move their operations to developing countries unless taxes were reduced, environmental regulations relaxed, and social programs pared back. Now that satellite and computer communications made it possible to transfer assets instantaneously around the world, 'transnational' corporations could easily defy any one government's efforts to control their activities. This pattern was nothing new to Atlantic Canadians, who for nearly a century had watched the head offices of their banks, factories, and railways move to Montréal and Toronto, but this time the entire country seemed to be at risk. Ottawa had to respond.

In 1982 the Trudeau government established a Royal Commission on Canada's Economic Union and Development Prospects, chaired by Donald Macdonald, a former Liberal finance minister. The commission's 1985 report supported neo-liberal demands for a more flexible economy capable of adjusting to global trends and new technologies, and recommended both free trade with the United States and an end to universal welfare state programs. The commission's suggestions for mitigating the human costs of economic restructuring were forgotten, and the principle of regional equity faded into the background. It was each province for itself in the brave new 'information age'.

Atlantic premiers made no coordinated effort to influence the Macdonald Commission's findings or the way its recommendations were implemented. Instead, they tried to reposition their provinces to compete in a global market place. Motivated by the expansion of the fisheries and the discovery of the Hibernia oil field in the late 1970s, Premier Brian Peckford asserted Newfoundland's ownership of offshore resources on the basis of its status in international law before 1949, and insisted that the province should have equal control with Ottawa over offshore developments. The Trudeau government refused to relinquish federal control of offshore resources, and the Supreme Court in 1984 supported his contention that Ottawa had both ownership and exclusive jurisdiction.

The Progressive Conservatives, who came to power in 1984, were willing to negotiate. With the assistance of John Crosbie, the colourful and outspoken Newfoundland member of the Mulroney cabinet, accords were signed in 1985

The Costs of Development

In the winter of 1982, 84 crew members lost their lives when Mobil Oil's rig *Ocean Ranger* capsized in a fierce storm on the Hibernia oil field. This tragedy underscored the reality that new sea-based industries were no less life-threatening than the ones they had replaced. As in previous periods, human resources in the region were sometimes sacrificed to the gods of corporate investment.

This was certainly the case for the workers at the Westray coal mine in Pictou County, Nova Scotia, whose complaints about rock slides, cave-ins, and dangerous levels of methane gas had been largely ignored. When an explosion destroyed the mine in 1993, eight months into its operation, 26 men were killed. The mine owners were not held responsible for their negligence.

Nor were company owners required to shoulder the environmental costs of their enterprises.

Among the worst legacies of industrial development in the Atlantic region are the Sydney tar ponds, reservoirs for the toxic brew of chemicals—benzene, kerosene, naphthalene, PCBs—produced as waste by the coke ovens and furnaces used in Sydney's steel processing industry for more than 80 years. The size of three city blocks, the tar ponds are especially troubling to the people living nearest to them, who have suffered a wide range of physical problems, including severe headaches, nosebleeds, breathing problems, birth defects, miscarriages, and cancer. Finally, in 2004 the federal and provincial governments announced that they would spend up to $400 million dollars on a 10-year plan to clean up the site.

with Newfoundland and Nova Scotia. While the agreements offered fewer benefits from offshore developments than Crosbie had hoped for, they signalled a less rigid attitude in Ottawa towards accommodating the interests of have-not provinces. The creation in 1987 of the Atlantic Canada Opportunities Agency (ACOA), which replaced the Department of Regional Industrial Expansion (DRIE) established in 1982, was a further indication of Ottawa's intention to decentralize regional development efforts.

Federalism in Crisis

Federal–provincial relations were further complicated by the seemingly endless constitutional talks that followed the 1980 Québec referendum on sovereignty-association. To blunt Québec's desire for independence, Trudeau had promised constitutional reform. Since any change to Canada's constitution still had to be passed by the British parliament, the power to amend the constitution had to be brought home to Canada, and an amending formula worked out between the federal government and the provinces. Trudeau also wanted the new constitution to include a Charter of Rights and Freedoms—a proposal that Québec and most other provinces perceived as an attempt to curtail provincial powers. Only Richard Hatfield in New Brunswick and William Davis in Ontario were initially prepared to support the legislation. Trudeau declared that he would proceed with or without provincial support, and the majority of premiers—fearing that Trudeau might get his reforms without making any concessions to the provinces—came to terms. The Constitution Act (1982) passed, and Québec cried betrayal.

Determined to better Trudeau, Mulroney set out to broker a deal that would 'bring Québec into the constitution'. Ultimately, the Meech Lake Accord (1987–90) and Charlottetown (1992) Accord (named after the places where they were negotiated) both failed, but Mulroney's efforts to secure a free trade agreement with the United States succeeded, ending more than a century of protectionism in Canadian trade policy.

The Atlantic premiers went their separate ways on constitutional and trade issues. By the time the deadline for ratifying Meech Lake was about to expire, Newfoundland's legislature had already accepted it. The new Liberal premier, Clyde Wells (elected in 1989) strongly opposed the accord, arguing that it trampled on provincial rights and failed to address regional disparities. The legislature rescinded its ratification and was preparing to hold a free vote when it became clear that Manitoba would not pass its legislation in time to save the accord from expiry.

Wells also opposed the Canada–United States Free Trade Agreement, but Maritime premiers took a different view. Indeed, New Brunswick's premier, Frank McKenna, defied the federal wing of his party by supporting the deal. Most Atlantic Canadians seemed to agree with Wells. In the 1988 federal election, voters in Atlantic Canada gave only 41 per cent of the popular vote and 12 of their 32 seats to the Progressive Conservatives. Once again the region was out of step with the rest of the country, and the agreement took effect on 1 January 1989.

The stranglehold of majority cultures on high political office in the region was broken in 1986 when Joe Ghiz, whose family came from Lebanon, was sworn in as Liberal premier of Prince Edward Island. He was a popular premier who, like Wells and McKenna, enjoyed the national stage. Ghiz welcomed first ministers to the Island for the talks that produced the Charlottetown Accord in 1992. This time Newfoundland and Alberta held out for Senate reform that would recognize the equality of the provinces. When Québec decided to submit the accord to a binding referendum, Mulroney declared that all Canadians would have a voice. A national referendum was held on 26 October 1992. The Charlottetown Accord was rejected by the majority in all provinces except Newfoundland, New Brunswick, and Prince Edward Island, where voters apparently had had enough of constitutional wrangling.

In 1993 the Liberals returned to power under Jean Chrétien and continued along the same neo-liberal path taken by their Progressive Conservative predecessors. Social programs were cut, unemployment insurance became more difficult to get, and transfer payments decreased. Most provinces were forced to carry the ever-increasing costs of Medicare while slashing education and social services budgets, and reducing public-sector employment.

In the Atlantic provinces, some governments contracted out school construc-

Bruce MacKinnon, 'Oh Please, Oh Please', 1992. As this award-winning cartoon, published in the *Halifax Herald*, suggests, regional fortunes were increasingly tied to those of the United States following the Free Trade agreements of 1989 and 1992. Republished with permission from The Halifax Herald Limited.

tion to private companies, built toll roads, and authorized universities to raise their fees to nearly double what students paid elsewhere in Canada. As a result the gap between rich and poor widened while the line-ups at food banks and welfare offices lengthened. Populations in the region's resource-based communities declined and local economies suffered; but this was the free market at work.

The Fisheries Gutted

Nowhere was the impact of restructuring more keenly felt than in the Atlantic region's many fishing communities. When a 200-mile (370 km) limit was declared in 1977, it looked as if the fisheries would have a bright future. With foreign vessels forbidden to fish within 200 miles of shore, governments had the opportunity to conserve and rebuild fish stocks. At that point scientific estimates of the stock's size were still overly optimistic, so instead of scaling back the Canadian fishery, governments encouraged it to expand. Political considerations no doubt played a role in this decision, along with inflated quotas.

The number of Atlantic Canadians engaged in the fishing industry rose from roughly 31,000 in 1974 to nearly 55,000 in 1980. By the early 1980s Canada was the world's most important fish-exporting country, up from third in 1976, with the Atlantic provinces providing 65 per cent of the national total. At the same time, fishing by foreign fleets outside the 200-mile limit, and in the case of France, inside the limit, intensified. During the 1980s both inshore and offshore fishers began to sound the alarm, and scientists reconsidered their estimates. With the collapse of the fish stocks in the late 1980s, Canadian quotas were cut and processing plants shut down. Meanwhile, two corporate giants, Fishery Products International and National Sea, swallowed up their hard-pressed competitors.

In 1992 Fisheries Minister John Crosbie announced a moratorium on cod fishing and stringent controls on the exploitation of other fish stocks. With 1,300 Atlantic communities almost entirely dependent on the fishery, its collapse precipitated a crisis of titanic proportions. In Newfoundland and Labrador, where much of the expansion in the fisheries had occurred, nearly 20,000 people were thrown out of work and the survival of dozens of communities became doubtful.

The crisis in the domestic fishery heightened Atlantic Canadians' resentment of what appeared to be irresponsible overfishing by foreign (mainly European) trawlers in international waters just outside the 200-mile limit. Spanish and Portuguese vessels in particular were increasing their catch of turbot—a species that, according to scientists, was now endangered. When Spain and Portugal, backed by the European Union, refused in 1995 to accept the reduced quotas set by the Northwest Atlantic Fisheries Organization (NAFO), the Canadian government—in which Newfoundlander Brian Tobin was fisheries minister—decided to move aggressively to conserve the stocks. Tobin's much-publicized efforts to protect the lowly turbot led the Spanish to talk of piracy and even war. Eventually an agreement was reached to control fishing on the Grand Banks more effectively, but overfishing persists.

Native Claims

A new factor in resource development was the assertion of Aboriginal claims both to land and to specific hunting and fishing rights. In the Maritimes such claims were based on treaties signed with the British in 1725–6 and 1760–1, and on the possession of Aboriginal rights that had never been extinguished. The Mi'kmaq and Maliseet, and Passamaquoddy found the courts receptive. The Inuit and Innu of Labrador have no treaty rights, and whether Newfoundland Mi'kmaq are covered by the eighteenth-century treaties remains in dispute. But they—and all First Nations—have been sustained in their resolve to redress past injustices by a series of Supreme Count decisions and by Section 35c of the constitution, which recognizes and affirms existing Aboriginal rights.

The Mi'kmaq and Maliseet had repeatedly raised questions about their treaty, land, and resource rights but without success. In 1928 a Nova Scotia judge convicted Chief Gabriel Syliboy for possessing pelts in contravention of the Lands and Forests Act, despite defence claims that he had 'by Treaty the right to hunt and trap at all times'.[1] The situation changed when the Supreme Court ruled in 1990 (*R. v. Sparrow*) that Aboriginal people had the right to fish for subsistence and ceremonial purposes unless the government could demonstrate why limitation was necessary. In response, Ottawa introduced an Aboriginal Fisheries Strategy whereby communal fishing licences were distributed to First Nations in Atlantic Canada

This cartoon by Josh Beutel, which appeared in the Saint John *Telegraph Journal*, 16 March 1985, captures some of the frustration that erupted over issues of official languages in the province of New Brunswick. PANB MC2806-1861.

and British Columbia. Two Mi'kmaq communities—Membertou and Afton—refused to sign licensing agreements, arguing that treaty rights secured in 1761 superseded federal fisheries legislation.

In 1993 the Department of Fisheries and Oceans (DFO) charged Donald Marshall Jr of Membertou for catching eels out of season, fishing without a licence, and selling eels without a licence. The case eventually reached the Supreme Court, which dismissed the charges. It was a landmark ruling, reaffirming the integrity of eighteenth-century treaties and confirming the Mi'kmaq right to make a moderate living from the fishery. By extension, the Mi'kmaq could claim access to other ocean resources and to hunting. The firestorm that followed this decision forced the Supreme Court to qualify its judgment to the extent of arguing that the federal government had the power to restrict even the right to a 'moderate livelihood' if the Crown could justify the regulation on the 'grounds of public importance'.

DFO officials would now be obliged to negotiate fisheries agreements rather than impose them on the Mi'kmaq. Since the DFO was slow to respond, the

Mi'kmaq in some areas began fishing lobster out of season. In St Mary's Bay, Nova Scotia, Native and non-Native fishers negotiated an agreement to jointly manage the lobster fishery. Elsewhere, though, conflict often prevailed. When the Mi'kmaq of Esgenoopetits (Burnt Church), New Brunswick, laid lobster traps in the fall of 1999, non-Natives responded by destroying their traps, attacking their property, and vandalizing fish plants that accepted lobsters from Native fishers. The federal government tried to establish quotas for both sides, but tensions continued.

Meanwhile, Thomas Peter Paul, a New Brunswick Maliseet, tested the right of Aboriginal people to take forest resources from Crown land for commercial purposes. The New Brunswick Court of Appeal upheld Paul's conviction, and the Supreme Court refused to accept an appeal. Undaunted, the Mi'kmaq continued to exercise what they saw as their treaty right to commercially exploit Crown timber resources. In July 2005 the Supreme Count handed down rulings in two cases relating to Mi'kmaq logging rights. The appeals by Stephen Frederick Marshall and 34 other Mi'kmaq in Nova Scotia and Joshua Bernard in New Brunswick were denied on the grounds that there was no connection between the commercial cutting of timber and Aboriginal trading activities at the time the treaties were signed.

The Conne River Mi'kmaq (Miawpukek) in Newfoundland also launched a claim to about 20 per cent of the island in 1996. The Newfoundland Supreme Court ruled in 2003 (in the case of *R. vs. Drew*) that there was insufficient evidence of a Mi'kmaq presence in the area before the arrival of Europeans to sustain the claim. The decision has been appealed and a ruling was still pending in 2005.

A complex situation developed in Labrador. In 1977 the Innu Nation and the Labrador Inuit Association (LIA) filed overlapping land claims. Negotiations with the LIA began in 1988, but an agreement in principle was not reached until 2001. The settlement was no doubt encouraged by the discovery in 1993 of huge nickel deposits at Voisey's Bay, just south of the Inuit town of Nain. In January 2005 a treaty was signed that gave the Labrador Inuit substantial control over the northern coast, an area named Nunatsiavut ('our beautiful land'). The Innu claim to a large part of Nitassinan (including Voisey's Bay)—their ancestral homeland in Labrador and Québec—has proceeded even more slowly.

Both of these cases have been complicated by the intervention of the Labrador Métis Nation, founded in 1985, which in 1991 filed its own claim to Labrador south of Nain. The Métis people's claim to distinct Aboriginal status has been rejected by the provincial and federal governments, and criticized by both Innu and Inuit. As a result, the validity of their land claim remains undecided.

Pulling Against Gravity

No matter what strategy its political leaders tried in this period, the region remained an area of high unemployment, low wages, and uncertain prospects. Governing a have-not province was, as the political scientist Donald J. Savoie has suggested, like pulling against the forces of gravity.[2] Capital investment and human resources were irresistibly attracted to established centres of economic development. Try as they might, political leaders usually lost the tug-of-war with national and global economic forces—and the support of voters to boot.

In 1987 New Brunswick voters annihilated Richard Hatfield's Conservatives, giving every seat in the legislature to Frank McKenna's Liberals. McKenna was particularly aggressive in his efforts to attract call centres to the province, but such low-paying operations did little to change the overall economic picture. In the next provincial election the Liberals held on to most of the seats, but the Confederation of Regions (COR) Party, which attacked official bilingualism, managed to become the official opposition. Internal bickering soon made COR ineffective on the political scene. Following McKenna's resignation in 1997, the party collapsed and a reorganized Progressive Conservative Party swept back to power in 1999 under Bernard Lord. Unable to slay the dragon of underdevelopment and reluctant to stand up to private corporations that hiked insurance rates to obscene levels, Lord managed only a one-seat majority in the 2003 election.

Prince Edward Island experienced similar swings from the Progressive Conservatives to the Liberals and back again. In 1979 J. Angus MacLean, who had served as a cabinet minister in the Diefenbaker government, led the Progressive Conservatives to victory on a platform of 'rural renewal'. His efforts to slow the tide of modernity included a moratorium on new shopping malls, breaking a contract with New Brunswick to purchase energy from its Point Lepreau nuclear power plant—the only such station in Atlantic Canada—and a Land Protection Act that restricted individual land holdings to 1000 acres (2471 ha) and corporate holdings to 3,000 acres (7413 ha). The latter policy was aimed specifically at another New Brunswick-based interest—the powerful Irvings—who were building up landholdings to support their processing operations.

When the Liberals, led by Catherine Callbeck, won the 1993 election, Prince Edward Island made history by becoming the first province in Canada to elect a woman as premier. (The leaders of both the other major parties were women as well.) Callbeck's victory was short-lived. Forced to deal with drastic federal cutbacks, she was blamed for the difficulties they caused in a province with a small tax base. In 1996 the Progressive Conservatives, under the leadership of Pat Binns, defeated the Liberals. A native of Saskatchewan, Binns was a farmer who managed to maintain voters' confidence in the primarily rural province through two more provincial elections.

Nova Scotia's political fortunes in the late 1990s suggest the difficulties facing politicians in the two mainline parties. While the good-natured Progressive Conservative Premier John Buchanan managed to hold onto power from 1978 to 1990, his successor Donald Cameron quickly lost ground to the Liberals led by Dr John Savage, who won the 1993 provincial election. Savage too found it impossible to satisfy voter demands in an era defined by government downsizing, and in the next election his party was defeated by the Progressive Conservatives under the leadership of another medical doctor, John Hamm. This time the election results were more complicated, with the NDP emerging as the official opposition. Hamm managed to hang on to power but had to walk a difficult tightrope.

Determined not to suffer the fate of Liberal premiers elsewhere in the Atlantic region, Roger Grimes in Newfoundland and Labrador decided to deflect criticisms of his government by establishing a royal commission to explore how best to renew and strengthen his province's place in Canada. Although the commission's report, tabled in the summer of 2003, clearly summarized the difficult economic situation and offered practical remedies, the response in Ottawa was a polite yawn. Grimes lost a provincial election later that fall to the Progressive Conservatives led by Danny Williams and the commission report was quietly buried.

Williams made national headlines in the fall of 2004 when he abruptly walked out of a federal–provincial conference on equalization policy, claiming that Liberal Prime Minister Paul Martin had reneged on his pre-election promise to give Newfoundland and Nova Scotia a better deal on royalties from offshore development. After three months of posturing, an agreement was finally reached in January 2005 that gave the two have-not provinces most of what they wanted. Newfoundland and Labrador would receive $2 billion and Nova Scotia $830,000 over eight years to compensate them for equalization clawbacks, and the agreement could be extended for a further eight years if the provinces were still receiving equalization payments.

Newfoundland and Nova Scotia collaborated in their efforts to wrest royalty concessions from Ottawa, but they battled each other in the courts to determine the undersea boundary between the two provinces. There was a lot at stake. In 2002 an arbitration tribunal handed down a ruling that gave most of the potentially rich area in dispute to Newfoundland and Labrador. Meanwhile, Ottawa's distribution of scarce fish quotas in the Gulf of St Lawrence produced tensions among competing fishers from Québec, Newfoundland, New Brunswick, and Prince Edward Island.

An Uncertain Future

As in the past, Atlantic Canadians adjusted as best they could to the economic and political forces swirling around them. Out-migration remained a common recourse for the unemployed, the young, and the upwardly mobile. During the 1990s Newfoundland actually declined in population for the first time in recorded history. Other provinces held their own, but unevenly: in areas such as northeastern New Brunswick and Cape Breton the losses were just as precipitous as in Newfoundland. In all four provinces, population and services alike increasingly gravitated towards urban centres; see Tables 15.1 and 15.2.

Three cities in particular were targeted as 'growth centres': St John's, Moncton, and, above all, Halifax. Prosperous, lively, and expanding, Halifax has become a genuine metropolis, home to numerous corporate headquarters, regional federal offices, military installations, educational institutions, and health care facilities, as well as a centre for film and television production. Its hinterland consists of all four provinces, and the other capitals are becoming more or less resentful outports.

Prince Edward Island was finally linked to the mainland with the completion of the Confederation Bridge in 1997. The structure is a magnificent engineering achievement and a rare example of a public service delegated to private initiative

Table 15.1 Population of the Atlantic Provinces, 2001

	Total	Urban		Rural	
Province	population	population	% of total	population	% of total
New Brunswick	729,498	367,902	50.4	361,596	49.6
Newfoundland	512,930	296,196	57.7	216,734	42.3
Nova Scotia	908,007	507,009	55.8	400,998	44.2
Prince Edward Island	135,294	60,675	44.8	74,619	55.2
Total	2,285,729	1,231,782	53.9	1,053,947	46.1

Source: Statistics Canada

Table 15.2 Cities with populations with over 20,000, 2001

Halifax, Nova Scotia	359,111
St. John's, Newfoundland	99,182
Saint John, New Brunswick	69,661
Moncton, New Brunswick	61,046
Fredericton, New Brunswick	47,560
Charlottetown, Prince Edward Island	32,245
Sydney, Nova Scotia	26,083
Corner Brook, Newfoundland	20,103

Source: Statistics Canada

that seems to have succeeded. It is still too soon to say what impact improved communications will have on the island province. Essentially a city-state built around Charlottetown, Prince Edward Island remains the most cohesive of the Atlantic provinces, and polls suggest that, of all Canadians, its people are among those most satisfied with their worldly condition.

What the future holds for the region as a whole is unclear. There are some who support Atlantic or Maritime union, but the preferred strategy, at least among political leaders, is to pursue closer collaboration while remaining separate entities. In 2000 the Council of Maritime Premiers evolved into the Council of Atlantic Premiers, with a renewed mandate for regional cooperation. The jury is still out on whether this strategy will pay dividends in negotiations with Ottawa and with capitalists eager to exploit what is left of the region's resources. Given the continuing strength of neo-liberal perspectives, it may be a long time before provincial governments, either singly or together, will be prepared to tackle the old problem of poverty in the midst of plenty.

The Confederation Bridge finally linked the mainland to Prince Edward Island in 1997. BMPstock.com.

Neo-liberal strategists remain critical of the state's handling of regional development. Demanding lower taxes, less bureaucratic regulation, and more power for private interests, they argue that the heavy hand of the state has stunted the region's growth and led it to focus too much energy on appealing to Ottawa for solutions to regional underdevelopment. Brian Lee Crowley, director of the Atlantic Institute for Market Studies (AIMS), a Halifax-based neo-liberal think tank, has urged business leaders to make the Atlantic provinces the hub of 'Atlantica': a North Atlantic economic zone that would include northern New England and southern Québec—but not Labrador.[3] In a globalized world it seems that all things are possible.

Most policy makers concede that Confederation remains the preferred framework in which to help the Atlantic provinces close the gap between national and regional living standards. Although the gap has not disappeared, it has narrowed considerably since the 1950s. Indeed, economic growth in the region has kept pace, if at a distance, with the spectacular growth of the nation as a whole, and that in itself is a major achievement. So too is the emergence of new industries, including high-tech operations to support offshore development, fish farming, and wineries whose products win international competitions. Whether they can maintain the pace in an increasingly competitive global context is difficult to predict.

Conclusion

Four centuries after the first permanent European settlements were established in the region, Atlantic Canadians face the prospect of responding yet again to forces centred elsewhere. Reform, retrenchment, and restructuring have been the mantra of the new world order, but Atlantic Canada has embraced them more out of necessity than conviction. While a few have been converted to the religion of the unshackled marketplace, many Atlantic Canadians regret the abandonment of the noble dream that made human welfare rather than corporate profits the measure of a civil society. 'Where are we,' asked the Newfoundland writer Moses Harvey in 1885, 'and whither tending?'[4] The answer remains obscure, but the region is undeniably at another turning point in its long history.

Selected Bibliography

The historical literature on Atlantic Canada is so vast that making a selection of sources is a difficult exercise. To conserve space, we have decided not to include the many fine biographies that have appeared in recent years; nor have we listed articles. Additional titles can be found in *Canadian History: A Readers' Guide*, 2 vols (Toronto: University of Toronto Press, 1994). *Volume 1: Beginnings to Confederation* (edited by M. Brook Taylor) is particularly useful for students of Atlantic Canada. Bibliographies are published regularly in the journals *Acadiensis* and *Newfoundland and Labrador Studies*, and the Atlantic Canada Portal (http://atlanticportal.hil.unb.ca) includes a searchable database of the *Acadiensis* bibliographies and an annotated list of websites devoted to Atlantic Canada history and culture. Articles on the region's history can be found in *Acadiensis* and *Newfoundland and Labrador Studies*, as well as *The Nova Scotia Historical Review*, *The Newfoundland Quarterly*, *Them Days*, *The Island Magazine*, *Les Cahiers de la Société historique acadienne*, and *The Cape Breton Magazine*.

General Works

Atlantic Geoscience Society. *The Last Billion Years: A Geological History of the Maritime Provinces*. Halifax: Nimbus Publishing, 2001.

Buckner, Phillip A., and John G. Reid, eds. *The Atlantic Region to Confederation: A History*. Toronto: University of Toronto Press, 1994.

Conrad, Margaret R. and James K. Hiller. *Atlantic Canada: A Region in the Making*. Toronto: Oxford University Press, 2001.

Forbes, E.R., and D.A. Muise, eds. *The Atlantic Provinces in Confederation*. Toronto: University of Toronto Press, 1993.

MacNutt, W.S. *The Atlantic Provinces: The Emergence of Colonial Society, 1712–1857*. Toronto: McClelland and Stewart, 1965.

Reid, John. *Six Crucial Decades: Times of Change in the History of the Maritimes*. Halifax: Nimbus, 1987.

General Essay Collections

Alexander, David. *Atlantic Canada and Confederation: Essays in Canadian Political Economy*, comp. Eric W. Sager, Lewis R. Fischer, and Stuart O. Pierson. Toronto: University of Toronto Press, 1983.

Bercuson, David Jay, and Phillip A. Buckner, eds. *Eastern and Western Perspectives, Papers from the Joint Atlantic Canada/Western Canadian Studies Conference*. Toronto: University of Toronto Press, 1981.

Bogaard, Paul A., ed. *Profiles of Science and Society in the Maritimes prior to 1914*. Fredericton: Acadiensis Press, 1990.

Brym, Robert J., and R. James Sacouman, eds. *Underdevelopment and Social Movements in Atlantic Canada*. Toronto: New Hogtown Press, 1979.

Buckner, P.A., and David Frank, eds. *Atlantic Canada Before Confederation: The Acadiensis Reader*, Vol. 1. 3rd edn. Fredericton: Acadiensis Press, 1999.

———, eds. *Atlantic Canada After Confederation: The Acadiensis Reader*, Vol. 2. 3rd edn. Fredericton: Acadiensis Press, 1999.

Candow, James E., and Carol Corbin, eds. *How Deep is the Ocean? Historical Essays on Canada's Atlantic Fishery*. Sydney: University College of Cape Breton Press, 1997.

Davies, Gwendolyn. *Studies in Maritime Literary History*. Fredericton: Acadiensis Press, 1991.

Fleming, Berkeley, ed. *Beyond Anger and Longing: Community and Development in Atlantic Canada*. Sackville and Fredericton: Centre for Canadian Studies, Mount Allison University and Acadiensis Press, 1988.

Forbes, E.R. *Challenging the Regional Stereotype: Essays on the 20th Century Maritimes.* Fredericton: Acadiensis Press, 1989.

Frank, David, and Gregory S. Kealey, eds. *Labour and Working-Class History in Atlantic Canada: A Reader.* St John's: Institute of Social and Economic Research, 1995.

Guildford, Janet, and Suzanne Morton, eds. *Separate Spheres. Women's Worlds in the 19th Century Maritimes.* Fredericton: Acadiensis Press, 1994.

Inwood, Kris, ed. *Farm, Factory and Fortune: New Studies in the Economic History of the Maritime Provinces.* Fredericton: Acadiensis Press, 1993.

McCann, Larry, ed. *People and Place: Studies of Small Town Life in the Maritimes.* Fredericton: Acadiensis Press, 1987.

————, and Carrie MacMillan, eds. *The Sea and Culture of Atlantic Canada: A Multidisciplinary Sampler.* Sackville: Centre for Canadian Studies, Mount Allison University, 1992.

Martin, Ged, ed. *The Causes of Confederation.* Fredericton: Acadiensis Press, 1990

Murphy, Terrence, and Cyril J. Byrne, eds. *Religion and Identity: The Experience of Irish and Scots Catholics in Atlantic Canada.* St John's: Jesperson Press, 1987.

Rawlyk, G.A., ed. *Historical Essays on the Atlantic Provinces.* Toronto: McClelland and Stewart, 1967.

————, ed. *The Atlantic Provinces and the Problems of Confederation.* St John's: Breakwater, 1979.

Samson, Daniel, ed. *Contested Countryside: Rural Workers and Modern Society in Atlantic Canada.* Fredericton: Acadiensis Press, 1994.

Toner, Peter, ed. *The Irish in Atlantic Canada, 1780–1900.* Fredericton: New Ireland Press, 1991.

Regional Monographs

MacEachern, Alan. *Natural Selections: National Parks in Atlantic Canada, 1935–1970.* Montréal: McGill-Queen's University Press, 2001.

Beattie, Betsy. *Obligations and Opportunity: Single Maritime Women in Boston, 1870–1930.* Montréal: McGill-Queen's University Press, 2000.

Burrill, Gary. *Away: Maritimers in Massachusetts, Ontario, and Alberta.* Montréal: McGill-Queen's University Press, 1992.

Buckner, P.A. *The Transition to Responsible Government: British Policy in British North America, 1815–1850.* Westport CT: Greenwood, 1985.

Kert, Faye. *Prize and Prejudice: Privateering and Naval Prize in Atlantic Canada in the War of 1812.* St John's: International Maritime Economic History Association, 1997.

Fingard, Judith. *Jack in Port: Sailortowns in Eastern Canada.* Toronto: University of Toronto Press, 1982.

Forbes, E.R. *The Maritime Rights Movement: 1919–1927: A Study in Canadian Regionalism.* Montréal: McGill-Queen's Press, 1970.

Howell, Colin D. *Northern Sandlots: A Social History of Maritime Baseball.* Toronto: University of Toronto Press, 1995.

Innis, Harold. *The Cod Fishery: The History of an International Economy.* 1940 rev. Toronto: University of Toronto Press, 1954.

Keefer, Janice Kulyk. *Under Eastern Eyes: A Critical Reading of Maritime Fiction.* Toronto: University of Toronto Press, 1987.

MacLeod, Malcolm. *Connections: Newfoundland's Pre-Confederation Links with Canada and the World.* St. John's: Creative Publishers, 2003.

Ommer, Rosemary. *From Outpost to Outport: A Structural Analysis of the Jersey–Gaspé Cod Fishery, 1767–1914.* Montréal: McGill-Queen's University Press, 1991.

Sager, Eric W., with Gerald E. Panting. *Maritime Capital: The Shipping Industry in Atlantic Canada, 1820–1914.* Montréal: McGill-Queen's University Press, 1990.

Sager, Eric. *Seafaring Labour: The Merchant Marine in Atlantic Canada.* Montréal: McGill-Queen's University Press, 1989.

Saunders, S.A. *The Economic History of the Maritime Provinces.* 1939 rept. Fredericton: Acadiensis Press, 1984.

Taylor, M. Brook. *Promoters, Patriots and Partisans: Historiography in Nineteenth-Century English Canada.* Toronto: University of Toronto Press, 1989.

Thomas, Peter. *Strangers from a Secret Land: The Voyages of the Brig 'Albion' and the Founding of the First Welsh Settlements in Canada.* Toronto: University of Toronto Press, 1986.

Aboriginal Peoples

Bailey, A.G. *The Conflict of European and Eastern Algonkian Cultures, 1504–1700.* 2nd edn. Toronto: University of Toronto Press, 1969.

Coates, Ken. *The Marshall Decision and Native Rights.* Toronto: General Publishing, 2000.

Davis, Stephen A. *The Micmac.* Tantallon: Four East Publications, 1991.

Deal, Michael, and Susan Deal. *Prehistoric Archaeology in the Maritime Provinces, Past and Present.* Research Reports in Archaeology No. 8. Fredericton: Council of Maritime Premiers Maritime Committee on Archaeological Cooperation, 1991.

Gould, G.P., and A.J. Semple, eds. *Our Land: The Maritimes.* Fredericton: Sainte Annes Point Press, 1980.

Henriksen, Georg. *Hunters in the Barrens: the Naskapi on the edge of the white man's world.* St John's: ISER, 1973.

Kleivan, Helge. *The Eskimos of Northeast Labrador: A History of Eskimo–White Relations, 1771–1955.* Olso: Norsk Polarinstitutt, 1966.

Mailhot, José. *The People of Sheshatshit: In the Land of the Innu.* St John's: Institute for Social and Economic Research, 1997.

Marshall, Ingeborg. *The History and Ethnography of the Beothuk.* Montréal: McGill-Queen's University Press, 1996.

McGhee, Robert. *The Last Imaginary Place: A Human History of the Arctic World.* Toronto: Key Porter Books, 2004.

———. *Ancient People of the Arctic.* Vancouver: University of British Columbia Press, 1996.

———. *The Native Peoples of Atlantic Canada: A History of Ethnic Interaction.* Toronto: McClelland and Stewart, 1974.

Pastore, Ralph T. *The Newfoundland Micmacs: A History of their Traditional Life.* St John's: Newfoundland Historical Society, Pamphlet no. 5, 1978.

Paul, Daniel N. *We Were Not the Savages: A Mi'kmaq Perspective on the Collision Between Europe and North American Civilizations.* Rev. ed. Halifax: Fernwood, 2000.

Prins, Harold E.L. *The Mi'kmaq: Resistance, Accommodation, and Cultural Survival.* Fort Worth: Harcourt Brace College Publishers, 1996.

Reid, Jennifer. *Myth, Symbol, and Colonial Encounter: British and Mi'kmaq in Acadia, 1700–1867.* Ottawa: University of Ottawa Press, 1995.

Tuck, James A. *Newfoundland and Labrador Prehistory.* Ottawa: National Museum of Man, National Museums of Canada, 1976.

———. *Maritime Provinces Prehistory.* Ottawa: National Museum of Man, National Museums of Canada, 1984.

Upton, L.F.S. *Micmacs and Colonists: A Study of Imperial Relations, 1713–1760.* Vancouver: University of British Columbia Press, 1979.

Whitehead, Ruth Holmes. *Micmac Quillwork.* Halifax: Nova Scotia Museum, 1982.

———. *The Old Man Told Us: Excerpts from Micmac History, 1500–1950.* Halifax: Nimbus 1991.

Wicken, William C. *Mi'kmaq Treaties on Trial: History, Land and Donald Marshall Junior.* Toronto: University of Toronto Press, 2002.

European Exploration and Early Settlement

Bumsted, J.M. *The People's Clearance: Highland Emigration to British North America, 1770–1815.* Winnipeg: University of Manitoba Press, 1982.

Cell, Gillian T. *English Enterprise in Newfoundland, 1577–1660.* Toronto: University of Toronto Press, 1969.

Conrad, Margaret, ed. *They Planted Well: New England Planters in Maritime Canada.* Fredericton: Acadiensis Press, 1988.

———, ed. *Making Adjustments: Change and Continuity in Planter Nova Scotia, 1759–1800.* Fredericton: Acadiensis Press, 1991.

———, ed. *Intimate Relations: Family and Community in Planter Nova Scotia, 1759–1800.* Fredericton: Acadiensis Press, 1995.

———, and Barry Moody, eds. *Planter Links: Community and Culture in Colonial Nova Scotia.* Fredericton: Acadiensis Press, 2001.

Cook, Ramsay. *1492 and All That: Making a Garden Out of A Wilderness.* Toronto: Robarts Centre for Canadian Studies, 1993.

Dunn, Brenda. *A History of Port-Royal/Annapolis Royal, 1605–1800.* Halifax: Nimbus, 2000.

Handcock, W. Gordon. *'Soe Longe as there comes noe women': Origins of English Settlement in Newfoundland.* St John's: Breakwater Press, 1989.

Head, C. Grant. *Eighteenth Century Newfoundland: A Geographer's Perspective.* Toronto: McClelland and Stewart, 1976.

Lewis-Simpson, Shannon, ed. *Vinland Revisited: The Norse World at the Turn of the First Millennium.* St. John's: Historic Sites Association of Newfoundland and Labrador, 2003.

McGhee, Robert. *Canada Rediscovered.* Hull: Canadian Museum of Civilization, 1991.

Pope, Peter E. *Fish into Wine. The Newfoundland*

Plantation in the Seventeenth Century. Chapel Hill: University of North Carolina Press, 2004.

———. *The Many Landfalls of John Cabot.* Toronto: University of Toronto Press, 1997.

Reid, John. *Acadia, Maine, and New Scotland: Marginal Colonies in the Seventeenth Century.* Toronto: University of Toronto Press, 1981.

Acadia and the Acadians

Arsenault, Georges. *The Island Acadians, 1720–1980.* Translated by Sally Ross. Charlottetown: Ragweed Press, 1989.

Basque, Maurice, et Jacques Paul Couturier, dirs, *Les Territoires de l'identité : perspectives acadiennes et françaises, XVIIe–XX siècles.* Moncton: Chaire d'études acadiennes, Université de Moncton, 2005.

Basque, Maurice, et al. *Acadie au féminin: Un regard multidisciplinaire sur les Acadiennes et les Canadiens.* Moncton: Chaire d'études acadiennes, Université de Moncton, 2000.

Brebner, John Bartlet. *New England's Outpost: Acadia Before the Conquest of Canada.* New York: Columbia University Press, 1927.

Clark, Andrew Hill. *The Geography of Early Nova Scotia to 1760.* Madison: University of Wisconsin Press, 1986.

Conrad, Margaret, ed. *Looking into Acadie: Three Illustrated Lectures.* Halifax: Nova Scotia Museum, 1999.

Couturier, Jacques Paul, and Phyllis E. LeBlanc, eds. *Économie et société en Acadie, 1850–1950.* Moncton: Éditions d'Acadie, 1996.

Daigle, Jean, ed. *Acadia of the Maritimes: Thematic Studies.* Moncton: Chaire d'études acadiennes, Université de Moncton, 1995.

Faragher, John Mack. *A Great and Noble Scheme: The Tragic Story of the Expulsion of the French Acadians from Their American Homeland.* New York: W.W. Norton, 2005.

Griffiths, N.E.S. *From Migrant to Acadian: A North American Border People 1604–1755.* Moncton and Montréal: Canadian Institute for Research on Public Policy and Public Administration, University of Moncton, and McGill-Queen's University Press, 2004.

———. *The Contexts of Acadian History, 1686–1784.* Montréal: McGill-Queen's University Press, 1992.

———. *The Acadians: Creation of A People.* Toronto: McGraw Hill-Ryerson, 1973.

Harvey, Fernand, and Gérard Beaulieu, dirs. *Les*

Relations entre le Québec et l'Acadie de la tradition à la modernité. Québec: Éditions de l'IQRC/Éditions d'Acadie, 2000.

Johnson, A.J.B. *Control and Order in French Colonial Louisbourg, 1713–1758.* East Lansing: Michigan State University Press, 2001.

———. *Life and Religion at Louisbourg, 1713–1758.* Montréal: McGill-Queen's University Press, 1984.

Jones, Elizabeth. *Gentlemen and Jesuits: Quests for Glory and Adventure in the Early Days of New France.* Toronto: University of Toronto Press, 1986.

Landry, Nicolas. *Les pêches dans la péninsule acadienne, 1850–1900.* Moncton: Éditions d'Acadie, 1994.

Landry, Nicolas, and Nicole Lang. *Histoire de l'Acadie.* Sillery: Septentrion, 2001.

LeBlanc, Ronnie-Gilles, dir. *Du Grand Dérangement à la Déportation : Nouvelles perspectives historiques.* Moncton: Chaire d'études acadiennes, Université de Moncton, 2005.

Magord, André, dir. *Les Franco-Terreneuviens de la péninsule de Port-au-Port Évolution d'une identité franco-canadienne.* Moncton: Chaire d'études acadiennes, Université de Moncton, 2002.

McNeil, John Robert. *Atlantic Empires of France and Spain: Louisbourg and Havana, 1700–1763.* Chapel Hill: University of North Carolina, 1985.

Moore, Christopher. *Louisbourg Portraits: Life in an Eighteenth-Century Garrison Town.* Toronto: Macmillan, 1982.

Reid, John G., et al. *The 'Conquest' of Acadia: Imperial, Colonial, and Aboriginal Constructions.* Toronto: University of Toronto Press, 2004.

Ross, Sally, and Alphonse Deveau. *The Acadians of Nova Scotia Past and Present.* Halifax: Nimbus, 1992.

Vanderlinden, Jacques. *Se marier en Acadie française, XVIIe et XVIIIe siècles.* Moncton: Chaire d'études acadiennes et Éditions d'Acadie, 1998.

New Brunswick

Acheson, T.W. *Saint John: The Making of an Urban Colonial Society.* Toronto: University of Toronto Press, 1985.

Bell, David G. *Early Loyalist Saint John: The Origins of New Brunswick Politics, 1783–1786.* Fredericton: New Ireland Press, 1983.

Condon, Ann Gorman. *The Loyalist Dream for New Brunswick: The Envy of the American*

States. Fredericton: New Ireland Press, 1984.

MacDonald, M.A. *Rebels and Royalists: The Lives and Material Culture of New Brunswick's Early English Settlers, 1758–1783.* Fredericton: New Ireland Press, 1990.

MacNutt, W.S. *New Brunswick: A History.* Toronto: Macmillan, 1984.

Savoie, Donald J. *Pulling Against Gravity: Economic Development in New Brunswick During the McKenna Years.* Montréal: Institute for Research on Public Policy, 2001.

See, Scott W. *Riots in New Brunswick: Orange Nativism and Social Violence in the 1840s.* Toronto: University of Toronto Press, 1993.

Spray, William, *The Blacks in New Brunswick.* Fredericton: Brunswick Press, 1972.

Toner, Peter, ed. *New Ireland Remembered: Historical Essays on the Irish in New Brunswick.* Fredericton: New Ireland Press, 1988.

Wright, Esther Clark. *The Loyalists of New Brunswick.* Wolfville: Wright, 1955.

Wynn, Graeme. *Timber Colony: A Historical Geography of Early Nineteenth Century New Brunswick.* Toronto: University of Toronto Press, 1981.

Newfoundland and Labrador

Bannister, Jerry. *The Rule of the Admirals: Law, Custom, and Naval Government in Newfoundland, 1699–1832.* Toronto, University of Toronto Press for the Osgoode Society, 2004.

Blake, Raymond B. *Canadians at Last: Canada Integrates Newfoundland as a Province.* Toronto: University of Toronto Press, 1994.

Cadigan, Sean T. *Hope and Deception in Conception Bay: Merchant–Settler Relations in Newfoundland, 1785–1855.* Toronto: University of Toronto Press, 1995.

Duley, Margot I. *Where Once Our Mothers Stood We Stand: Women's Suffrage in Newfoundland, 1890–1925.* Charlottetown: gynergy books, 1993.

Fitzhugh, Lynne D. *The Labradorians: Voices from the land of Cain.* St John's: Breakwater, 1999.

Hiller, James, and Peter Neary, eds. *Newfoundland in the Nineteenth and Twentieth Centuries: Essays in Interpretation.* Toronto: University of Toronto Press, 1980.

———, eds. *Twentieth-Century Newfoundland: Explorations.* St John's: Breakwater Books, 1994.

Kealey, Linda, ed. *Pursuing Equality: Historical Perspectives on Women in Newfoundland and Lab-*

rador. St John's: Institute for Social and Economic Research, 1993.

MacKenzie, David. *Inside the Atlantic Triangle. Canada and the Entrance of Newfoundland into Confederation, 1939–1949.* Toronto: University of Toronto Press, 1986.

McDonald, Ian D.H. *'To Each His Own': William Coaker and the Fishermen's Protective Union, 1908–1925.* St John's: ISER, 1987.

Macpherson, Alan G., and Joyce Brown Macpherson. *The Natural Environment of Newfoundland, Past and Present.* St John's: Department of Geography, Memorial University of Newfoundland, 1981.

Mannion, John J., ed. *The Peopling of Newfoundland: Essays in Historical Geography.* St John's: Institute of Social and Economic Research, 1977.

Neary, Peter. *Newfoundland and the North Atlantic World, 1929–1949.* Montréal: McGill-Queen's University Press, 1988.

———, and Patrick O'Flaherty. *By Great Waters: A Newfoundland and Labrador Anthology.* Toronto: University of Toronto Press, 1974.

Noel, S.J.R. *Politics in Newfoundland.* Toronto: University of Toronto Press, 1971.

O'Flaherty, Patrick. *The Rock Observed: Studies in the Literature of Newfoundland.* Toronto: University of Toronto Press, 1979.

———. *Old Newfoundland: A History to 1843.* St John's: Long Beach Press, 1999.

———. *Lost Country: the Rise and Fall of Newfoundland, 1843–1933.* St John's: Long Beach Press, 2005.

Overton, James. *Making A World of Difference: Essays on Tourism, Culture and Development in Newfoundland.* St John's: Institute of Social and Economic Research, 1996.

Porter, Marilyn. *Place and Persistence in the Lives of Newfoundland Women.* Aldershot: Avebury, 1993.

Rompkey, Bill. *The Story of Labrador.* Montréal: McGill-Queen's University Press, 2003.

Rowe, Frederick W. *History of Newfoundland and Labrador.* Toronto: McGraw Hill-Ryerson, 1980.

Ryan, Shannon. *The Ice Hunters: A History of Newfoundland Sealing to 1914.* St John's: Breakwater Press, 1994.

———. *Fish Out of Water: The Newfoundland Saltfish Trade, 1814–1914.* St John's: Breakwater, n.d.

Thompson, F.F. *The French Shore Problem in New-*

foundland. An Imperial Study. Toronto: University of Toronto Press, 1961.

Nova Scotia

Barman, Jean. *Sojourning Sisters: The Lives and Letters of Jessie and Annie McQueen.* Toronto: University of Toronto Press, 2003.

Bickerton, James P. *Nova Scotia, Ottawa, and the Politics of Regional Development.* Toronto: University of Toronto Press, 1990.

Beck, J. Murray. *The Politics of Nova Scotia.* 2 vols. Tantallon, NS: Four East Publications, 1985/88.

Brebner, John Bartlet. *The Neutral Yankees of Nova Scotia.* Toronto: McClelland and Stewart, 1969.

Bruce, Harry. *An Illustrated History of Nova Scotia.* Halifax: Nimbus, 1997.

Campbell, D., and R.A. MacLean. *Beyond the Atlantic Roar: A Study of Nova Scotia Scots.* Toronto: McClelland and Stewart, 1974.

Conrad, Margaret, Toni Laidlaw, and Donna Smyth. *No Place Like Home: The Diaries and Letters of Nova Scotia Women, 1771–1938.* Halifax: Formac, 1988.

Cuthbertson, Brian. *Johnny Bluenose at the Polls: Epic Nova Scotian Election Battles, 1758–1848.* Halifax: Formac, 1994.

Donovan, Kenneth, ed. *Cape Breton at 200: Historical Essays in Honour of the Island's Bicentennial, 1785–1985.* Sydney: University College of Cape Breton Press, 1985.

———, ed. *The Island: New Perspectives on Cape Breton's History, 1713–1975.* Fredericton: Acadiensis Press, 1990.

Fingard, Judith. *The Dark Side of Life in Victorian Halifax.* Porters Lake, NS: Pottersfield Press, 1989.

———, and Janet Guildford, eds. *Mothers of the Municipality: Women, Work and Social Policy in Post-1945 Halifax.* Toronto: University of Toronto Press, 2005.

———, ———, and David Sutherland. *Halifax: The First 250 Years.* Halifax: Formac, 1999.

Frost, James D. *Merchant Princes: Halifax's First Family of Finance, Ships and Steel.* Toronto: James Lorimer, 2003.

Gwyn, Julian. *Ashore and Afloat: The British Navy and the Halifax Naval Yard Before 1820.* Ottawa: University of Ottawa Press, 2004.

———. *Frigates and Foremasts: The North American Squadron in Nova Scotia Waters, 1745–1815.* Vancouver: UBC Press, 2003.

———. *Excessive Expectations: Maritime Commerce and the Development of Nova Scotia, 1740–1870.* Montréal: McGill-Queen's University Press, 1998.

Hornsby, Stephen. *Nineteenth-Century Cape Breton: A Historical Geography.* Montréal: McGill-Queen's University Press, 1992.

Macgillivray, Donald, and Brian Tennyson, eds. *Cape Breton Historical Essays.* Sydney: University College of Cape Breton Press, 1980.

MacKinnon, Neil. *This Unfriendly Soil: The Loyalist Experience in Nova Scotia, 1783–1791.* Montréal: McGill-Queen's University Press, 1989.

McKay, Ian. *The Quest of the Folk: Antimodernism and Cultural Selection in Twentieth-Century Nova Scotia.* Montréal: McGill-Queen's University Press, 1994.

Morgan, Robert. *Early Cape Breton: From Founding to Famine.* Cape Breton: Breton Books, 2000.

Morton, Suzanne. *Ideal Surroundings: Domestic Life in a Working-Class Suburb in the 1920s.* Toronto: University of Toronto Press, 1995.

Neal, Rusty. *Brotherhood Economics: Women and Cooperatives in Nova Scotia.* Sydney: University of Cape Breton Press, 1999.

Pachai, Bridglal. *Beneath the Clouds of the Promised Land: The Survival of Nova Scotia's Blacks,* 2 vols. Halifax: Black Educators Association, 1987/90.

Pryke, K.G. *Nova Scotia and Confederation, 1864–74.* Toronto: University of Toronto Press, 1979.

Rawlyk, G.A. *Nova Scotia's Massachusetts: A Study of Massachusetts–Nova Scotia Relations, 1630 to 1784.* Montréal: McGill-Queen's University Press, 1973.

Sandberg, L. Anders, and Peter Clancy. *Against the Grain: Foresters and Politics in Nova Scotia.* Vancouver: UBC Press, 2000.

Tennyson, Brian, and Roger Sarty. *Guardian of the Gulf: Sydney, Cape Breton and the Atlantic Wars.* Toronto: University of Toronto Press, 2000.

Walker, James W. St G. *The Black Loyalists: The Search for a Promised Land in Nova Scotia and Sierra Leone.* 2nd ed. Toronto: University of Toronto Press, 1992.

Prince Edward Island

Baldwin, Douglas, and Thomas Spira, *Gaslights, Epidemics and Vagabond Cows: Charlottetown in the Victorian Era.* Charlottetown: Ragweed Press, 1988.

Bolger, Francis. *Canada's Smallest Province: A His-*

tory of PEI. Charlottetown: Prince Edward Island Centennial Commission, 1973.

Bumsted, J.M. *Land, Settlement, and Politics in Eighteenth-Century Prince Edward Island.* Montréal: McGill-Queen's University Press, 1987.

Clark, Andrew Hill. *Three Centuries and the Island: A Historical Geography of Settlement and Agriculture in Prince Edward Island.* Toronto: University of Toronto Press, 1959.

Hornby, Jim. *Black Islanders.* Island Studies Series No. 3. Charlottetown: Institute of Island Studies, 1991.

MacDonald, Edward. *If You're Stronghearted: Prince Edward Island in the Twentieth Century.* Charlottetown: Museum and Heritage Foundation, 2000.

Robertson, Ian Ross. *The Tenant League of Prince Edward Island: Leasehold Tenure in the New World.* Toronto: University of Toronto Press, 1996.

Smitheram, Verner, David Milne, and Satadal Dasgupta, eds. *The Garden Transformed: Prince Edward Island, 1945–1980.* Charlottetown: Ragweed Press, 1982.

Notes

Chapter 1: Beginnings

1. Ruth Holmes Whitehead, *Stories from the Six Worlds: Micmac Legends* (Halifax: Nimbus Publishing, 1988), 166–7.
2. Atlantic Geoscience Society, *The Last Billion Years: A Geological History of the Maritime Provinces* (Halifax: Nimbus Publishing, 2001), 62.
3. A useful summary of recent scholarship on this period of the region's history can be found in Stephen A. Davis, 'Early Societies: Sequences of Change', in Phillip A. Buckner and John G. Reid, eds, *The Atlantic Region to Confederation* (Toronto and Fredericton: University of Toronto and Acadiensis Press, 1994), 3–21.
4. James A. Tuck, 'The Archaic Period in the Maritime Provinces', in Michael Deal and Susan Blair, eds., *Prehistoric Archaeology in the Maritime Provinces: Past and Present Research* (Fredericton: Council of Maritime Premiers, 1991).
5. Bruce J. Bourque, *Diversity and Complexity in Prehistoric Maritime Societies* (New York: Plenum Press, 1995).
6. Robert McGhee, *Ancient Peoples of the Arctic* (Vancouver: University of British Columbia Press, 1996).

Chapter 2: Aboriginal Peoples

1. Olive Patricia Dickason, *Canada's First Nations: A History of Founding Peoples from Earliest Times* (Toronto: McClelland and Stewart, 1992), 12.
2. For various perspectives on the numbers of Mi'kmaq at the time of contact see: Daniel N. Paul, *We Were Not the Savages*, 2nd edn (Halifax: Fernwood Publishing, 2000), 45–6; Virginia P. Miller, 'Aboriginal Micmac Population: A Review of the Evidence', *Ethnohistory* 23, 2 (Spring 1976): 117–27, and 'The Decline of the Nova Scotia Micmac Population, AD 1600–1850', *Culture*, 2, 3 (1982): 107–20; Harald E.L. Prins, *The Mi'kmaq: Resistance, Accommodation, and Cultural Survival* (Fort Worth: Harcourt Brace College Publishers, 1996), 27; Ralph Pastore, 'The Sixteenth Century: Aboriginal Peoples and European Contact', in Phillip A. Buckner and John G. Reid, eds, *The Atlantic Region to Confederation: A History* (Toronto: University of Toronto Press, 1994), 24; See also John D. Daniels, 'The Indian Population of North America in 1492', *The William and Mary Quarterly*, 3rd series, 49, 2 (April 1992): 298–320.
3. Nicolas Denys, *The Description and Natural History of the Coasts of North America*, ed. William F. Ganong (Toronto: Champlain Society, 1908), 401.
4. Cited in Ruth Holmes Whitehead, *The Old Man Told Us: Excerpts from Micmac History, 1500–1950* (Halifax: Nimbus Publishing, 1991), 11–12; translated by Margaret Anne Hamelin from a 'Lettre à Madame de Drucourt', n.d [c. 1750], in *Les Soirées Canadiennes* (Québec: Brousseau Frères, 1863), 300–1.

5. Father Chrestien Le Clercq, *New Relation of Gaspesia With the Customs and Religion of the Gaspesian Indians*, 2nd edn, ed. and trans. William F. Ganong (Toronto: Champlain Society, 1910), 239.

6. Prins, *The Mi'kmaq*, 39–41.

7. Nain station diary, 5 November 1772. Quoted in J.K. Hiller, 'The Foundation and the Early Years of the Moravian Mission in Labrador, 1752–1805' (MA thesis, Memorial University, 1967), 163.

8. Pastore, 34–5.

9. Translation from W.C. Sturtevant, 'The First Inuit Depiction by Europeans', *Études/Inuit/Studies* 4, 1–2 (1980), 47–9.

Chapter 3: European Encounters, 1000–1598

1. Josiah Jeremy to Silas Rand, 26 September 1869. Cited in Ruth Holmes Whitehead, *The Old Man Told Us: Excerpts from Micmac History* (Halifax: Nimbus, 1991), 8.

2. Birgitta Wallace, 'The Norse in Newfoundland: L'Anse aux Meadows and Vinland'. *Newfoundland Studies* 19, 1 (2003), 5–43.

3. James Axtell, 'At the Water's Edge: Trading in the 16th Century,' in Axtell, *After Columbus: Essays in the Ethnohistory of Colonial North America* (New York: Oxford University Press, 1988), 145.

4. Cited in Harald E.L. Prins, *The Mi'kmaq: Resistance, Accommodation, and Cultural Survival* (Fort Worth: Harcourt Brace College Publishers, 1996), 50.

5. As translated in Sally Ross and Alphonse Deveau, *The Acadians of Nova Scotia, Past and Present* (Halifax: Nimbus, 1992), 3–4.

6. Axtell, 'At the Water's Edge', 177.

7. D.B. Quinn, *North American World*, vol. 4 (New York: Arno Press, 1979), 64–5.

Chapter 4: Colonial Experiments, 1598–1632

1. Cited in Patrick O'Flaherty, *The Rock Observed: Studies in the Literature of Newfound-land* (Toronto: University of Toronto Press, 1979), 10.

2. Elizabeth Jones, *Gentlemen and Jesuits: Quests for Glory and Adventure in the Early Days of New France* (Toronto: University of Toronto Press, 1986), 29.

3. Ibid., 76.

4. Cited in ibid., 92–3.

5. Peter Pope, 'Six Letters from the Early Colony of Avalon,' *Avalon Chronicles*, 1 (1996), 6.

6. George Calvert to King Charles I, 19 August 1629, in Gillian Cell, *Newfoundland Discovered: English Attempts at Colonization, 1610–1630* (London: Hakluyt Society, 1982), 295–6.

7. Ramsay Cook, '1492 and All That: Making a Garden out of a Wilderness,' in Chad Gaffield and Pam Gaffield, eds, *Consuming Canada: Readings in Environmental History* (Toronto: Copp Clark, Ltd., 1995), 62–80.

8. Cited in Ruth Holmes Whitehead, *The Old Man Told Us: Excerpts from Micmac History, 1500–1950* (Halifax: Nimbus, 1991), 39.

9. Cited in Peter Neary and Patrick O'Flaherty, *By Great Waters: A Newfoundland and Labrador Anthology* (Toronto: University of Toronto Press, 1974), 10.

Chapter 5: Colonial Communities, 1632–1713

1. Andrew Hill Clark, *Acadia: The Geography of Early Nova Scotia to 1760* (Madison: University of Wisconsin Press, 1968), 90.

2. Sieur de Dièreville, *Relation of the Voyage to Port Royal in Acadia or New France*, ed. John Clarence Webster (Toronto: Champlain Society, 1933), 94–5.

3. N.E.S. Griffiths, 'The Acadians,' *Dictionary of Canadian Biography IV*, xviii. For a more detailed discussion, see Naomi E.S. Griffiths, *The Contexts of Acadian History, 1686–1784* (Montréal and Kingston: McGill-Queen's University Press, 1992), and *From Migrant to Acadian: A North American Border People, 1604–1755* (Montréal and Kingston:

McGill-Queen's University Press, 2005).

4. Peter E. Pope, *Fish into Wine: The Newfound-land Plantation in the Seventeenth Century* (Chapel Hill: University of North Carolina Press, 2004), 300.

5. Gordon Handcock, '*Soe longe as there comes noe women': Origins of English Settlement in Newfoundland* (St John's: Breakwater Press, 1989), 37.

6. Maurice Basque, 'Family and Political Culture in Pre-Conquest Acadia', in John G. Reid et al., *The Conquest of Acadia, 1710: Imperial, Colonial and Aboriginal Constructions* (Toronto: University of Toronto Press, 2004), 58.

7. William C. Wicken, *Mi'kmaq Treaties on Trial: History, Land, and Donald Marshall Junior* (Toronto: University of Toronto Press, 2002), 56–7.

8. John G. Reid, '1686-1720: Imperial Intrusions', in Phillip A. Buckner and John G. Reid, eds, *The Atlantic Region to Confederation: A History* (Toronto and Fredericton: University of Toronto Press and Acadiensis Press, 1994), 94.

Chapter 6: Renegotiating the Atlantic Region, 1713–63

1. John G. Reid et al., *The 'Conquest' of Acadia, 1710: Imperial, Colonial, and Aboriginal Constructions* (Toronto: University of Toronto Press, 2004), 208.

2. Jerry Bannister, *The Rule of the Admirals: Laws, Custom, and Naval Government, 1699–1832* (Toronto: University of Toronto Press, 2003).

3. Kenneth Donovan, 'Slaves and Their Owners in Île Royale, 1713–1760', *Acadiensis*, 25, 1 (Autumn 1995), 3–32.

4. Brenda Dunn, *A History of Port-Royal/ Annapolis Royal, 1605–1800* (Halifax: Nimbus, 2004),106.

5. N.E.S. Griffiths, 'The Golden Age: Acadian Life, 1713–1748', *Histoire Sociale*, 17, 33 (May 1984): 21–34.

6. Cited in John G. Reid, 'Imperial Intrusions, 1686–1720', *The Atlantic Region to Confederation: A History*, ed. Phillip A. Buckner and John G. Reid (Toronto and Fredericton: University of Toronto Press and Acadiensis Press, 1994), 100.

7. Public Record Office, London, Colonial Office Series 217/5: 3r-5r. Cited in William C. Wicken, *Mi'kmaq Treaties on Trial: History, Land, and Donald Marshall Junior* (Toronto: University of Toronto Press, 2002), 61–2.

8. Public Record Office, London, Colonial Office Series 217/4: doc 321. Cited in William C. Wicken, *Mi'kmaq Treaties on Trial: History, Land, and Donald Marshall Junior* (Toronto: University of Toronto Press, 2002), 63–4.

9. Cited in G.F.G. Stanley, *New France: The Last Phase, 1744–1760* (Toronto: McClelland and Stewart, 1968), 65.

10. Stephen A. White, 'The True Number of Acadians,' in Ronnie-Gilles LeBlanc, dir., *Du Grand Dérangement à la Déportation: Nouvelles perspectives historiques* (Moncton: Chaire d'études acadiennes, Université de Moncton, 2005), 21–56; Earle Lockerby, 'The Deportation of the Acadians from Ile St.-Jean, 1758', *Acadiensis* 27, 2 (Spring 1998), 45–94.

11. Stephen E. Patterson, 'Colonial Wars and Aboriginal Peoples, 1744–1763', in Buckner and Reid, eds, *The Atlantic Region to Confederation: A History*, 147.

12. Cited in M.A. MacDonald, *Rebels and Royalists: The Lives and Material Culture of New Brunswick's Early English-Speaking Settlers, 1758–1783* (Fredericton: New Ireland Press, 1990), 21.

13. G.P. Gould and A.J. Semple, eds., *Our Land: The Maritimes* (Fredericton: Sainte Annes Point Press, 1980), 177.

Chapter 7: Community Formation, 1749–1815

1. Julian Gwyn, *Excessive Expectations: Maritime*

Commerce and the Development of Nova Scotia, 1740–1870 (Montréal and Kingston: McGill-Queen's University Press, 1998).

2. J. Garth Taylor, 'The Two World of Mikak'. *The Beaver* 314, 3 (1984), 4–13; and 314, 4 (1984): 18–25. See also entries on Francis Lucas in *Dictionary of Canadian Biography*, vol. 3, 411–12; and on Mikak and Tuglavina in *Dictionary of Canadian Biography*, vol. 4, 536–7, 740.

3. Quoted in C. Grant Head, *Eighteenth Century Newfoundland: A Geographer's Perspective* (Toronto: McClelland and Stewart, 1976), 198.

4. Michael Francklin to Lord George Germaine, 21 November 1780; cited in *Source Materials Relating to the New Brunswick Indian*, ed. W.D. Hamilton and W.A. Spray (Fredericton: Centennial Press and Litho Ltd, 1976), 58–9.

5. Ann Gorman Condon, '1783–1800. Loyalist Arrival, Acadian Return, Imperial Reform', in Phillip A. Buckner and John G. Reid, eds, *The Atlantic Region to Confederation: A History* (Toronto and Fredericton: University of Toronto and Acadiensis Press, 1994), 192.

6. Edward Winslow to Ward Chipman, 7 July 1783, University of New Brunswick Archives, Harriet Irving Library, Winslow Family Papers, MG H2, Vol. 2, Part 2, p. 104.

7. Graeme Wynn, *Timber Colony: A Historical Geography of Early Nineteenth Century New Brunswick* (Toronto: University of Toronto Press, 1981).

Chapter 8: Maturing Colonial Societies, 1815–60

1. Joseph Howe, 'The Blue Nose', in M.G. Parks ed., *Joseph Howe: Poems and Essays* (Toronto: University of Toronto Press, 1973), 145–6.

2. Douglas F. Campbell and David Niece, *Ties that Bind: Structure and Marriage in Nova Scotia* (Port Credit ON: Scribblers' Press, 1979), 41; Ralph Nelson et al., 'Canadian Confederation as a Case Study in Community

Formation', in Ged Martin, ed., *The Causes of Canadian Confederation* (Fredericton: Acadiensis Press, 1990), 70.

3. Cited in D.C. Harvey ed., *Journeys to the Island of St. John* (Toronto: Macmillan, 1955), 105.

4. 'Statement of the Indian Delegation, 23 June 1842', cited in *Source Materials Relating to the New Brunswick Indian*, ed. W.D. Hamilton and W.A. Spray (Fredericton: Centennial Print and Litho Ltd., 1976), 112.

5. Cited in Jennifer Reid, *Myth, Symbol, and Colonial Encounter: British and Mi'kmaq in Acadia, 1700–1867* (Ottawa: University of Ottawa Press, 1995), 36.

6. Eric W. Sager with Gerald E. Panting, *Maritime Capital: The Shipping Industry in Atlantic Canada, 1820–1914* (Montréal: McGill-Queen's University Press, 1990) 17.

7. T.W. Acheson, 'The 1840s: Decade of Tribulation', in *The Atlantic Region to Confederation: A History*, 307–32.

8. Cited in J.G. Millais, *Newfoundland and its Untrodden Ways* (London, 1907), 41.

9. A.J. Sandy Young, *Beyond Heroes: A Sport History of Nova Scotia*, Vol. 2 (Hantsport: Lancelot Press, 1991), 15.

Chapter 9: Confronting Confederation, 1860–73

1. Ian Ross Robertson, ed., *The Prince Edward Island Land Commission of 1860* (Fredericton: Acadiensis Press, 1988), 69–70.

2. Phillip A. Buckner, 'The 1860s: An End and a Beginning', in Phillip A. Buckner and John G. Reid, eds, *The Atlantic Region to Confederation: A History* (Toronto and Fredericton: University of Toronto Press and Acadiensis Press, 1994), 377.

3. C.M. Wallace, 'Sir Samuel Leonard Tilley', *Dictionary of Canadian Biography*, vol. XII (Toronto: University of Toronto Press, 1990), 1051–9.

4. Cited in Kenneth G. Pryke, *Nova Scotia and Confederation, 1864–74* (Toronto: University

of Toronto Press, 1978), 41.

5. Donald Warner, *The Idea of Continental Union: Agitation for the Annexation of Canada to the United States, 1849–1893* (University of Kentucky Press, 1960), 814.

6. David G. Alexander, 'Economic Growth in the Atlantic Region, 1880–1940', in Alexander, Atlantic *Canada and Confederation: Essays in Canadian Political Economy*, comp. Eric W. Sager, Lewis R. Fischer, Stuart O. Pierson. (St John's and Toronto: Memorial University and University of Toronto Press, 1983), 74.

7. Ian Ross Robertson, *The Tenant League of Prince Edward Island, 1864–1867: Leasehold Tenure in the New World* (Toronto: University of Toronto Press, 1996), 273.

Chapter 10: The Industrial Challenge, 1873–1901

1. T.W. Acheson, 'The National Policy and the Industrialization of the Maritimes, 1880–1910', *Acadiensis*, 1, 2 (Spring 1972), 3–28.

2. Greg Kealey, ed., *Canada Investigates Industrialism* (Toronto: University of Toronto Press, 1973), 395–6.

3. Judith Fingard, 'The 1880s: Paradoxes of Progress', in E.R. Forbes and D.A. Muise, eds, *The Atlantic Provinces in Confederation* (Toronto: University of Toronto Press, 1993), 97.

4. Naomi Griffiths, 'Evangeline: A Tale of Acadie', *The Canadian Encyclopedia*, 2nd edn (Edmonton: Hurtig, 1988), II, 729.

5. Moniteur Acadien, 10 June 1880, cited in Georges Arsenault, *The Island Acadians, 1720–1980* (Charlottetown: Ragweed Press, 1989), 155.

6. Ronald Rompkey, *Grenfell of Labrador: A Biography* (Toronto: University of Toronto Press, 1991).

Chapter 11: The Promise and Peril of a New Century, 1901–19

1. David Frank, 'The Cape Breton Coal Industry and the Rise and Fall of the British Empire Steel Corporation', in Don Macgillivray and Brian Tennyson, eds, *Cape Breton Historical Essays* (Sydney: College of Cape Breton Press, 1980), 114–15.

2. Mary Rubio and Elizabeth Waterston, eds, *The Selected Journals of L.M. Montgomery*, 5 vols (Toronto: Oxford University Press, 1987–2004).

3. Ian McKay, 'The Five Ages of Nova Scotian Tourism', *New Maritimes* 5, 11–12 (1987): 8.

4. Gerald L. Pocius, 'Tourists, Health Seekers and Sportsmen: Luring Americans to Newfoundland in the Early Twentieth Century', in James Hiller and Peter Neary, eds, *Twentieth-Century Newfoundland: Explorations* (St John's: Breakwater Books, 1994), 47–78.

5. Major A. Rayley, 'Beaumont Hamel', Veterans', *Magazine* 1, 3 (1921): 37.

6. Ian McKay, 'The 1910s: The Stillborn Triumph of Progressive Reform', in E.R. Forbes and D.A. Muise, eds, *The Atlantic Provinces in Confederation* (Toronto and Fredericton: University of Toronto Press and Acadiensis Press, 1993), 229.

7. Extract from Periodical Accounts relating to the Missions of the Church of the United Brethren, 1919, in Helge Kleivan, *The Eskimos of Northeast Labrador: A History of Eskimo–White Relations, 1771–1955* (Oslo: Norsk Polarinstitutt, 1966), 181.

8. Sylvia Bashevkin, *Toeing the Lines: Women and Party Politics in English Canada*, 2nd edn (Toronto: University of Toronto Press, 1993), 5.

Chapter 12: Between the Wars, 1919–39

1. S.A. Saunders, *The Economic History of the Maritime Provinces*, ed. T.W. Acheson (Fredericton: Acadiensis Press, 1984), 38.

2. E.R. Forbes, *The Maritime Rights Movement, 1919–1927: A Study in Canadian Regionalism* (Montréal: McGill-Queen's University Press, 1979), 176.

3. Douglas O. Baldwin, *She Answered Every Call: The Life of Public Health Nurse, Mona Gordon Wilson (1894–1981)* (Charlottetown: Indigo Press, 1997), 299.

4. Ian McKay, 'Among the Fisherfolk: J.F.B. Livesay and the Invention of Peggy's Cove', *Journal of Canadian Studies* 23, 1–2 (1988): 23–45.

5. Gwendolyn Davies, 'Frank Parker Day's Rockbound', in Davies, *Studies in Maritime Literary History* (Fredericton: Acadiensis Press, 1991), 174.

6. James Overton, 'Brown Flour and Beri-beri: The Politics of Dietary and Health Reform in Newfoundland in the First Half of the Twentieth Century', *Newfoundland Studies* 14, 1 (1998): 15.

Chapter 13: The Emergence of an Atlantic Region, 1939–49

1. Georges Arsenault, *The Island Acadians, 1720–1980*, trans. Sally Ross (Charlottetown: Ragweed Press, 1989), 242.

2. J.R. Smallwood, 'An Appeal', 31 May 1948, cited in Peter Neary, ed., *The Political Economy of Newfoundland, 1929–1972* (Toronto: Copp Clark, 1973), 142.

3. Quoted in Jeff A. Webb, 'The Responsible Government League and the Confederation Campaigns of 1948', *Newfoundland Studies* 5, 2 (1989), 214.

Chapter 14: The Real Golden Age? 1949–75

1. Eric Hobsbawm, *Age of Extremes: The Short Twentieth Century, 1914–1991* (London: Abacus, 1995), 6.

2. W.S. MacNutt, 'The Atlantic Revolution', *Atlantic Advocate* (June 1957): 11–13.

3. Della Stanley, M.M. Stanley, *Louis Robichaud: A Decade of Power* (Halifax: Nimbus Publishing, 1984) 93.

4. Edward MacDonald, *If You're Stronghearted: Prince Edward Island in the Twentieth Century* (Charlottetown: Prince Edward Island Museum and Heritage Foundation, 2000), 297–307.

5. Africville Genealogical Society, *The Spirit of Africville* (Halifax: Formac, 1992), 70.

6. Labrador Inuit Association, 'Nunatsiavut News', accessed 15 July 2005 at www.nunatsiavut.com/en/windsofchange.php.

Chapter 15: The Atlantic Region in a Global Context, 1975–2005

1. Ken S. Coates, *The Marshall Decision and Native Rights* (Montréal: McGill-Queen's University Press, 2000), 83.

2. Donald J. Savoie, *Pulling Against Gravity: Economic Development in New Brunswick During the McKenna Years* (Montréal: Institute for Research on Public Policy, 2001).

3. Brian Lee Crowley, *Atlantic Institute for Market Studies* (aims) http://www.aims.ca/library/atlanticapart1.pdf.

4. Moses Harvey, *Where Are We and Whither Tending? Three Lectures on the Reality and Worth of Human Progress* (Boston: Doyle and Whittle, 1886).

Index

Abenaki peoples, 17, 52, 56, 66, 84
Aboriginal peoples, *see* Native peoples
Aborigines' Protection Society, 98
Academy of Arts and Sciences, *see* College of New Brunswick
Acadia, 39, 55, 66–7, 152, 154; Anglo-French wars, 62, 64–70; British acquisition of, 60; Dutch attack on, 52; dykeland agriculture, 49–50, 57; First World War, 158–9; 'golden age' of, 64, 69; hostilities with New England, 52, 57; neutrality, 56; Roman Catholic clergy, 38–9, 50–1; settlement, 35–40, 43–5, 46–53; social organization, 62, 64; Treaty of Utrecht, 62; *see also* Acadie, Grand Pré, New France
Acadians, 102, 196, 200; 'Ave Maris Stella', 140; British administration, 60, 84; education, 106; English settlers, 80, 86; expulsion, 61, 70–2, 77, 139; flag, 140; identity, 140–1; language, 133–43; music, 207; Native peoples, 64, 68–71; neutrality, 67, 69; newspapers, 106, 140; political activism, 139–41, 192, 202–3; population, 60, 62, 64, 71–2; return, 78, 80–1; settlements 39, 57–8, 174; 'Société Nationale l'Assomption', 140; Société Nationale de l'Acadie', 140; *see also* Acadia, Grand Pré
Acadia University, Wolfville, NS, 106

Acadie, vii, 48; *see also* Acadia
Adena peoples (Ohio), 20–1
Africadia, vii; *see also* Africville
African Americans: Black Panthers, 204; Black Power movement, 203; immigrants, 88, 94, 96, 104; *see also* Black peoples
African United Baptist Association, 95, 104–5
Africville, 105, 192, 203–4; Halifax Harbour Explosion, 159; *see also* Africadia, Black peoples
agriculture, 27, 40, 49, 109, 119–21, 128, 133, 145, 156–9, 162, 176, 199
Albion Mines (Stellerton), NS, 95, 101
Albert County, NB, 3, 6, 101
Alexander, David, 7
Alexander, Sir William, 35, 40
Algonkian peoples, 18, 84
Allain River, NS, 37
Allen, John, 84
Alline, Henry, 85
Amalgamated Mine Workers of Nova Scotia, 182
American Civil War (1861–5), 102, 112–14, 119, 123; *see also* United States
American Revolution, 78, 83–5, 87, 89, 94, 109; Saratoga, 85; *see also* United States
Amherst, NS, 132, 150, 160
Amherst, General Jeffrey, 73
Amherst, Colonel William, 74
Amulree, Lord, 163, 173–4
L'Anse Amour, NL, 7
L'Anse aux Meadows, NL, 23–5
Anglicans, 104; *see also* Church of England

Anglo-Dutch war (1672–4), 55
Anglo-French entente cordiale (1904), 154
animals; beaver, 16, 31; bison, 5; caribou, 6, 18–9; great auk, 96; mammoths and mastadons, 5; moose, 14, 16, 31, 96; reindeer, 145; seals, 7, 18, 31; whales, 7, 10–11, 18, 29, 32; *see also* sealing industry; whaling industry
Annapolis Royal, NS, vii, 60, 65–8, 70, 80, 199; *see also* Port-Royal
Annapolis Valley, NS, 128
Annexation League, 122
Anspach, Reverend Lewis, *History of the Island of Newfoundland*, 109
Anticosti Island, 32, 76
Antigonish, NS, 174
Antigonish Movement, 174–5; *see also* Cooperatives
Antwerp, 20
Anville, Duc d', 61, 68
Appalachians Mountains, 3, 76
apples, 128, 145, 159, 164, 175, 182, 186, 199
Aquaforte, NL, 41
Arabella, 83
archaic cultures, 6–8, 10; burial mounds, 8; European contact, 8
Argall, Samuel, 35, 39
Arguimaut, Chief (L'kimu), 15
Argyle, NS, 80
Aroostook, NB, 94
Arsenault, Joseph-Octave, 141
Asia, 22, 24–5, 27
Associated Press, 107
Atholville, NB, 164
'Atlantica', 222

Atlantic Accord (1985), 211
Atlantic Advocate, 195
Atlantic Canada, 3, 11, 22, 76, 219; cartoon, 215; defining, vii–viii, 178, 180; economy, 94, 100–5, 191–201, 214, 222–3; government, 94, 201–203; immigration, 77; population, 97, 119, 220–2
Atlantic Canada Opportunities Agency (ACOA), 213, 215
Atlantic Development Board (ADB), 192, 194
Atlantic Institute for Market Studies (AIMS), 222
Atlantic Ocean, 3, 22, 26, 43, 77, 84, 96, 112, 153; fisheries, 28–9, 163
Atlantic Provinces Adjustment Grant, 192, 194, 198
Atlantic Provinces Economic Council (APEC), 192–3
'Atlantic Revolution', 195–6
Augsberg, Germany, 20
Aulnay, Charles de Menou d', 46–8, 52
automobiles, 146, 154, 196
Avalon Peninsula, NL, 7, 30, 40–2, 45, 53, 55, 57, 96, 136, 188
aviation, 146, 153; Aerial Experiment Association, 153; *Silver Dart*, 153; *see also* Bell, Alexander Graham
Axtell, James, 46
Aylesford, NS, 86
Azores, 24, 26–7

Baddeck, NS, 155
Baffin Island, 22
Baie des Chaleurs, NB, 31, 46, 72–3
Baker, Carol, 207
Baldwin, F.W., 153
Balfour, James, 84
Baltimore, Lord, 41–2
banks, 101, 144, 212; Bank of Commerce, 150; Bank of Montréal, 135, 150; Bank of New Brunswick, 95, 101; Bank of Nova Scotia, 129, 132; Farmer's Bank of Rustico (PEI), 102
Banks, Harold 'Hal', 179, 186

Baptist Church, 69, 106; missionaries, 22, 98, 105
Bardot, Brigit, 207
Basque, Maurice, 56
Basque peoples, 23, 28–31, 33, 62, 70
Bates, Stewart, 183
Bathurst, NB, 141, 164
Battle of the Boyne, 106
Baxter, J.B.M., 167
Bay of Fundy, 1, 3, 5–6, 29, 36, 45, 49, 56, 60, 80, 87
Bear, Ned and Shirley, 209
Beaubassin, NB, 49, 51, 56
Beckwith, Julia Catherine, *St Ursula's Convent*, 95, 109
Bedford Basin, NS, 105, 180–1, 204
Bélanger de Rouen, Étienne, 31
Belcher, Governor Jonathan, 73
Belcourt, Father George-Antoine, 102
Bell, Alexander Graham, 153; *see also* aviation
Bell Island, NL, 131, 135, 150, 170, 179–80
Bengough, J.W., 124
Bennett, Charles Fox, 125
Bennett, R.B., 174–5
Beothuk, 12, 18–19; Beothick Institution, 98; contact with Europeans, 31, 40; decline of, 80, 98; origins, 11
Bermuda, 89, 180, 198
Bernard, Joshua, 218
Beutel, Josh, 217
Biard, Père Pierre, 38, 45
Biencourt, Charles de, 36, 38–9
Binns, Pat, 219
Black Cultural Centre, Dartmouth, NS, 204
Black peoples, 62, 175, 200; First World War, 152, 156; Loyalists, 78, 88, 96; music, 207; political activism, 200, 202–4; settlement, 105; sports, 153; *see also* Africville, African Americans, Sierra Leone, slavery
Black United Front, 192, 204
Blaine, James, 138
Blair, Andrew G., 137
Blanc Sablon, Labrador, 98
Bluenose, 163, 171
Bonavista Peninsula (North

Falkland), 41
Bond, Robert, 138, 152–3
Bordeaux, France, 28
Borden, PEI, 199
Borden, Robert, 152, 157, 167
Boston, MA, 52, 57, 60, 66–8, 70, 77, 80, 83–4, 92, 108, 123, 135, 153
Botwood, NL, 179
Bourque, B.J., 7
Bowring, Benjamin, 101
Boyd Creek, NB, 50
Bradley, F. Gordon, 187–9
Bridgewater, NS, 198
Bristol, England, 24–6, 32, 35, 40
Bristol's Hope (Harbour Grace), NL, 40
British Columbia, 152, 216
British Empire, 35, 88, 94–5, 105, 111–3, 128, 138, 142–4, 153, 155, 180
British military, 116; Rangers, 73; Royal Navy, 73, 92
British North America Act (1867), 116, 122; *see also* Confederation
Brittany, France, 28, 46
Broad Point (Susquehanna) peoples, 7
Brothers and Sisters of Cornelius Howatt, 201
Brown, George, 113
Brunel, I.K., 107
Buchanan, John, 219
Buckner, Philip, 116
Burgeo, NL, 201
Burin Peninsula, NL, 200
Burke, Bishop Edmund, 105
Burnt Church (Esgenoopetits) reserve, 218
Burpee, Reverend Richard, 105
Burrill, Gary, 4
Bush, George, 211
Busy East of Canada, 147
Butler, Edith, 207
Butler, Nat, 153
Byers, George, 153
Byrne, Edward G., 192

Cabot, John (Zuan Caboto), 12, 41, 143; *Matthew*, 25; voyages of, 23, 25–8, 142
Cabot, Sebastian, 23, 27
Cabot Strait, viii, 3, 9, 18, 106, 144

Cabot Trail, NS, 172
Callbeck, Catherine, 219
Callbeck, Phillips, 85
Calvert (Caplin Bay), NL, 41
Calvert, Sir George (Lord
    Baltimore); Ferryland settle-
    ment, 35, 41–2, 54
Campbell, Alexander, 196
Cameron, Donald, 219
Cameron, John Allan, 207
Canada, vii, 4, 29, 31, 36, 40, 49,
    54–9, 62–3, 71, 84, 98, 112,
    128–9, 131–39, 141–2, 147,
    150, 153–4, 160, 167, 170–2,
    186–9, 191, 197, 206, 210–11,
    214–15, 219–21; elections,
    137; First World War, 155–9,
    House of Commons, 119,
    122, 152, 167, 182; marine
    boundaries, 146, 200, 211,
    215; Second World War,
    178–9, 181, 184–5; Senate,
    205, 214; Supreme Court,
    216–18; the United, 89, 94,
    115–16, 119, 120, 122–3; *see
    also* Confederation, Lower
    Canada, Upper Canada
Canadian Broadcasting Corpora-
    tion, 204; *This Hour Has 22
    Minutes*, 208
Canadian Food and Allied
    Workers Union, 201
Canadian High Commission,
    179, 187
Canadian military, 201; Royal
    Canadian Air Force, 179;
    Royal Canadian Navy, 179
Canadian Seamen's Union, 186
Canso Causeway, 192, 198;
    Canso, NS, 46, 48, 60, 65, 145,
    201
Cape Bauld, NL, 29
Cape Bonavista, NL, 26–7, 31,
    41, 57, 59, 62, 72, 142–3
Cape Breton County, NS, 147
Cape Breton Island, vii, 3, 23,
    26–7, 29, 35, 40, 59, 78–81,
    86, 91, 103, 123, 128, 175,
    186, 202, 207, 220; annexation
    by Nova Scotia, 95, 109; and
    federal programs, 198; mining,
    101, 133, 163, 165–6, 182;
    naming, 74; *see also* Île Royale
Cape Breton Development Cor-

poration, 192, 198
Cape Breton Highlands National
    Park, 198
Cape Charles, Labrador, 29, 82
Cape Cod, MA, 36
Cape Harrison, Labrador, 98
Cape North, NS, 106
Cape of Good Hope, 24
Cape Race, NL, 29, 106
Cape Ray, NL, 85, 135
Cape Sable (Cap de Sable), NS,
    39, 46, 48, 65–6
Cape St John, NL, 29, 85, 135
Cape Spear, NL 29, 32
Cape Tormentine, NB, 107
Cape Verde Islands, 26
Cap Nègre (Cape Negro), NS,
    39, 49
Capuchins, 46, 50
Caraquet, NB, 140; riots, 129,
    139, 153
Cardinal Richelieu, 46
Caribbean, 23, 25, 28, 89, 92,
    129–30, 162–4, 170, 180,
    206–8
Carbonear Island, NL, 57, 74
Caribou, 179–80
Carman, Bliss, 153
Carmichael, Stokeley, 204
Carroll, W.F., 182
Carrol's Cove, NL, 29
Carson, Dr William, 108
Carson, Rachel, *Silent Spring*, 207
Carter, Frederic, 125
Carter, Wilf, 207
Cartier, Jacques, 97; Mi'kmaq fur
    trade, 31; voyages of, 23, 27, 30
Cartier, George-Étienne, 113
Cartwright, George, 78, 83, 85
Cartwright, John, 80
Carvary, Aaron, 204
Cashin, Richard, 201
Cavendish, PEI, 155
celtic music, 207
Chalmers, Robert, 195
Champagne, France, 36
Champlain, Samuel de, 19, 35–8,
    54, 94, 172; map by, 37
Chapel Island, NS, 65
Charitable Irish Society, 91
Charles I, 40, 42, 53–4
Charles Robin and Company,
    131
Charlottetown Accord (1992),

211, 214
Charlottetown Conference (1864),
    113, 119, 208
Charlottetown Festival Theatre,
    208
Charlottetown (Port LaJoie),
    PEI, 64, 79, 85, 96, 118, 168,
    171, 179, 199, 221
Chateau Bay, Labrador, 82
Chatham, NB, 96, 179, 183
Chebucto Bay, NS, 69
Chedabucto Bay, NS, 24
Chesapeake, USS, 92
Cheticamp, NS, 80
Chicago Exhibition, 137
Chignecto Bay, NS, 1, 57
Chipman, Ward, 87
Chrétien, Jean, 214
Church, Benjamin, 56–7
Churchill Falls hydro develop-
    ment, 147, 192–3, 196, 206
Churchill River, NL, 147
Churchill, Winston, 180
Churchill, Jr., Winston, 193
Church of England, 84, 89, 106,
    121, 139; *see also* Anglicans,
    Society for the Propagation of
    the Gospel
Church Point (Point de l'Église),
    NS, 140–2
Clare, NS, 80
Coady, Father Moses, 174
Coaker, William, 146, 151,
    163–4, 170
Coal, 1, 62, 79, 123, 127,
    131–33, 139, 146–7, 150,
    165–7, 175, 181–3, 194, 198;
    Cumberland Coal and Rail
    Company, 150; decline of,
    200; Nova Scotia Steel and
    Coal Company, 129, 131, 150,
    165; mining, 10, 114, 122, 145,
    156, 159, 213
Cobequid Bay, NS, 6, 57
Cochrane, Sir Thomas, 110
Coercive Acts, 83
Coffin, Captain Isaac, 81
Colchester County, NS, 81
Cold War, 191, 200, 206–7
Coles, George, 117
College of New Brunswick,
    Fredericton, NB, 89, 106
College St-Joseph, NB, 106, 140
Collins, Enos, 93, 101

colonization, 34–6, 41–5, 48; *see also* settlements

Columbus, Christopher, 23, 25, 27

Come By Chance, NL, 198

Comingo, Joseph Brown, 86

Compagnie des Cent-Associés, 46

Company of Adventurers to Newfoundland, 53

Conception Bay, NL, 40–1, 43, 56, 84, 89, 93, 103, 110, 135

Confederate, The, 189

Confederation (1867), 112–14, 118–25, 136–8, 152, 222; anti-confederates, 113, 120, 122–3, 125; cartoon, 124, 189; dissatisfaction with, 152; J.A. Macdonald, 121, 123–7; Newfoundland, 110–11, 187–9, 209; poets, 153; *see also* British North America Act

Confederation Bridge, 211, 221–2

Congregational church, 80, 89

Congregation of the Holy Cross, 51

Connelly, Archbishop T.L., 122

Conne River, NL, 138, 218

Conroy, Nicolas, 115

Constitution Act (1982), 211, 213–14, 217; Charter of Rights and Freedoms, 205, 213

Continental Congress, 83–4

Cook, James, 79–80

Cook, Ramsey, 44

Cooperatives, 143, 165, 174, 182, 191; *see also* Antigonish Movement

Cooper, William, 110

copper, 101, 200; *see also* mining

Cormack, William, 95, 98, 101

Cornor Brook, NL, 163–4, 170, 180, 221

Cornwallis, Edward, 69

Corte-Real, Gaspar, 23, 26

Corte-Real, Miguel, 26

Cotton industry, 131–33, 179, Canadian Coloured Cotton Company, 133; Dominion Cotton Mills, 133

Coughlan, Reverend Laurence, 89

Council of Atlantic Premiers, 221

Council of Maritime Premiers, 192, 199, 221

Courtney Bay, NB, 100

Crieghton, Helen, 171

Cromwell, Oliver, 48, 54

Crosbie, John, 212–13, 216

Crowley, Brian Lee, 222

Crow's Nest Pass, AB, 167

Cullen, Joseph, 209

Cumberland County, NS, 84, 112

Cunard, Edward, 113–14

Cunard, Samuel, 95, 101, 113, 125

Cupid's Cove, NL, 35, 40–1

Cuyler, Abraham, 86

Dalhousie, NB, 164–5

Dalhousie University, Halifax, NS, 106, 155

Daniel, Captain Charles, 40

Davidson, Sir Walter, 156

Davidson, William, 81

Davies, Brian, 207

Davis Inlet, Labrador, 136, 206

Davis, William, 166, 214

Dawson, Robert McGregor, 185

Dawson, Sir J. William, 1, 3, 5

Day, Frank Parker, *Rockbound*, 171

'Day of Concern' (NB, 1972), 202

Debert, NS, 2, 6, 179

Deerfield Massacre (1703), 57

Demasduit (Mary March), 98

Denson, Henry Denny, 81

Denys, Nicholas, 14, 46, 48

Department of: Fisheries and Oceans (DFO), 217; Regional Economic Expansion (DREE), 194, 202; Regional Industrial Expansion (DRIE), 213

DesBarres, Joseph F.W., 79, 81; *The Atlantic Neptune*, 79

Desmond, Viola, 202

Deutsch, John, 192, 199

Diefenbaker, John, 182, 194, 219

Diereville, Sieur de, 49

Digby, NS, 86, 171

Dingle Bay, Ireland, 24

divorce, 185

Dixon, George, 153

Doiron, François-E., 186

Dominion Fuel Act (1927), 168

Donovan, Kenneth, 63

Dorset (Paleo-Eskimo) peoples, 2; tools, 10

Doucett, Captain John, 66

Doyle, Gerald S., 171

'draft dodgers', 206

Drucour, Governor, 73

Duchambon, Governor Louis Du Pont, 68

Du Gua, Pierre, 35

Duncan, Norman, 153

Duncan, Sir Andrew Rae, 163, 166, 168

Duquesnel, Jean Baptiste-Louis Le Prévost, 68

Dutch peoples, 43, 52–3, 55; immigrants, 206

Duvivier, Captain François Du Pont, 68

Eastern Chronicle, 122

Eastern Townships, QC, 94

Easton, Peter, 40

Eaton, Cyrus, 207

Eaton, Timothy, 133

Echaniz, Joanes de, 29

Eddy, Jonathan, 84

Edinburgh, Scotland, 108

Edmundston, NB, 162, 179

Education, 108, 144, 175, 186–7, 205, 207, 209, 214; and denominationalism, 106, 139; Dominion Schools Act (1871), 139; Mechanics Institutes, 108; post-secondary, 106, 201, 215; public schools, 95, 106, 186, vocational schools, 201; *see also* Literacy

Edward Augustus, Prince, 81, 88

Eel Ground Reserve, 91

Eiriksson, Leif, 22–3

Eirik the Red, 22, 25

Electricity, 186; Beechwood power project, 192, 194; British Newfoundland Corporation (BRINCO), 192, 196; hydro-, 147, 164–5; International Power and Paper, 164

Elizabeth I, 34–5

England, 25–7, 34–5, 40, 46, 48, 53–5, 79, 81–2, 164, 210; abolishes slavery, 95; acquisition of Acadia/Nova Scotia, 60; American Revolution, 84–5, 87–8; Colonial Office, 97, 109–10, 113, 120; Confederation, 120–2, 123, 188; First World War, 155, 160; Imperial War Cabinet, 160; Parliament, 53, 78, 88; Second World War, 178, 180; wars with France, 55–7, 59, 64–8, 74, 91–2; United States, 92–3, 112, 117; West Country, 29–30, 33, 43, 53–5, 72, 98

English peoples: immigrants, 77, 89, 96

environment, 207, 213

equalization legislation, 192–3, 220

Essex County, MA, 80

Europe, 12, 19–20, 22–3, 25, 30, 34, 43, 45, 48, 54, 77, 107, 112, 132, 138, 170, 178, 184–5, 206–8, 210

Europeans: and contact with Aboriginal peoples, 9–12, 14–21, 33; exploration, 22, 24–7; population, 47; settlement, 7, 27, 31, 35, 40–1, 43, 45, 97

European Union, 216

Évangeline, 140

Exploits River, NL, 80, 147

exploration: English, 23–6; French, 23, 27; Norse, 22–5; Portuguese, 23–4, 26–7; Spanish, 26; see also maps and mapping

Fagundes, Joao Alvarez, 27

Family Allowance legislation, 179, 185–6, 201

Feast of the Assumption, 140

Fédération Acadienne de la Nouvelle-Écosse, 202

Fédération francophone de Terre-Neuve et du Labrador, 202

Federation of Newfoundland and Labrador Indians, 206

Fenerty, Charles, 109

Fenians, 119–21; raids, 113

Fergusson, Muriel, 206

Fernandes, João, 26

ferries, 137–8, 144, 151, 168, 179–80

Ferryland, NL, 29, 32, 53–6; plantation 35, 41–3; *see also* Newfoundland and Labrador

Field, Cyrus W., 107

Fielding, W.S., 137

film industry; *L'Acadie, l'Acadie*, 202; *Goin' Down the Road*, 208; *John and the Missus*, 208; *Evangeline*, 154

Fingard, Judith, 136

First World War (1914–18), 145–7, 150, 155–9, 160–2, 164; American Army Nursing Corps, 168; Battle of the Somme, 156; Beaumont Hamel, 146, 156–7; Black peoples, 152, 156; Canadian Expeditionary Force, 156; Canadian Forestry Corps, 156; casualties, 157–9; conscription, 146, 157–8, 164; enlistment rates, 156; First Canadian Division, 156; Imperial War Conference, 160; Mi'kmaq, 156; No 2 Construction Battalion, 156; nurses, 156, 168; Versailles Treaty, 160; veterans, 160

Fischer, Peter, *First History of New Brunswick*, 109

Fisher, Charles, 117

fisheries, 27, 31–3, 40, 43, 45–6, 49, 63, 73–5, 80–1, 94, 104, 121, 122, 129–31, 133–5, 145, 159–64, 175–6, 183, 188, 193, 199–201, 212; Aboriginal Fisheries Strategy, 216; Basques, 23, 28–9; bye-boat, 54–5, 93; canneries, 140; cod, 19, 28–9, 32, 55, 62, 64, 130–1, 137, 164; cod moratorium, 211, 216; collapse of, 215–16; 'dry' cure, 30, 85; English, 29–30, 72, 74; Europe, 27–8; fish farming, 222; fishing banks, 4; fishing room, 53; French, 28–30, 39, 46, 48; herring, 154; inshore, 53, 131; lobster, 130–32, 176, 218; map of, 4; migratory, 43, 53, 55, 60, 74, 83, 93, 99, 103, 110; offshore, 72, 130; Portuguese, 23, 28–30; resident, 43,

93; salmon, 19, 72, 81, 131; saltfish, 30, 55, 101, 130–1, 146, 162, 183, 200; Spanish, 23, 30; sport, 154, 171; turbot, 216; US inshore rights, 146; 'wet' ('green') cure, 30; weir, 14; *see also* sealing industry, whaling industry

Fisheries Products International, 216

Fishermen's Protective Union (FPU), 146, 151, 164, 170

Fléché, Jessé, 37–8

Fleming, Bishop Michael, 116

Flemming, Hugh John, 192–4

Forbes, E.R., 168

Foreign Protestants, 78

forest industries, 94, 128, 132–3, 136, 199–200; *see also* lumber industry, timber industry

Fort: Anne, 37; Beauséjour, 61, 69–70; Cumberland (formerly Fort Beauséjour), NS, 84; Duquesne (Ohio Valley), 70; Edward (Windsor), NS, 69; Howe, 84; Lawrence, 61, 70; Niagara, 70

Fortune Bay, NL, 29

fox farming, 128, 145, 159

France, 27, 34–40, 46–9, 135, 152, 215; American Revolution, 85; Louisbourg, 60–3, 68–9; wars with England, 54–7, 59, 64–8, 74, 85, 91–2

Francklin, Michael, 84

Franks, David, 150

Fraser River, NB, 91

Fredericton, NB, 87, 89, 109, 202, 206, 221

French peoples, 19, 35, 37, 43, 60, 62, 69, 73

French Revolution, 78, 91

free trade, 94–5, 102, 112–15 121, 127, 137, 210–12, 214–15

Frontenac, Comte de, 56

Funk Islands, NL, 97

fur trade, 28, 31, 33, 35–40, 43, 45–9, 72, 98, 136, 205

Gabarus Bay, NS, 68

gaelic language, 91, 172

Gagetown, NB, 86, 121, 200

Gallagher, Del, 197
Galt, Alexander, 113
Gander, NL, 179–80
Gaspé Peninsula, 16–17, 29, 31, 48, 73, 81, 179
Gastaldi, Jacoma di, 30
Gaultois, NL, 11
Geddie, Reverend John, 106
General Mining Association, 95, 101
Geological Survey of Canada, 101, 135, 147
George I, 66–7
George II, 73
George III, 79
Georgetown, PEI, 79
Georgia, USA, 72, 83
German peoples: immigrants, 62, 77, 80
Gesner, Abraham, 1, 97–8, 109
Ghiz, Joseph, 214
Gilbert, Sir Humphrey, 34–5, 45
Gillis, Clarie, 182
Gilpin, Dr J.P., 104
Gisbourne, Frederick Newton, 106
Glace Bay, NS, 146–7, 150, 153, 182
glassworks, 131, 133; Diamond Glass, 133
globalization, 210–11
Gloucester, MA, 130
Godfrey, George, 153
gold mining, 101
Gomes, Estevão, 27
Goose Bay, Labrador, 179–80, 183, 206
Gordon, Arthur Hamilton, 122
Gordon, Walter, 193
Grand Banks, 29, 145, 216
Grand Falls, NB, 164
Grand Falls, NL, 146–7, 151
Grandfontaine, Governor Hector d'Andigné de, 49, 52
Grand Ole Opry, 207
Grand Pré, NS: Battle of, 61; Massacre of, 68; *see also* Acadia, Acadians
Granton, NS, 198
Gray, John Hamilton, 116, 120
Great Britain, *see* England
Great Depression, 162–4, 172–4, 184, 189; stock market crash, 162

Great Eastern, 107
Great Lakes, 6, 70
Greenland, 22–7
Greenleaf, Elisabeth, 171
Greenock, Scotland, 89, 92
Greenpeace, 207
Greenwood, NS, 179, 183
Grenfell, Dr Wilfred, 129, 142–3; Royal National Mission to Deep Sea Fishermen, 143, 205
Griffiths, Naomi, 52, 64
Grimes, Roger, 220
Gros Morne National Park, NL, 3
Guercheville, Marquise de (Antoinette de Pons), 38
Gulf of St Lawrence, 3, 7–8, 21, 23, 27, 29, 31, 33, 55, 79, 85, 130, 220
Guy, John, 40
Guy, Ray, 8
Guysborough County, 172; Guysborough, NS, 86
Gypsum, 79, 101

Hague, The, 146, 153
Haliburton, Thomas Chandler, 109
Halifax, NS, viii, 8, 65, 70, 73–4, 81, 84, 87, 92–3, 100–1, 103, 106, 109, 117–20, 125, 132–4, 152, 160, 168, 171, 221–2; Black people, 203–4; economy, 116, 131, 136, 138, 145, 163, 181–2, 198, 220; First World War, 156–9; founding, 61, 69, 77–8; Pier 21, 184; riots (1945), 179; Second World War, 180–2, 183–4; settlement, 77, 86, 91, 96; sports, 153; theatre, 207
Halifax Harbour Explosion, 146, 157
Halifax Herald, 171, 215
Halifax Magazine Explosion, 180
Halifax Shipyards Limited, 181
Hamilton Inlet, Labrador, 18, 82, 98, 136, 147
Hamm, John, 219
Hammonds Plains, NS, 96
Happy Valley, Labrador, 183
Harbour Grace, NL, 74
Harmony, 160
Harmsworth, Harold and Alfred, 147

Harvard University, 87
Harvey, Moses, 223
Harvey, Sir John, 110
Hatfield, Richard, 196, 198, 202, 214, 219
Haven, Jens, 82
Hay, Gilbert, 209
Haythorne, Robert, 125
Hazen, J.D., 152
Hazen, Lieutenant Moses, 73
Hazen, William, 80
Health care, 157, 186; federal legislation, 201, 214; reform, 142, 151, 168–9
Hébert, Louis, 36
Hebron, Labrador, 99, 205
Hector, 78, 81
Helluland, 22
Henry IV, 35
Henry VII, 25–6
Henry VIII, 27
Herjolfsson, Bjarni, 22
Hillsborough, NB, 80
Hiroshima, Japan, 157
Histoire de la Nouvelle France, 37
Hobsbawm, Eric, 191
Holland, Samuel, 78–9, 81; map by, 79
Hopedale, Labrador, 99
Hopewell, NB, 6, 80
Hopkins, Lady Frances, 54
Hopson, Peregrine Thompson, 70
Howatt, Cornelius, 199
Howe, Joseph, 94, 97, 114–15, 120–2, 123; democratic reform, 110; 'The Blue Nose', 94
Howley, James P., 101
Hoyles, Hugh, 117, 120
Hudson Bay, 10, 57, 59; Company, 85, 98–9, 113, 160, 163, 167, 171, 183
Huguenots, 35, 43
Huron peoples, 84

Iberia, 29–30
Iberville, Pierre Le Moyne d', 47, 56–7
ice age, 2, 4–5
ice boats, 138
iceland, 24; fisheries, 28, 162
Île Madame, NS, 80
Île Royale, 59–60, 62–3, 69, 74;

map of, 65; *see also* Cape
Breton Island; Louisbourg
Île Saint-Jean, 59, 68, 70; settlement, 61, 63–4, 73;
Compagnie de, 64; *see also*
Prince Edward Island, Saint
John's Island
Îles de la Madeleine, 64, 71, 76,
79–80, 85
immigration, 117, 121; in 17th
century, 48, 77–8, 80–3, 85–9,
91; in 19th century, 104, 136,
206
Imo, 157
Imperial Federation Movement,
142
India, 24, 105
Industrial Estates Limited, 192,
197
inflation, 212
influenza epidemic (1918),
145–6, 160
Inglis, Bishop Charles, 89
Ingstad, Helge and Anne, 24
Innu (Montagnais-Naskapi), 12,
54, 185, 189, 205–6, 216, 217;
contact with Europeans, 18, 21,
31, 33, 98, 136; origins, 11;
women, 18
International Fisherman's Trophy,
173
International Fund for Animal
Welfare, 205
Inuit (Eskimo), 12, 83, 160, 183,
189, 205–6, 217–18; and contact with Europeans, 18–21,
31, 98–9, 136; Inuktitut, 99;
origins, 10; shamans, 19
Ireland, 24, 91, 104, 121; famine,
95–6
Irish peoples, 140; immigrants,
62, 72, 81, 83, 89, 91, 96; sectarian conflict, 106
iron, 3, 101, 133, 135, 200; *see
also* mining, steel industry
Ironbound Island, NS, 171
Iroquois peoples (Houdenosaunee), 31, 52, 56–7
Irving, K.C., 198, 219
Isthmus of Chignecto, 65, 69–70,
81

James I, 35, 40
James Bay, 147

Jefferson, President Thomas, 92
Jemseg, NB, 49, 56
Jeremy, Josiah, 22
jesuits, 38–9, 50
Jodrey, R.A., 198
Joggins, NS, 1, 139
Johns Hopkins University, 168
Johnstone, Walter, 96
Jones, John, 89
Jones, Walter 'Farmer', 186
J. Rhodes, Curry, and Co, 132,
150
Jukes, James, 101
Julien, John, 91
Juno Awards, 207

Karlsefni, Thorfinn, 23
Karpeles, Maud, 171
Kavanagh, Lawrence, 105
Keddy, Betty, 207
Kentville, NS, 206
King's College, Windsor, NS, 89,
106
King, William Lyon Mackenzie,
167, 185, 191
King William's Act (1699), 55,
61, 110
King William's War (1689–97),
55–6
Kirke, Lady Sara, 54
Kirke, Sir David, 40, 47, 53–4
Kji-kinap (Mi'kmaq deity), 1
Kluskap (Glooscap), 1
Korean War, 200

labour, 201; legislation, 134, 146,
151, 198, 210; unemployment
insurance, 179, 185, 193, 201,
214; unrest and strikes, 139,
145–6, 150–1, 158, 160,
162–3, 165–6, 173, 179, 181,
186, 192, 194, 201–202
Labrador, vii–viii, 2–4, 6, 12, 14,
18–22, 27, 29–31, 59, 74–6,
78–80, 82–5, 93, 94, 129–30,
136, 142–3, 171–3, 177–9,
188, 193, 216, 217, 222;
boundary with Québec, 147,
163; economy, 195, 205–6;
flag, 199; Geological Survey,
147; naming, 26; political parties, 199; population, 98–9;
prehistory, 7, 10–11, 25; *see also*
Newfoundland and Labrador

Labrador City, 195
Labrador Inuit Association (LIA),
205–6, 218
La Hève (La Have), NS, 39, 46–7
Lake Champlain, 70
Lake Melville, Labrador, 98, 143
Landry, Israel J-D, 106
Lane, Michael, 79
Langford, Sam, 153
L'Anse Amour, NL, 18, 19
L'Anse-aux-Meadows, NL, 9, 37
Larkins, Joseph, 134
La Rochelle, France, 28, 39
La Tour, Charles de Saint-
Etienne de, 36, 39, 46–8
La Tour, Claude de Saint-
Etienne de, 39–40
La Tour, Françoise-Marie
Jaquelin, 48
Lattimer, Dr J.E., 185
Laurent, Jean Baptiste, 63
Laurier, Sir Wilfrid, 137, 152
Lawrence, Governor Charles, 70,
78; letter expelling Acadians,
71
League of Nations, 161
Le Borgne de Belle-Isle, Alex-
andre, 54
Le Borgne, Emmanuel, 47–8
Le Clerq, Chrestien, 16, 51
Le Loutre, Abbé Jean-Louis,
64–5, 68–70
Lennox Island, PEI, 91, 98
Lescarbot, Marc, 36–7, 43
Lewis, Maud, 206
literacy, 108, 114, 144, 187; *see
also* Education
literature: in 17th century, 37–8;
in the 19th century, 109; in
the 20th century, 153–4, 171
Liverpool, England, 101
Liverpool, NS, 92–3, 164
Liverpool Packet, 93
Livingstone, 'Red Dan', 166
Loch Lomond, NB, 96
London and Bristol Company,
40
London Conference (1866), 115
Londonderry, NS, 81, 101, 182
London, England, 35, 42, 53, 83,
97, 108–10, 123–5, 128, 138,
152, 159, 162, 173–5, 188
Longfellow, Henry Wadsworth,
Evangeline (1847), 139

Longley, J.W., 142
Loppinot, Jean Chrysostome, 63
Lord, Bernard, 219
Lord's Day Act (1907), 146, 151
Louisbourg (Havre L'Anglois),
    NS, 60–2, 68–9, 71, 73, 77–8;
    restoration of, 198; slavery at,
    63
Louis XIII, 46
Louis XIV, 48–9, 56
Lovelace, Bernard and Sandra,
    205
Low, A.P., 147
Lowell, Reverend R.T.S., *The
    New Priest in Conception Bay*,
    109
Lower Canada (Canada East), 78,
    115; *see also* Canada, Québec
Loyalists, 85–8, 121, 141; settle-
    ments, 86; *see also* Black peo-
    ples
Lucas, Francis, 82
lumber industry, 46, 128–9, 156,
    175; *see also* forest industries,
    pulp and paper industry, news-
    print industry, timber industry
Lunenburg County, NS, 81;
    Lunenburg, NS, 9, 77, 131, 162
Lunenburg Progress-Enterprise, 171
Lyell, Charles, 1, 3

McCain family, 198
McCullough, Thomas, 91; *The
    Stepsure Letters*, 95, 109
McCurdy, John A.D., 146, 153
Macdonald, Angus L., 172, 175,
    185–6
Macdonald, Donald, 212
Macdonald, Douglas, 182
MacDonald, John, 83
Macdonald, John A., 113, 121,
    123–7, 137
MacDonald, Margaret, 156
Macdonald, Reverend Ewan, 153
McGill University, Montréal,
    QC, 185
MacGregor, James, 91
McKay, Ian, 159
McKenna, Frank, 214, 219
Mackenzie, Norman A.M., 185
MacKinnon, Bruce, 215
McLachlan, James B., 150, 166,
    182
MacLean, J. Angus, 219

MacLellan, Gene, 207
MacLeod, Reverend Norman,
    104
MacMaster, Natalie, 207
McNair, J.B., 186, 194
McNutt, Alexander, 81
MacNutt, W.S., 193
Madawaska, NB, 86, 94
Magdalen Islands, 103
Maillard, Abbé Pierre-Antoine-
    Simon, 15, 64, 69
Maine, 7, 17, 31, 33, 39, 52, 92,
    114–15
Malli, Chief Joseph, 97
Maliseet (Malecite,
    Wulstukwiuk), 12, 16, 51, 56,
    68, 80, 91, 136, 216, 218;
    Acadians, 51–2, 84, 86; British
    authorities, 65, 97–8; cultural
    practices, 17; European trade,
    33; treaties with British, 61,
    65–6, 69; Woodland (Ceramic)
    peoples, 8; *see also* Native peo-
    ples
Manitoba, 152, 167, 214
maps and mapping, 30, 41,
    79–80; *see also* exploration
Marchand, Jean, 202
Marconi, Guglielmo, 153; *see also*
    Telegraph
Maritime Freight Rates Act
    (1927), 168
Maritime Provinces, 1, 3–4, 6–7,
    14, 43, 89, 90–2, 112, 128–9,
    144, 160, 178; economy,
    100–1, 103–4, 131–3, 147,
    150, 162–5, 167, 172, 176,
    181–3, 191–3; First World War,
    155–7; folklore, 171; govern-
    ment, 110–11, 137–8, 152,
    175–6; 'home children', 136;
    population, 8, 94–7, 135–6,
    140, 145, 164; religious activi-
    ty, 105–6, 140–2; sports, 153;
    trade, 145
Maritime Provinces Higher
    Education Commission, 201
Maritime Rights movement,
    167–8
Maritime Union, 120, 123, 137,
    192
Markland, 22, 25
Marshall, Donald, 211, 217
Marshall, Stephen Frederick, 218

Marshall, Teresa, 209
Maryland, USA, 43, 72
Matheson, Alexander, 192
Martin, Paul, 220
Mascarene, Paul, 68
Mason, John, 26, 41
Massachusetts, USA, 34, 43, 52,
    57, 65, 68, 72, 80, 83–4, 87,
    156; General Court, 56
Massé, Énemond, 38
Mauger, Joshua, 77, 80
Maximilian, Archduke, 112
May, Elizabeth, 207
Mediterranean, 30
Meech Lake Accord (1987), 211,
    214
Meighen, Arthur, 167
Membertou reserve, 216–7
Memramcook, NB, 140–1
Merchant marine, 100
Métis peoples, 218
Methodist church, 81, 89, 105–6,
    139
Mexico, 27, 112, 200, 210
Michelin Tire, 197–8
Mikak (Inuk), 82
Mi'kma'ki, vii, 60
Mi'kmaq (Micmac), 1, 36–7, 56,
    62, 68, 84, 91, 106, 136,
    216–18; Acadians, 39–40,
    51–2; British authorities, 65,
    69, 84, 97–8; creation stories,
    1; cultural practices, 14–18, 65;
    dictionary, 98; European con-
    tact, 15–18, 22, 43, 47;
    European trade, 31, 33; First
    World War, 156;
    Newfoundland, 80, 189; oral
    traditions, 15, 17–18, 98; pop-
    ulation, 60; Port-Royal, 36, 38;
    spiritual beliefs, 12, 16, 51;
    treaties with British, 61, 66–7,
    70, 73; women, 16; Woodland
    (Ceramic) peoples, 8; *see also*
    Native peoples
Minas Basin, NS, 49, 57, 81
mining, 95, 100–1, 133–5,
    199–200, 205; *see also* coal,
    copper, iron
Minister's Island, NB, 150
Mira (Riviere de Miré), NS, 62
Mirimachi River, NB, 8, 73, 81,
    84, 91–2, 160; Great Fire, 95–6
Miscou Island, 64

Miscouche, NB, 140–1
Missaguash River, NS, 69
Missionaries, 54, 64, 84, 98–9;
  evangelical churches, 105–6;
  see also Capuchins; Jesuits;
  Moravians; Récollets
Mohawk peoples, 68
Monckton, Colonel Robert, 70
Moncton, NB, 3, 80, 132, 147,
  179, 202, 220–1
Moniteur Acadien, 106
Mont Blanc, 157
Montgomery, Sir James, 83, 91
Montgomery, Lucy Maud, 153,
  155; *Anne of Green Gables*,
  146, 153, 155; 'The Island
  Hymn', 155
Montigny, Testard de, 56, 58
Montréal, QC, 57, 73, 106, 113,
  131–5, 150, 166, 180, 212
Monts, Pierre Du Gua, Sieur de,
  35–7
Moores, Frank, 198
Moravians (Unitas
  Fratrum/United Brethren), 19,
  78–9, 82–3, 98, 160, 183, 205
Morning Chronicle, 122
Morse, Samuel, 109
Morris, Patrick, 110
Morris, Sir Edward, 156, 159
Motin, Jeanne, 48
Mount Allison University, Sack-
  ville, NB, 106, 208
Mount Carleton, NB, 7
Mount Caubvick, Labrador, 7
Mount Desert Island (Saint-
  Sauveur), 39
Mount Saint Vincent University,
  Halifax, NS, 106
Mulroney, Brian, 210, 212, 214
mummering, 108; mummers'
  Troupe, 207–8
Murray, Alexander, 101
Murray, Anne, 207
Murray, George, 151
Murray, Rear-Admiral L.W., 184
Musquodoboit Harbour (Mous-
  coudabouet), NS, 49

Nain, Labrador, 19, 78, 82–3, 98,
  218
Napoleon III, 114
Napoleonic Wars, 77–8, 86,
  91–3, 101, 110

Nashwaak, NB, 56
National Energy Policy, 210
National Farmers Union, 199
National Film Board, 202
National Policy, 121, 129, 131,
  133, 147
National Sea Products Ltd, 179,
  183, 216
Native peoples: Acadians, 64,
  68–71, 200; alliances, 56, 64–5,
  71; British authorities, 60, 76,
  77, 84, 97–8; cartoon, 217;
  Confederation, 136, 189; contact with Europeans, 12–13,
  15, 27, 33–4; cultural practices
  of, 12, 15–16; diseases, 45, 160;
  European trade, 14; French
  clergy, 35–6, 64–5; Indian
  Affairs, 121; Indian Act (1876),
  136, 189, 204–5; Indian
  Commissioners, 97–8; land
  claims, 218; political activism
  of, 204–5; prehistory of, 5–11;
  reserves, 8, 91, 97–8, 205; slavery, 63; suffrage, 192; treaties
  with British, 66–7, 73, 75;
  White Paper (1969), 192,
  204–5; *see also* Abenaki peoples, Algonkian peoples,
  Archaic cultures, Beothuk,
  Dorset, Huron, Innu, Inuit,
  Iroquois, Maliseet, Mi'kmaq,
  Mohawk, Ottawa, Paleo-
  Indians, Passamaquoddy, Thule,
  Woodland (Ceramic)
Navigation Acts, 91
Nepisiquit, NB, 46
Neptune Theatre, 207
New Brunswick, vii, 6, 16, 25,
  60, 85, 107, 159, 203, 207,
  214, 218–20; banks, 95; bilingualism, 192, 196, 202–3, 217,
  219; boundary dispute, 94;
  Confederation, 115, 118,
  120–2; 'Day of Concern'
  (1972), 202; education, 106,
  139; economy, 114–15,
  198–200, 202; environment,
  207; founding, 78; geology, 3;
  government, 110, 117, 161,
  192, 197; Land Protection Act,
  219; population, 117, 145, 221;
  prehistory 7–8; prohibition,
  95; railways, 149; religious

activity, 105–6; rights to natural resources, 216–18; settlement, 80, 87–8, 91; shipbuilding, 92; as timber colony, 92
New Dublin, NS, 81
New England, 6, 8, 14, 46, 49,
  52, 55, 57, 61, 64–6, 68–9, 80,
  92, 128, 130, 222; American
  Revolution, 83–5, 87
New England Planters, 78, 80,
  85
Newfoundland, 154
Newfoundland and Labrador, vii;
  12, 14, 17, 19, 54, 79–80, 86,
  89, 99, 211, 214, 220, 223;
  American Revolution, 83, 85;
  Anglo-French wars, 70–1;
  bilingualism, 202; as British
  colony, 61, 75, 95, 110,
  169–71; Commission
  Government, 174–5, 180,
  187–8, 194; Confederation
  (1949), vii, 114–15, 120,
  124–5, 127, 138, 174, 179,
  187–9, 191, 194, 209; Dutch
  attack on, 55; economy,
  128–9, 131, 133, 135, 137–8,
  147, 162, 176, 178, 191–97;
  education, 106, 139; elections,
  106; English Shore, 31, 44,
  53–5, 57; European exploration, 22–7, 45; First World
  War, 146, 159–60; fisheries, 23,
  40, 47, 54–6, 59, 72, 74, 83,
  85, 93, 99, 130, 143, 146–7,
  152–3, 160, 162–4, 169–70,
  172–3, 175, 183, 188, 201,
  211, 215–16; French invasion,
  73–4; French Treaty Shore, 60,
  74–6, 85, 111, 135, 146, 152;
  geology, 2–4; Geological
  Survey, 101, 133; government,
  95, 109–110, 119–20, 161,
  163, 173–5, 201–2, 205–6;
  'Grant of', 53; map, 41; literature, 109; mummering, 108;
  National Convention
  (1946–8), 187–8; newspapers,
  106; 'Ode to Newfoundland',
  154; offshore oil, 212–13, 220;
  outport resettlement, 196–7;
  'Policy of Progress', 135, 147;
  population, 72–3, 83, 119,
  136–7, 221; prehistory, 7,

10–11; railways, 147–8; religious activity, 89, 105–6; sealing, 102–3; Second World War, 178–9, 184–5; settlement, 22–5, 29, 34–5, 40–3, 46, 53–5, 91, 96; social reform, 142–4, 168–9; Supreme Court, 78, 89; Term 29, 194; tourism, 154; *see also* Ferryland; Labrador
Newfoundland Electric Telegraph Co., 107
Newfoundlander, The, 106
Newfoundland Fishermen, Food, and Allies Workers, 201
Newfoundland Industrial Workers Association, 158
Newfoundland Outport Nursing and Industrial Association (NONIA), 168
Newfoundland Patriotic Association (NPA), 156, 159
Newfoundland Ranger Force, 175
Newfoundland Regiment, 156–8
New France (Nouvelle France), 36–7, 46, 56, 70, 74; map of, 30; *see also* Acadia
New Glasgow, NS, 122, 129
New Hampshire, USA, 66, 81, 87–8
New Hebrides, 106
New Relation of Gaspésia, 51
New Scotland 48; *see also* Nova Scotia
newspapers, 94, 106, 108, 147, 151
newsprint industry, 163–4, 170, 176, 181; *see also* pulp and paper industry
New Waterford, NS, 179, 184
New York, USA, 72, 74, 79, 85, 87, 89, 107–8, 135
Nicholson, General Francis, 57
Nobel Peace Prize, 207
Normandy, France 28, 30
Norris, Joseph, 209
Norse, 22–5
North America, 7, 14, 18–19, 24, 26–7, 33–4, 37, 43, 52, 57, 60, 64, 68, 70–3, 81–3, 91–2, 101, 107, 121, 135, 162, 176–80, 186, 206, 211
Northern Peninsula, NL, 4, 23

Northumberland Strait, 9, 138
Northwest Atlantic Fisheries Organization (NAFO), 216
Northwest Rebellion, 137
North West River, Labrador, 134
Notre Dame Bay, NL, 72, 101, 151
Nova Scotia, vii, 1, 6, 24, 29, 36, 49, 64–6, 69–70, 74, 76, 207, 218–19; American Revolution, 83–5; annexation of Cape Breton, 95; bilingualism, 202; British acquisition of, 60; coat of arms and flag, 40; Confederation, 115, 119–23, 129, 137; economy, 93, 116, 163–6, 172, 174, 181–3, 192, 197–200; education, 89, 106, 139, 151; geology, 3, 5; government, 95, 78, 105, 110–11, 161, 165, 167–8; naming, 40; offshore oil, 211, 213, 220; population, 119, 145, 221; prehistory, 7–8; railways, 95, 149; religious activity, 89, 105–6; Scottish heritage, 172; settlement, 35–40, 77–8, 80–8, 90; sports, 108; surveyed, 79; *see also* New Scotland
Nova Scotia Association for the Advancement of Coloured People, 202–3; *see also* Black peoples
Nova Scotia Technical College, 151
Nunatsiavut agreement (2005), 211, 218
Nutak, Labrador, 205

Oak Island, 24
Oblates of Mary Immaculate, 98
Ocean Ranger disaster, 211, 213
Ochiltree, Lord, 40
O'Donnell, Father James, 89
Official Languages Act, 202
oil: crisis, 210–11; Hibernia, 212–13; Mobil Oil, 213; natural gas, 3, 101, 191, 198, 200, 222
Okak, Labrador, 98, 160
Ontario, 113, 119, 128, 136, 141, 152, 155, 167, 178, 182, 194, 208, 214
Order of Good Cheer (Ordre de

Bon Temps), 35, 37, 172, 195
Organization of Petroleum Exporting Countries (OPEC), 210
Orwell-Point Prim, PEI, 91
Osborne, Captain Henry, 61–2
Ottawa (as federal government), 123, 125, 128, 137–9, 152, 159, 162, 167, 172–5, 178, 185, 187–8, 191–4, 198–9, 210, 212–13, 220–2
Ottawa peoples, 84

Paleo-Indians, 2, 5–7, 11
Palliser, Jonathan, 82
Palliser, Sir Hugh, 78, 82–3
Palmer, Edward, 115–16
Paris, France, 36, 38, 40, 46, 53, 153; custom of, 48; peace conference, 160
Parkhurst, Anthony, 29
Parkin, George, 142
Parmenius, Stephen, 45
Partridge Island, NB, 96
Passamaquoddy Bay, 8
Passamaquoddy peoples, 52, 56, 61, 65–6, 69, 73, 97, 216
Patriot, The, 106
Patterson, Stephen E., 72
Paul, Leonard, 209
Paul, Thomas Peter, 218
Pearson, Lester B., 194
Peckford, Brian, 212
Peggy's Cove, NS, 5, 171
Penobscot people, 52, 56
Penobscot River, Maine, 31, 39, 66
Pennsylvania, USA, 72, 80–1
Pentagouet, NB, 49, 52
Pepperrell, William, 68
Perley, Moses, 97
Peters, Thomas, 122
Petit, Father Louis, 51
Petit Nord, NL, 59
Philiadelphia, USA, 81, 83
Philipps, Governor Richard, 65
Phips, Sir William, 47, 56
Pickersgill, J.W., 191, 193
Pictou Academy, 109
Pictou County, NS, 1, 81, 101, 133, 213; Pictou, NS, 91, 95, 100, 116, 139, 171, 186
Pisiquid Bay, NS, 57
Pitts, Herbert H., 141
Placentia, NL, 29, 32, 41, 62; *see*

also Plaisance
Plaisance, NL, 47, 55–8, 62
Point Lepreau nuclear power
  plant, 219
Point Revenge, NL, 11
Point Riche, NL, 59
Poitou, France, 47, 49
political parties: Communist,
  175, 186; Conservative, 113,
  115–16, 119, 125, 161, 167,
  192–6, 198, 210, 212–14,
  219–20; Cooperative
  Commonwealth Federation
  (CCF), 175, 182, 196, 201;
  Confederation of Regions
  Party (COR), 219; Farmer, 161,
  165; Labour, 161, 165; Liberal,
  111, 119–20, 125, 137, 161,
  165, 167, 192, 194, 196, 219;
  New Democratic Party (NDP),
  201, 219; New Labrador Party,
  199; Parti Acadian, 192, 202;
  Parti Québécois, 210–11;
  Progressive, 161, 167;
  Reconstruction, 175; Reform,
  115, 210
Poor, Joseph Alfred, 115
Pope, James, 125
Pope, Peter, 54
population, 221; growth, 164;
  out-migration, 135–6, 141,
  161–3, 186, 191, 220
Port au Choix, NL, 7, 10, 70
Port-aux-Baleines, NS, 40
Port aux Basques, NL, 71, 180
Porter, Gladys, 206
Port Hawkesbury, NS, 198
Porland Point, NB, 80
Port Lomeron, NS, 39
Port-Royal, NS, 35–40, 44, 46–9,
  51, 57, 60, 172; Champlain's
  map, 37; *see also* Annapolis
  Royal
Portugal, 26, 29–30, 216; King
  Manoel, 26
Portuguese peoples: exploration,
  24, 26–7; fishery, 28–9
Port Union, NL, 151
potatoes, 104, 130, 145, 164
Pouch Cove, NL, 8
Poutrincourt et de Saint-Just,
  Jean de, 36–9
Presbyterian church, 91, 106
Preston, NS, 96

Preston, Reverend Richard,
  104–5
Prince Edward Island, vii, 15, 27,
  59, 95–6, 98, 101, 107, 152,
  163, 167–8, 214, 219–22;
  bilingualism, 202;
  Confederation, 113, 122,
  124–5; education, 106, 186–7;
  economy, 93, 103, 164, 172,
  192, 196–7; First World War,
  158; geology, 3, 5; horse racing, 153; Land Commission,
  113, 115; Land Purchase Act
  (1853), 115; naming, 78; population, 119, 141, 145, 221; prehistory, 6, 8; proprietors, 78,
  106, 110, 117–9; railways, 148;
  religious activity, 105–6; settlement, 91; social reform, 129,
  151, 168–8; soils, 3; surveyed,
  79; Tenant League, 113,
  117–18, 127; *see also* Île Saint-
  Jean, Saint John's Island
Prince Madoc, 24
Prince of Wales College,
  Charlottetown, PEI, 106, 155
Princetown, PEI, 79
privateers, 43, 54, 56–7, 68, 85,
  92–3, 101
Programme of Equal
  Opportunity, 196
prohibition, 95, 105, 129, 141,
  146, 151, 159, 163, 170; Scott
  Act (1878), 142; *see also* temperance
protectionism, 123, 214
Protestants, 35, 41, 89, 96, 106,
  119; Reformation, 43; Orange
  Order, 106, 188
Provincial Workman's Association
  (PWA), 129, 139, 150
Public Ledger, The, 106
Pubnico (Pobomcoup), NS, 49
Pugwash Conference on Science
  and World Affairs, 206–7
pulp and paper industry, 146–7,
  164, 199; *see also* newsprint

Quakers, 83
Québec, 14, 40, 48–9, 51, 54–5,
  60, 68–9, 72, 78–80, 83–5,
  97–8, 103, 105, 113, 119, 128,
  131, 141, 147, 152, 156, 159,
  165, 167, 171, 178, 180, 185,

194–5, 218, 220, 222;
  Confederation, 119, 120–3;
  Hydro-Québec, 192, 196; ref-
  erendums, 211, 213–14; *see also*
  Lower Canada
Québec Act, 75
Québec City, 27, 114, 136, 141
Québec Conference (1864), 113
Queen's University, 199
Quidi Vidi Lake, NL, 108

Railways, 95, 109, 112, 116–175,
  122, 125, 131, 165, 170, 195;
  1914 (maps), 148–9; Canadian
  National, 163; Canadian
  Pacific, 133, 135, 137; Grand
  Trunk, 120; Intercolonial,
  113–175, 119, 122–3, 129,
  132–3, 147, 163–7;
  Newfoundland, 144, 147–8;
  Québec Railway Company,
  116
Ramah Bay, Labrador, 7
Ramezay, Sieur de, 68
Rand, Chief Justice Ivan, 198
Rand, Silas, 22, 98
Rawdon, NS, 86
Razilly, Isaac de, 46–8
Reagan, Ronald, 210
Recent Indians, 11
Reciprocity, 137–8, 152; Treaty
  (1854), 95, 102, 122, 123, 128,
  131; *see also* free trade
Récollets, 40, 50
Red Bank reserve, 8
Red Bay, Labrador, 28–9
Red Cross, 159, 168–97, 172
Red Indian Lake, NL, 80, 98
Reid, John, 59
Reid Newfoundland Company,
  158, 164
Reid, Robert G., 135
Renews, NL, 41, 53–4
representative government, 95,
  109–10
responsible government, 94–5,
  110–11, 119, 121, 127, 163,
  174, 187–8
Restigouche River, NB, 97
Rhodes, E.N., 167
Richard, Father Marcel-François,
  140
Richelieu, Cardinal, 46
Ritchie, J.W., 116

roads, 171, 186, 196, 215
Roberts, Charles G.D., 153
Robertson, Ian, 125
Robichaud, Louis J., 196, 199
Roche, Marquis de la, 35
Rogers, Malcolm, 198
Rogers, Stan, 207
Roma, Jean-Pierre, 64, 68
Roman Catholics, 35, 41, 89, 91, 96, 106, 119–20, 125, 139–42, 175; emancipation, 95, 105
Roman Catholic church, 48, 50–1, 63, 175; convents, 119; *see also* Capuchins; Jesuits; Récollets
Rose, Marie Marguerite, 63
Rouen, France, 35
Rous, Captain John, 70
Royal Canadian Legion, 184
Royal Canadian Mounted Police (RCMP), 194
Royal Commission on: Canada's Economic Prospects (1955), 192–4, 211; Canada's Economic Union and Development Prospects/Macdonald Commission (1985), 212; Coal (1960), 198; Coal Mining Industry (1925), 163, 166–7; Dominion-Provincial Relations/Rowell-Sirois Commission (1940), 175, 185; Fisheries of the Maritime Provinces/Maclean Commission (1927), 163; Labour and Capital (1889), 134; Maritime Claims/Duncan Commission (1926), 163, 168; Municipal Finance and Taxation/Bryne Commission (1960), 196; Newfoundland/Amulree Commission (1933), 163, 173–4; Newfoundland and Labrador's Place in Canada, 211, 220; Provincial Development/Dawson Commission, 187; Reconstruction/Bates Commission (1944), 183; the Status of Women (1970), 192, 206
rum, 78; rum-running, 170
Rupert's Land, 113, 125
Russia, 121; Bolshevik Revolu-
tion, 160; *see also* Soviet Union
Russell, John, 82
Russell, Lord John, 110
Rut, John, 27

Sable Island, NS, 35
Saco River, Maine, 17
Saglek Bay, Labrador, 3, 7, 11
St Andrew's, NB, 86, 92, 96, 150
St Ann's, NS, 104, 172
St Anthony, NL, 143
St Brendan, 24
Saint-Castin, Bernard-Anselme d'Abbadie de, 52
St Dunstan's University, 106
Ste-Croix River, NB, 35–6, 40, 94
St Francis Xavier Univerity, Antigonish, NS, 106, 174
St George's Bay, NL, 71
St-Jean-Baptiste Day, 141
Saint John, NB, 66, 86–7, 91–2, 106–7, 110, 115, 121, 128, 132–3, 136, 159, 168, 171, 184, 217, 221; commission government, 146, 151; economy, 198; fire, 129; lumbering, 129; shipbuilding, 98–100
Saint John River, 17, 46–8, 56, 72–3, 79, 84, 92, 94, 96, 128; settlement, 80, 86–7
St John's, NL, 29, 34, 43, 55–7, 82, 89, 91, 93, 98, 100–1, 103, 107–8, 110, 119, 146–7, 151, 153–5, 170–1, 187–8, 208, 220–1; fire, 129; First World War, 156–7; French attack on, 61, 74; labour unrest, 150–1, 170, 172–5; riot (1932), 173; newspapers, 106–7; Second World War, 179–80, 184; sports, 108
St John's Island, 72, 74, 78–81, 83–4, 86, 91; *see also* Île Royale, Prince Edward Island
St Laurent, Louis, 191–2
St Laurent, Madame de, 88
St Lawrence River, 27, 29, 37, 40, 46, 49, 60, 62, 94, 114, 131, 180
St Margaret's Bay, NS, 8
St Martins, NS, 100
St Mary's Bay, NS, 218
St Mary's University, Halifax, NS, 106
Saint Paul's Church, Halifax, NS, 74
St Paul River, Labrador, 29
Saint-Pierre, Comte de, 61, 64
Saint-Pierre (St Peter's), NS, 46, 49, 62, 64, 128, 135
St Pierre et Miquelon, 71, 74, 76, 85, 170
St Stephens, NB, 133
Saint-Vallier, Bishop, 51
Salvation Army, 142
Sandwich Bay, Labrador, 85
San Juan, 29
Saskatchewan, 156, 167, 196, 219
Saunders, Margaret Marshall, *Beautiful Joe*, 153
Saunders, S.A., 165
Savage, John, 219
Savoie, Donald J., 6–7, 218
Scandanavia, 3, 22
Scotland, 34, 81, 91, 108
Scottish peoples: immigrants, 62, 81, 83, 89, 91, 96
sealing industry, 19, 72, 93, 101–3, 130, 146–7, 154, 207–8; *see also* animals
Second World War, 162–3, 169–70, 175, 171, 178, 191, 204, 212; Battle of the Atlantic, 180; Battle of the St Lawrence, 180; U-Boats, 179–80
Sedgewick, Robert, 47–8
Selkirk, Earl of, 91
Sellar's Cove site, NS, 8
settlement, 90; Acadian, 39, 57–8; English, 40–1, 77; French, 36–40; Irish, 81, 89; late 18th century, 77–8; Loyalist, 85–8; New England, 80; Norse, 22–5; Scottish, 40, 81, 89, 91; Yorkshire, 81; *see also* colonization
Seven Years' War (1756–63), 61, 72–4, 78–80, 83
Seward, William (US Secretary of State), 121
Shaheen, John, 198
Shanawdithit (Beothuk), 19, 95, 98
Shannon, HMS, 92
Shediac, NB, 106, 115
Shelburne, NS, 86, 92, 179

Sherbrooke, Sir John, 92

Sheshatshiu, Labrador, 205

Shirley, Governor, 68

shipbuilding, 77, 81, 89, 91–3, 100–1, 129, 137, 181

Ship Harbour, NS, 86

Short, Richard, 74

Shubenacadie, NS, 65

Sierra Leone, 78, 88; *see also* Black peoples

Signal Hill, NL, 153

Sillutalik, Labrador, 160

Simmonds, Mary, 87

Simonds, Charles, 110

Simonds, James, 80

Sinclair, Henry, 24

Skora, NS, 8

slavery: 62–3, 88; Act to Abolish (1833), 95; Code Noir, 63; *see also* Black peoples; Native peoples

Smallwood, Joseph R., 191, 195, 198–9; Churchill Falls hydro project, 193, 196; Confederation, 187–9, 194; labour unrest, 194

Smith, Albert J., 122

Snow, Hank, 207

Sobey, Frank, 198

'Social Gospel', 142

Société Saint-Thomas-d'Aquin, 202

Society for the Propagation of the Gospel, 89; *see also* Church of England

South America, 162

South Carolina, USA, 72

Southern Cross, 154

Southampton, England, 34

Soviet Union, 207; *see also* Russia

Sovereignty referendum, 210

Spain, 26–7, 29–30, 216

Spanish Armada, 29

Springhill, NS, 139, 146, 150; mining disasters, 200

Squires, Helena, 206

Squires, Richard, 170, 172–3, 187

Stanfield, Robert, 192, 197–8

Steele, Harry, 198

steel industry, 127, 131, 145, 147, 150, 156, 159, 165–64, 181, 198, 213; British Empire Steel

Corp (BESCO), 163, 165–6; Dominion Iron and Steel Company, 129, 131–2, 150, 163; Dominion Steel and Coal Corporation (DOSCO), 181, 186; Dominion Steel Company, 146, 150; Scotia and Dominion Steel, 163; Sydney Steel Corporation, 198; *see also* iron, mining

Stephenville, NL, 180, 183

Stewart, J.D., 167

Stewart, Captain Robert, 83

Stora Forest, 197

Strait of Belle Isle, 3, 6–7, 11, 23, 26–9, 79, 83, 103

Strait of Canso, 9

Subercase, Governor Daniel d'Auger de, 57

sugar industry, 129, 131, 133

Sullivan, Laurence, 125

Summerside, PEI, 179, 183

Swiss peoples: immigrants 62

Sydney (Baie-des-Espagnols), NS, 62, 86, 131, 133–4, 145, 160, 166, 179, 184, 221; Tar Ponds, 213

Sydney Mines, NS, 129, 131

Syliboy, Alan, 209

Syliboy, Chief Gabriel, 214

Tadoussac, NB, 33

Tansley, Donald, 196

Tatauk (Inuit), 82

telegraph, 95, 107, 109, 153; New York, Newfoundland, and London Telegraphy Company, 107; *see also* Marconi, Guglielmo

Telegraph Journal, 217

temperance, 105, 123, 142, 144; sons of, 122, 142; *see also* prohibition

Temple, Sir Thomas, 48

Ternay, Charles-Henry d'Arsac de, 74

Thatcher, Margaret, 210

theatre, 207–8; 'They Club Seals, Don't They?', 207

Le Théâtre de Neptune en la Nouvelle France, 37–8

Thom River, 91

Thule peoples, 2, 10–11

Tignish, PEI, 117

Tilley, Samuel Leonard, 121–2

timber industry, 80–1, 86, 91–3, 100–1, 104, 135, 147; *see also* forest industries, lumber industry

Tobin, Brian, 216

Tobique Reserve, 205

Torbay, NL, 61, 179

Toronto, ON, 129, 132–3, 135, 150, 168, 212

tourism, 15–24, 171–2, 197

Transtlantic: steamship service, 95, 101

Treaty of: Aix-la-Chapelle (1748), 61, 68; Breda (1667), 47–8; Paris (1763), 60–1, 74–5, 78; Paris (1783), 75, 78, 85; Peace and Friendship (1752), 61; Ryswick (1697), 47, 57; Saint-Germain-en-Laye (1632), 35, 40, 46, 54; Tordesillas (1494), 26; Utrecht (1713), 47, 59–62, 64, 66, 69, 72, 75; Versailles (1763), 75; Washington (1871), 113, 126, 129–31

Trent Affair, 114–15

Trenton, NS, 133

Trepassey, NL, 29, 154

Trinity Bay, NL, 56, 74

Trinity Church (NY), 89

Trois Rivières, QC, 64, 68

'truck system', 104

Trudeau, Pierre Elliott, 194, 210, 212–14

Truro, NS, 132

Tuck, James, 7, 42

Tupper, Charles, 114, 120, 122–4

Tusket, NS, 7

Ullman, Stephen, 5

Ungava Bay, 98

Uniacke, James Boyle, 111

United Fishermen and Allied Workers' Union, 200

United Mineworkers of America, 146, 150, 166, 182

United Nations, 205

United States: 3, 85–6, 89, 92, 95, 101–2, 104, 108, 112–14, 116–17, 129, 131, 137, 140, 143, 153–4, 160, 163–4, 170, 182, 207–8, 212, 215; boundary with New Brunswick, 94;

civil rights movement, 202;
Confederation, 119, 121–3;
'draft dodgers', 206; Free Trade
Agreement, 121, 210–12, 214;
'Manifest Destiny', 120; neu-
trality, 92; Newfoundland, 180,
187; Second World War,
179–80, 185; Smoot-Hawley
tarriff, 172; World Trade
Centre attack (2001), 211; *see
also* American Civil War,
American Revolution
Union of New Brunswick
Indians, 205
Union of Nova Scotia Indians,
205
Université de Moncton, 196,
202–3
University of New Brunswick,
Fredericton, NB, 185
University of Toronto, 185
Upper Canada (Canada West),
113; *see also* Canada, Ontario

Valdmanis, Alfred, 195
Van Horne, Sir William, 150
Vaughan, Sir William, 41; *The
Golden Fleece*, 41
Venice, Italy, 25, 30
Verrazano, Giovanni da, 23, 27
Victoria (Queen), 142
Vietnam War, 206
Villiers, Captain Louis Coulon
de, 68
Vinland, 23, 25
Virginia colony, 39
Voisey's Bay, Labrador, 218

Wabanaki ('Dawnland')
Confederacy, 52, 56, 66

Wabanaki-New England War, 61
Wallace, Birgitta, 25
Wallace, Frederick William,
Wooden Ships and Iron Men,
171
Waipu, New Zealand, 104
War of 1812, 78, 92–3, 96
War of the Austrian Succession
(1744), 57, 59, 61, 64, 67–8
War of the League of Augsburg
(1689–97), 47, 56
War of the Spanish Succession
(1702–13), 57
Washington DC, 122; Pentagon,
211
Washington, George, 84
Waterford, Ireland, 72
Waterville, NS, 198
Webster-Ashburton Treaty
(1842), 94–5
Wells, Clyde, 214
Welsh peoples: immigrants, 96
Wentworth, Sir John, 88
Western Charter, 47, 53, 55
West Indies, 43, 57, 62–3, 71, 78,
84, 89, 92–3, 162
Westray Mine disaster (1993),
211, 213
whaling industry, 23, 28–9, 31–3;
see also animals
Whitbourne, Richard, 33, 41
White, James, 80
White, Portia, 207–8
Whiteway, Sir William, 133, 135
Whitney, Henry M., 131–2, 150
Whitney Pier, NS, 166
Wicken, William, 56
Williams, Arch, 209
Williams, Danny, 205, 220
Williams, William Fenwick, 121

Wilson, Mona, 168–9
Windsor (Pisiquid), NS, 69–70,
81, 89, 100, 114, 132
wine, 53–4, 222
Winslow, Edward, 87–8
Winton, Henry, 107
Wolfe, General James, 73, 79
Woman's Christian Temperance
Union (WCTU), 142
women, 206, 219; capture of
aboriginal, 19–21, 82, 98; First
World War, 156–7, 159; health
care, 168–9; population, 72;
rights, 142, 151, 200, 206;
Second World War, 184, 206;
slavery, 63; suffrage, 129,
141–2, 146, 158, 161, 163
Women's Patriotic Association
(WPA), 156–7
Woodland (Ceramic) peoples,
8–9, 14
Woodstock, NB, 106
World War I, see First World War
World War II, see Second World
War
Wynne, Edward, 42

Yarmouth, NS, 7, 100, 131,
131–2, 179
Yonge, James, 53
Yorkshire peoples: immigrants,
78, 81
Young, John, *Letters to Agricola*,
95, 109
Young Men's and Young
Women's Christian
Associations (YMCA/ YWCA),
142